D1457559

MAY – 2018

By

NO LONGER PROPERTY OF
SEATTLE PUBLIC LIBRARY

The Science of Couples
and Family Therapy

A Norton Professional Book

THE SCIENCE OF COUPLES

AND FAMILY THERAPY

Behind the Scenes at the Love Lab

JOHN M. GOTTMAN

JULIE SCHWARTZ GOTTMAN

W.W. NORTON & COMPANY

Independent Publishers Since 1923

New York • London

Note to Readers: Standards of clinical practice and protocol change over time, and no technique or recommendation is guaranteed to be safe or effective in all circumstances. This volume is intended as a general information resource for professionals practicing in the field of psychotherapy and mental health; it is not a substitute for appropriate training, peer review, and/or clinical supervision. Neither the publisher nor the authors can guarantee the complete accuracy, efficacy, or appropriateness of any particular recommendation in every respect.

Copyright © 2018 by John M. Gottman and Julie Schwartz Gottman

All rights reserved
Printed in the United States of America
First Edition

For information about permission to reproduce selections from this book, write to Permissions, W. W. Norton & Company, Inc., 500 Fifth Avenue, New York, NY 10110

For information about special discounts for bulk purchases, please contact W. W. Norton Special Sales at specialsales@wwnorton.com or 800-233-4830

Manufacturing by LSC Harrisonburg
Production manager: Christine Critelli

Library of Congress Cataloging-in-Publication Data
Names: Gottman, John Mordechai, author. | Gottman, Julie Schwartz, author.
Title: The science of couples and family therapy: behind the scenes at the "love lab" / John M. Gottman, Ph.D., Julie Schwartz Gottman, Ph.D.
Description: First edition. | New York: W. W. Norton & Company, [2018] | Series: A Norton professional book | Includes bibliographical references and index.
Identifiers: LCCN 2017019910 | ISBN 9780393712742 (hardcover(
Subjects: LCSH: Family psychotherapy. | Couples therapy.
Classification: LCC RC488.5 .G684 2018 | DDC 616.89/1562—dc23 LC record available at https://lccn.loc.gov/2017019910

ISBN: 978-0-393-71274-2

W. W. Norton & Company, Inc., 500 Fifth Avenue, New York, N.Y. 10110
www.wwnorton.com

W. W. Norton & Company Ltd., 15 Carlisle Street, London W1D 3BS

1 2 3 4 5 6 7 8 9 0

To
Dr. Richard McFall
John Gottman's mentor

Contents

CONTENTS

Preface

A CALL FOR A NEW 4SD SYSTEMS THERAPY

In this informal book, we are going to present what we think is the ful-fillment of the original general systems theory. From our new theory has sprung new therapies that have now been applied to change the emotional world of a couple or a family system. We are going to describe this new the-ory and the new therapy that follows from it. This book is new in ways that are both theoretical and practical. We are both working therapists, and what we care most about is having a therapy that is practical and effective.

The original GENERAL SYSTEM THEORY, written by the biol-ogist Ludwig von Bertalanffy in 1968, began a set of world-shattering, innovative changes in psychotherapy. More than just one client was to be invited into the therapist's consulting room. That was shocking. There was much nail biting and hand wringing at the time. Many journals actu-ally decried the catastrophic and sudden loss of confidentiality when more than one patient entered the consulting room. Academics and therapists trembled at the horrifying prospect that the sacred transference neurosis would now never take place. They worried that total deep cures that changed the unconscious would be replaced by only superficial symptom change. They worried that new symptoms would spring up to substitute for the old ones.

None of those imagined catastrophes ever occurred. But psychotherapy was changed forever. The therapist became active, instead of quiet. The therapist became real and personal, instead of distant and removed. No longer was the therapist just a blank slate for the patient's projections. The therapist could now say things like, "How do you react to what she just said?" The entire interpersonal system unfolded right in front of the therapist's eyes. The focus of therapy jumped from one client free-associating what he or she recalled, to actual directly observable and lively social interaction.

After 1968 the therapeutic repertoire exploded into a cornucopia of new and exciting psychotherapeutic techniques. The new therapies even became a social movement. It was an exciting and heady time. The next several decades witnessed the emergence of new therapies such as structural family therapy, strategic family therapy, narrative family therapy, intergenerational family therapy, and many more. Charismatic and articulate figures emerged who have become legends in psychotherapy: Gregory Bateson, Jay Haley, Virginia Satir, Don Jackson, Paul Watzlawick, Carl Whittaker, Murray Bowen, Salvador Minuchin, and many others. General systems therapy swept the entirety of what young therapists wanted to learn from these new gurus.

That was then. It's now been 50 years since this revolution occurred in psychotherapy. The smoke has now cleared. The revolution has passed. It's time to evaluate, to take stock, to take a look around at where we are now, and the news after 50 years is not good. Unfortunately, even after these five decades of intense work on the topic, general systems theory remains only a loose set of vague metaphors, and, from a scientific basis, it remains a confused nonempirical muddle. The infrastructure of new therapeutic techniques has crumbled. The scaffolding has fallen. The old systems theory has been a failure. The theory needs to be overhauled.

The good news is that we have now done exactly that.

As we look around we also see that systems thinking hasn't presented us with a set of useful clinical tools. Sure, these general systems ideas are covered today in many introductory graduate courses on psychotherapy, but they don't really affect how clinicians work day to day. There is no guiding theory, and no set of reliable tools that therapists use on an every-day basis. General systems theory is a piece of history, but that's about it.

This is not to say that family systems therapy hasn't progressed or demonstrated some degree of effectiveness. It has. Yet, no specific methods appear to have been shown to be better than any others. There's no technology of change. Worse yet, we really haven't achieved a truly effective system of family treatment. Sure, research has shown us that the effects of family therapy are slightly better than doing absolutely noth-ing. However, by and large the effect size of couples and family therapy appears to be quite modest, about half of a standard deviation (Pinsof & Wynne, 1995). Okay, we agree, that is something, and we think we can be proud of that accomplishment. However, it's just not a very large effect clinically.

Let us explain using this unit called the "standard deviation." Remember the normal curve, that bell-shaped curve you studied when you read about intelligence testing? You learned that the population aver-age IQ is 100 and that the standard deviation is 15. The majority of the population (68%) have IQs between 85 and 115, that is, within one stan-dard deviation below or above the mean of 100. If we had an interven-tion that could increase people's intelligence one standard deviation, we would be able to increase someone's IQ from 85 to 100. Then we could say the effect size of that intervention is 1.0. If we had an intervention that increased intelligence two standard deviations, we would be able to increase someone's IQ from 70 to 100. The effect size of that intervention would be 2.0.

In the area of couples therapy, the scale most commonly used to mea-sure therapy outcome is called the Dyadic Adjustment Scale (DAS). It's a version of a very old scale of marital satisfaction devised in 1959 by two researchers, Locke and Wallace. Like the IQ test, this scale was devised so that the population mean for this scale is 100.0, with a standard devi-ation of 15.0. The hopes were that it would make this scale easier to understand. It led to an operational definition of unhappy marriage: At least one partner has a score of 85 or lower, that is, a score one standard deviation below the population mean of 100.

There are two problems with our research on couples therapy. First, in many university-based outcome studies, particularly in couples therapy, the population of clinical couples across studies before they begin treatment have an average DAS score of around 93, half a standard deviation below the mean. However, many couples we see in couples therapy have DAS scores of about 40.0, 60 points below the mean or four standard deviations below it. Therefore, the university-based outcome studies of couples therapy usually don't include the kinds of couples we see everyday in therapy. They have sampled only the worried well, not the severely distressed couples that are the bill of fare of our practices.

Here's the second problem. Now let us explain what we mean by weak effect sizes. The typical effect size of couples therapy interventions is one-half of a standard deviation, or about 7 points. That means the therapy would take a couple whose initial dyadic adjustment score was 93 to about 100. Okay, that doesn't sound too bad. However, if you move a couple from 40 to 47, you have moved them from miserable, at the brink of divorce, to a wee bit less miserable. That is just pitiful.

These so-called evidence-based small-effect treatments just don't do much to help our clients. The American Psychological Association may have given them their seal of approval, but that certification is small consolation to our everyday clients, who are still ailing after therapy. We are not crying wolf when there's no wolf out there. This average effect size of half a standard deviation would still leave many couples very, very unhappy.

Do you see the problem?

That's why we are saying that our field has a long, long way to go. We have to admit our evidence-based therapies really suck, and try to not oversell our interventions. An APA approval of evidence-based treatment might be awarded to interventions that are still nothing to brag about. This 0.5 standard deviation effect size is pitiful because it's just not clinically good enough. Figure P.1 dramatizes what we're talking about.

Another critique one must make of most couples and family outcome studies is the one positive psychology has leveled. This point is that we need theory and techniques that help get our clients into healthy, fulfill-

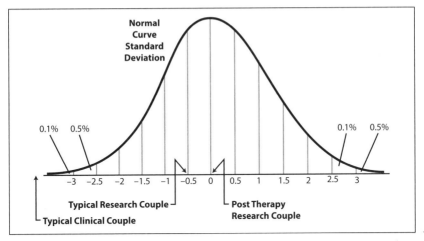

Figure P.1. The effect size is explained as the number of standard deviation units the experimental group changes after intervention.

ing, and joyful relationships. We would love to start with a couple who maybe are at the brink of divorce and end treatment with them when they are happy, in love again, enjoying their time with one another, and having great sex.

We also have a third problem to solve. As our colleague Neil Jacobson pointed out when he was still alive, when you follow couples after they've completed therapy, between 35% and 50% of them have relapsed to pre-therapy levels of marital satisfaction at two years post-therapy. But these days, no one is talking much about our huge relapse problem.

Things get a lot worse when we add in the usual comorbidities that we therapists encounter every day. Most of these comorbidities get screened out in a typical university-based study. In sum, we can applaud evidence-based treatments, but the effect sizes are paltry, there is lots of relapse, and we don't do very well when the everyday comorbidities show up in our consulting rooms.

For example, behavioral marital therapy for treating marital distress AND alcoholism (O'Farrell; McCrady) seems to really work well. Sure, it is evidence based. But it has a success rate of 30% at best, and that's without looking at long-term follow-up. Now admittedly, that's about twice the purported success rate of AA (because of AA's 60% dropout rates).

We think these two stalwart investigators have done some great work. But it still isn't ultimately very impressive. A 30% success rate means a 70% failure rate. How would you react to a surgeon who told you that your pending operation has a 70% chance of failing?

THEREFORE, in this book we issue a call:

> We need to develop family therapies with an effect size of at least four standard deviations, and these effects need to be on outcome measures we totally trust. We will call these family treatments 4SD INTERVENTIONS.

WE CANNOT RELY ON SELF-REPORT MEASURES OF TREATMENT OUTCOME

We want to make another point. We have said we need outcome measures that we can trust. Let's call them GOLD STANDARD MEASURES. We cannot continue to rely only on self-report measures. Most of the outcome literature on couples therapy, for example, is based on only two measures of self-reported marital satisfaction that are nearly identical to each other, the Locke-Wallace scale (Locke & Wallace, 1959), and the Dyadic Adjustment Scale (Spanier, 1979). (Only a few items differ between these two.) One or the other is usually used in every couples therapy outcome study. These measures are marginally okay, but they are also highly flawed. For example, both scales will rate couples higher in marital satisfaction if they avoid conflict. But that doesn't make sense, because when the dynamics of relationships are studied, couples who don't avoid conflicts but instead talk about conflicts and manage them well report higher marital satisfaction. But these measures will penalize them for having any conflicts at all.

We also need to directly observe couples and families. The Oregon OSLC group established over 50 years ago by Gerry Patterson quickly discovered yet another problem. They were getting what they thought were really great results in treating oppositional kids. At the time they were only using parent satisfaction measures to measure the success of their treatment. But they found that the kids weren't changing at all when observational measures were used. According to these measures the same awful kid behavior persisted. The puzzled researchers went to the parents and asked them why they were reporting such high satisfaction on their self-report scales when their kids weren't changing at all. The parents essentially replied, "We wanted to thank you guys. At least you tried." Since then, the OSLC group has stayed faithful to including observational outcome measures in every study they do. In studies of couples we have been giving ourselves a break by just relying on self-report measures. They are a good start, but they aren't enough (Campbell and Fiske, 1959).

We can also be dramatically misled if we rely only on questionnaires. That problem exists in therapy studies of couples suffering from domestic violence. Neil Jacobson and John Gottman discovered that many self-report measures of violence are tainted by shame, and also by fear. People will report being in the happily married range until you interview them and discover that they are getting seriously beaten on a regular basis. They are either too afraid or too ashamed to put this down on paper. On a self-report measure, people cannot be relied on to tell the whole story. In the outcome study our lab just conducted on treating domestic violence, we decided to include archival police records, observational data of couples dealing with a marital conflict, and physiological data in addition to self-report data. And we also collected data 18 months after treatment to make sure our therapy effects were more or less lasting.

OUR NEW GENERAL SYSTEMS THEORY

We believe that researchers in our field have tolerated such small effect sizes in their studies because of the general systems theory itself. The original theory is simply broken. That's our best guess, and that's why we are writing this book. In the area of couples and family work it is now possible to propose the true completion of von Bertalanffy's original ideas, with credible empirical backup and useful tools for both assessment and treatment. We believe that this new theory will prove useful for everyday clinicians, even though many of its ideas will seem somewhat exotic. Maybe this theory will eventually even get us to 4SD INTERVENTIONS.

Following von Bertalanffy's lead, this new work is a combination of empirical and mathematical ideas. And yes, we know that math is not very appealing to most people. A lot of us kids have suffered from bad math teaching in school, so it's nobody's fault. The good news is that the math we use can be presented visually and dramatically in fun graphics, and that is what we will do. We'll also put the algebra in math sidebars in an appendix, so people can skip the math if they want to. Or, who knows? Maybe some of you will enjoy the math parts.

THE NEW THERAPIES

We want to give you good news about a new systems *theory*. But that's only half the story. Our book is also about new empirical science that we think completes von Bertalanffy's work and helps us to know what needs to change in a dysfunctional couple or family system. With this refined theory and science, we can redefine the goals of systems family therapy and generate new therapeutic tools to reach them, tools that begin to build a 4SD therapy for treating couples and families. If you practice couples or family therapy, we hope that you will find this book to be a breath of fresh air that will help you to be even more effective in your everyday work.

John Gottman, PhD
Julie Gottman, PhD
Orcas Island, WA

The Science of Couples and Family Therapy

CHAPTER 1

The Old General Systems Theory and the Old Family Therapy

A little bit of history (but not too much).

THE OLD THEORY

The old general systems theory was invented by a biologist named Ludwig von Bertalanffy in his now-classic 1968 book entitled *General System Theory*. It summarized his life's work and centered on an important observation: interacting parts in nature often create a harmonized whole, a system that is "more than the sum of its parts."

Fortunately, von Bertalanffy was also writing during the cybernetic revolution, a time when there was a lot of excitement about regulating machines through feedback. The cybernetic revolution began during World War II. A former child prodigy, an MIT mathematician named Norbert Wiener, was asked by the Army to design a gun that could automatically adjust to, and ANTICIPATE, its target. In other words, through feedback the gun could adjust to where its target would be at a given time and thereby improve its accuracy. In the process Wiener invented cybernetics. This cybernetic theory of Wiener's became popularized through the Macy cybernetics conferences (held from 1946 to 1953). Cybernetics also kick-started industrial automation, which is sometimes called the second industrial revolution.

The Macy conference organizers even invited Norbert Wiener to attend. This was a surprise, because Wiener's lectures were legendary at MIT for being impossible to follow. Yes, he was the genius who invented the term cybernetics, and derived a lot of the necessary math for it (called time-series analysis), a truly brilliant pioneer, but he was very hard to follow. Here's one story John heard about Wiener when he was a math grad student at MIT. A student asked Wiener if he could show the class how he derived the math formula he had just written on the blackboard. Wiener erased the formula, paused for a minute, and then wrote the same formula again. The baffled student again said, "Professor Wiener, I still don't understand." Wiener erased the formula again, now paused for a longer time, and then wrote the same formula again. The student still persisted and said, even louder, "Professor Wiener, I *still* don't understand." Wiener again erased the formula, now paused for a very long time, and then wrote the same formula again. Exasperated, the student persisted and once again said, "Professor Wiener, I *still* have no understanding at all of this formula." Wiener's response was rumored to have been, "Damn it, I just derived it in three entirely different ways!"

Wiener's contribution was to describe the math of systems that reacted to feedback, systems that did not just perform a task, but instead were RESPONSIVE and could ADAPT to changing inputs, and adjust their outputs accordingly. That was a huge breakthrough in thinking about what a machine was capable of. Von Bertalanffy's systems theory echoed perfectly this understanding about the adaptive complexity of how natural systems worked. Together their work gave precise definition to what systems theory was all about.

As it turned out, the time was just right, and von Bertalanffy's book created huge changes in many fields, including psychiatry and psychotherapy—which is what we care about—through its influence on a small group of brilliant maverick therapists, people like anthropologist Gregory Bateson, and also Murray Bowen, Salvador Minuchin, Don Jackson, Paul Watzlawick, and Virginia Satir, all of whom went on to revolutionize psychotherapy.

Okay, that's the group of SYSTEMS innovators we are most interested in. Von Bertalanffy's book refocused psychotherapy from being about individuals lying on a couch and free-associating, to interactive groups of people talking to each other as well as to the therapist. YIKES! That was a bit like opening up a doorway and suddenly finding yourself holding a tiger by the tail. You've got hold of something big, and you'd better not let go or all hell could break loose. This was a major revolution in psychotherapy.

With this new systems therapy, the therapist became much more active, and much more real too. The therapist started trying to disrupt and challenge old DYSFUNCTIONAL patterns and create new patterns, not in a single individual, but in social groups of people. The new therapies also focused on BEHAVIOR, primarily behavior involved in communication. Suddenly everyone in the room was talking at the same time! Sometimes the therapist even had trouble getting them all to be quiet and listen to his brilliant interpretations. No wonder one of their mottoes was, "You cannot not communicate." These therapists were trying to view social interaction as a system, with organized patterns and FEEDBACK LOOPS. Figure 1.1 shows von Bertalanffy's basic idea. It was just a sketch, really. It doesn't seem like much, does it? Yet it compelled therapists to focus on the communication of messages and their complex meanings both verbally and nonverbally, rather than just one individual's intrapsychic world.

Early in his career, the great systems thinker Gregory Bateson had studied play in zoo animals. As a result, he was keenly aware of nonverbal behavior as an observer. So he and others also placed importance on nonverbal interaction in the consulting room, which was a first.

Of course, being the new kids on the block, these new therapists started getting handed the worst cases imaginable. It was as if the old guard was saying, "Oh, you think you're so smart? Well, have I got a case for you." For example, they started working with families that had a psychotic kid as a patient. Try that!

Undaunted, these dazzling guys proposed and developed the famous double bind hypothesis—which was the idea that some interaction patterns cause, or (as later turned out to be true) sustain psychopathology,

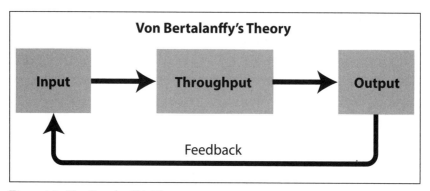

Figure 1.1. Von Bertalanffy's Theory

and may cause schizophrenics to relapse. The systems theorists noticed how one psychotic kid's mother, during a hospital visit, communicated two contradictory messages to the kid at the same time. Her *language* said one thing: "I love you. I'm so glad to see you. Come here and give me a kiss." But her *body* language was frozen and conveyed the opposite: "Ugh! Go away! Disappear."

So, these thinkers—people like Gregory Bateson, Don Jackson, Jay Haley, Virginia Satir, and Salvador Minuchin—boldly suggested that this double message of opposites was crazy making because it put the kid in a double bind. No matter what he did, he was doomed. It was just like an old joke that Freud once told. A mother gives her son two ties as a birthday present. He goes right upstairs to his room and puts on one of the ties. As he comes downstairs his mom says, "What's the matter, you didn't like the other tie?" The poor kid can't win. So these therapists boldly suggested that some forms of communication in families MAKE people psychotic.

Bateson thought that the kid with the double-binding mom is screwed unless he communicates about communication, or "metacommunicates." If in the Freud joke he says, "Mom, I can't win with you. Why the heck didn't you just give me one tie?" then he rises above the fray. It's like he's suddenly in his own hot air balloon and mom is disappearing far below him. He beat the system! Systems thinkers called this new idea metacommunication—or communication about communication. The therapist teaches this to the kid. It's his ticket out of Madville. The way out of madness is clear communication and feedback, even communication about THE PROCESS OF COMMUNICATION. Wow. For many of us at the time, these new ideas were breathtaking. They really got us thinking about how we communicate badly in our relationships. Communicating about communication, or metacommunication is the way out of the double bind. META became the new touchstone.

META, META

So in the meantime, these revolutionary family therapists got busy building these great feedback loops in the dysfunctional family system, changing old crazy-making interaction patterns into healthy patterns, and teaching the world how to observe the INTERACTION PROCESS. They also legitimized themselves by starting a new journal called *Family Process* and a new professional organization.

A whole new range of therapeutic techniques opened up once the therapist invited more than one person into the room. The therapist could now ask, "How do you react to what he just said?" and also, "How do you react to that reaction?" Whoa! New therapeutic techniques were sprouting heads like the Hydra. And just when these methods were getting hot, John was attending the University of Wisconsin's clinical and developmental psychology grad program. So he learned all about them. The famous developmental psychologist E. Mavis Hetherington was his teacher. And John's own mentor, Richard McFall, was a great observer who taught him how to integrate observations into a training program in order to evaluate it. In gratitude we dedicate this book to him.

With these new therapies the whole family system could now be **observed** in therapy, not merely get reported about by just one neurotic and highly biased client. Therapists were now doing couples therapy, an old idea for marriage counselors, but a new idea for systems thinkers, and they were also seeing whole families together. By the way, Freud once tried his version of couples therapy by analyzing each partner in a marriage (seeing each one separately, of course), and subsequently he wrote an article in 1919 forbidding that practice among analysts. Apparently it was a somewhat traumatic experience even for this giant thinker to try to understand a couple. What the heck was actually true? She says, he says, who says? What's the truth?

To give you an idea of how revolutionary all this seeing the whole system was, if you look back at the journals in those days, debates were raging endlessly about how seeing more than one client at a time fundamentally violates confidentiality. How so? It's simple. There's more than just one client in the room with the therapist. The identified patient's confidentiality is getting violated. In hindsight, these discussions seem silly, but they were deadly serious at the time, and a lot of this early therapy was done IN SECRET. No kidding. Well, remember, Freud's group even had secret signet rings.

Part of what was so exciting is that the focus evolved to be the observation of process. And these pioneers were brilliant at it, really gifted. They could even analyze the late Edward Albee's play *Who's Afraid of Virginia Woolf?* which most people, up to then, couldn't even understand. Also, because cameras and videotape recorders suddenly became affordable, videotape feedback emerged as an amazing technique for changing systems. No one really knew what they were doing, but, as someone once said, "If we knew what we were doing it wouldn't be called research." They showed clients their own tapes and said, "So what do you see?" and then, "Here's what I see." A whole cornucopia of new therapeutic techniques emerged.

These guys also studied language, nonverbal behavior, and even emotion (a little bit), and could see all of it as the source of potential crazy-making manipulation in dysfunctional families. They exclaimed, "The whole is greater than the sum of its parts!" They declared war on "linear thinking" in deference to "circular" and "nonlinear" thinking.

What they noticed most of all was that these disturbed families were darned rigid, and also there was a whole lot of conflict! Not anywhere near as calm as a guy on the couch free-associating, someone the therapist didn't even have to look at. It was exhausting working with these dysfunctional families, and getting them to change was probably a freaking nightmare. They were rigid AND their emotions seemed out of control. Volatile and rigid? What a combination!

Murray Bowen wound up essentially declaring war on being emotional. John once saw a video of Bowen saying to a woman, "I don't want to know how you feel. I want to know how you THINK. Your feelings always get you into trouble with your husband." These client families must have been in such negative places that they overwhelmed their therapists. Yet some of these therapists must have been very confident. Murray Bowen even tried changing *his own family!* And he even wrote about it. Not too many people picked up on his bold lead. When John tried it with his family, it was a total failure. No wonder Bowen thought emotionality was a culprit. Many people still think that. Bowen's initial definition of "differentiation" was that people were differentiated if they could control their emotions with their ability to reason. This was an anti-emotion therapy!

We have forgotten to tell you about HOMEOSTASIS, a key ingredient of von Bertalanffy's that wasn't in Figure 1.1. It is all about balance. Homeostasis as an idea came from the field of physiology (breakthroughs made by Claude Bernard in 1865, and later Walter Cannon in 1926). These pioneer physiologists suggested that biological systems have a "set point," that they use an error signal to readjust with feedback, so the system is actually regulated, just like a thermostat in your room regulates the set point of the room's temperature. Then, with homeostasis, the system stays stable. In the brain, the hypothalamus balances many of these biological functions in our bodies. These followers of von Bertalanffy, particularly one of our heroes, Salvador Minuchin, suggested that functional families had a functional homeostatic set point, and dysfunctional families had a dysfunctional homeostatic set point. But both types of families would try to maintain their own particular set point, for better or worse. Both types of families were regulated, one toward health, the other toward illness. Here was the concept of the homeostatic set point in the old general systems theory.

This was a great idea, but . . . there was a serious problem with this idea applied to families. Therapists took the homeostasis idea and generalized it from biology to social interaction. Okay, good, so they suggested that there may also be patterns in families that get protected and regulated. These patterns can be functional in healthy families or dysfunctional in crazy families, and family systems will defend their homeostatic setpoints and be resistant to change, even if it's crazy making! Okay, that was a neat theory about psychopathology.

Yet there was still a problem . . .

WHAT'S REGULATED?

In biology set points are very real variables. Biological set points are measurable, such as body temperature, blood glucose, calcium ions, blood oxygen, and arterial blood pressure. These are real variables. There are even norms for them, like 98.6 for body temperature and 120/80 for blood pressure, or numbers related to the regulation of blood sugar, which involves the liver and the pancreas, with sugar and insulin in balance, and so on. These are precise mechanisms.

But what variables in families were supposed to be regulated? Some said "family rules," some said "differentiation," but no one measured anything! Bateson, Watzlawick, Bowen, Jackson, Haley, et al. never identified a variable that was regulated or dysregulated in relationships. So, how could systems theory have any meaning other than as a freakin' metaphor?

This was metaphor, not science. What the heck was actually getting regulated in couples and families?

There was another problem, pointed out by master therapist Daniel Wile in his book *Couples Therapy* (1981). Dan Wile argued that the homeostasis concept created an adversarial relationship between the therapist and the dysfunctional homeostatic set point of the family. Like the knight Don Quixote de la Mancha who tilted at windmills, the new systems therapist was supposed to gallantly battle against the family's dysfunctional set point and was entitled to use any trick in the book to undermine the family system. As a result the therapist was entitled to play tricks on the family, like giving them paradoxical messages. For example, the therapist could instruct the family to keep doing something clearly dysfunctional, hoping they would rebel against the therapist and do something healthy instead. This method of using tricks to change families was called "Strategic Therapy". Some therapists were strongly drawn toward this strategic tactical psycho-judo approach. Tricks sprang up like weeds in the books these systems therapists authored. No judgment here, that's just what happened.

"But wait a minute!" Dan Wile said. The therapist claims to be attempting to change the sick homeostatic set point, so that the norm now becomes clear communication, with healthy feedback loops and metacommunication. Yet tricks are not clear communication. That was one of Dan Wile's points. What a mess this "social homeostasis" was! Instead, Dan argued, sometimes the family itself was against its own dysfunction, and then the therapist could join the family in rooting for health. It need not be adversarial.

Along with these problems with the homeostasis concept, these guys never collected much data. It's easy to think you're 100% right if you don't collect data.

Even worse than collecting data, von Bertalanffy also envisioned using math to fully describe a system, how the parts interacted to create a whole that was greater than the sum of its parts. In fact, he suggested using linear differential equations to describe this whole interacting system, with only one homeostatic set point. His book actually has a whole chapter filled with equations, and his math is totally correct. He even talks about eigenvalues, which we will do as well (see Appendix 2). Unfortunately, the linear equations he suggested don't work very well to create homeostasis—they are usually quite unstable. But, we'll talk a little more about the math later. We are completing his work, so we will use math as well, that is, real—not imagined—math.

SOCIAL EPIDEMIOLOGY, OR: WHY CARE SO MUCH ABOUT UNDERSTANDING LOVE?

In 2005, 14 scholars got together to review what the benefits of marriage might be, as determined by social science research (Wilcox, Doherty, Glenn, & Waite, 2005). Their 2012 report was cautious and quite lengthy. They wrote that it was happy marriage itself that predicted very positive life outcomes for men, women, and their children. That report was a resounding endorsement of marriage, and yet these conclusions were only part of the story. The results were only a small part of a much larger scientific literature linking the quality of people's closest relationships to health, longevity, and well-being.

Ignoring what is cause and what is effect, there is no doubt that people in happy, stable, committed relationships live significantly longer, are healthier physically and psychologically, become wealthier, and have children who do better in most aspects of living than people who are either alone, in uncommitted relationships, or in unhappy or unstable relationships. Therefore, there is no question that we can precisely identify successful and unsuccessful relationships, and measure the effects of both. Relationship success or failure has enormous consequences for people everywhere on the planet.

In the past four decades there has been a major breakthrough in the study of physical and mental health and longevity. This breakthrough created a new field called Social Epidemiology. Epidemiologists study disease patterns, and try to ferret out the causes of illness and sometimes the causes of epidemics. What more and more epidemiologists were discovering 45 years ago was that the secret to a successful and healthy, long, and prosperous life was the quality of people's closest relationships. This was a startling discovery, and it emerged over and over in many now classic studies. For example, at University of California, Berkeley, Leonard Syme and Lisa Berkman conducted the Alameda County Study in which they followed 9,000 people, taking blood samples, and studying diet, exercise, and personal habits, as well as measuring serum cholesterol to predict life and death. People who had close friendships and love relationships lived longer, while people who were more socially isolated died younger. This was true everywhere on the planet it was studied (for example, House 2001). If you would like to read a summary of some of this work, see Berkman and Kawachi's *Social Epidemiology* (or the second edition: Berkman, Kawachi, & Glymour, 2014).

So what we have learned is that good relationships matter a great deal.

SUMMARY, SO FAR

In all there were some great ideas here that were, in part, by von Bertalanffy . . . But what in families might be regulated? Let's explore this next.

CHAPTER 2

What Might Be Regulated in Family Homeostasis?

CONCEPT #1: Homeostasis in families is the balance between positive and negative affect

In our general systems theory, the rescue from this pesky question of what gets regulated in families comes from a strange place. . . . It's called game theory.

MATH TOOL 1: GAME THEORY

What the heck is game theory? We are anxious to tell you about it. It was invented by John von Neumann. Who was this second "von"? What is it with all these vons? A lot of very talented foreigners moved to the United States during World War II, including Albert Einstein, Leo Szilard, and Enrico Fermi. And Johnny von Neumann (pronounced FON NOI-MAHN).

Johnny von Neumann was a pretty amazing guy. He was a theoretical physicist who was central in the Manhattan Project, the secret project to beat the Nazis to make an atomic bomb and thus win the war. Von Neumann had a photographic memory. He wrote a major book about quantum mechanics. He was a Hungarian Jew—and very anti-Russian—who escaped from Nazi Europe. In fact, he designed Fat Boy, the Manhattan Project's second atomic bomb, the one that was dropped on the unfortunate people of Nagasaki. Von Neumann also designed and built one of the first electronic computers in the world, and many of his (and Alan Turing's) ideas for the design of computers are what we still use today. But, more important for us therapists is that he also invented a new branch of math and applied it to the study of economic behavior in his groundbreaking book with Oscar Morgenstern called *Theory of Games and Economic Behavior* (1949). This book transformed the entire field of economics.

It was not much use for psychology yet. But a decade later two social psychologists, Harold Kelley and John Thibaut, brought game theory into social psychology in their now-classic book, *The Social Psychology of Groups* (1959). They also had a brilliant student named Caryl Rusbult, but more about her later. Her contributions were enormous. We want to introduce therapists to her fabulous work, but not yet.

Here comes the main idea of game theory, that social interaction may be viewed as a set of behavior exchanges with associated payoffs, and maybe even with rules. Game theory views a relationship as if a behavior exchange, for example,

Jane smiles and Harry frowns,

As if this exchange . . .

Was selected from a matrix (of Harry-by-Jane behaviors), selected strategically.

Wait a minute! What do we mean by using the term "strategically"? Strategically for what? And what "matrix" are we talking about?

And here comes John von Neumann's brilliance: he says that the exchange was selected . . . to maximize (or minimize) a particular payoff, or some "function of the payoff," which we will call "a payoff metric." The payoff could be negative (a cost), or positive (a gain), or neutral. For example, as one exchanges pieces in a chess game, the metric is for one to win **and** for one's opponent to lose. It's a win-lose contest, with a win-lose metric. That's called a zero-sum game.

So, armed with game theory . . .

Maybe what we might measure is how the people each feel about a behavior exchange. Aha! Yes, now that's a thought. Now we were cooking with gas. That's what Thibaut and Kelley thought. For example,

> If John smiles warmly at Julie, and she looks sad instead of giving him a full-hearted return smile, she might evaluate his smile as very positive, but he may be disappointed, and evaluate her sad look as very negative. They could keep going through the whole interaction like that, exchanging actions and payoffs.

So, in line with this thinking, back in the 1970s Levenson and Gottman invented a gizmo. . . . It followed an older version John had used, which he called "the talk table." Same general idea.

THE LEVENSON-GOTTMAN VIDEO RECALL RATING DIAL GIZMO GIVES VALID PAYOFFS

Their dial is a scale that goes from "Very Negative" on the left to "Very Positive" on the right. After their videotaped interaction, they had people turn this dial to tell them what they were feeling during the interaction, as they watched the video replay of their interaction. They also collected physiological data from them as they watched.

John and Robert also collected physiology data during the interaction, and again as the couple watched the video replay and turned their little rating dial gizmo. You can also collect physiology data from your clients as you do couples therapy, if you buy two inexpensive pulse oximeters that the couple wear as they talk to one another. But more about that later.

Back to the gizmo. Robert Levenson and his student Anna Ruef also had people do this rating dial procedure twice: once, telling us what they were feeling during the interaction, and then again, guessing how their partner had been feeling during the interaction. Levenson and Ruef

(1992) found that people were good at guessing how their partner had been feeling to the extent that, while watching, they actually relived their partner's original physiology during the interaction. That is, if their hearts beat faster, their blood flowed faster, and they sweated more just at roughly the same times that their partner did in the actual interaction, they were good at guessing their partner's affect.

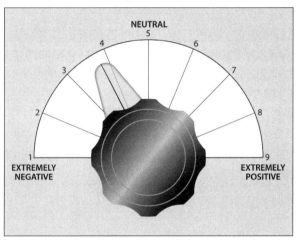

Pretty cool little dial, eh? This rating dial can measure empathy physiologically. And it's cheap to get these data. Robert always said that the powerpoint slide of the rating dial cost more than the actual rating dial. Yet it is now being used by many social psychology researchers because it gives very good numbers, reliable and valid ones.

This brings us to our Concept #1. What might be regulated? Well, Robert and John suggested:

Concept #1. What might get regulated in families is the *BAL-ANCE* between positive and negative emotions.

Yes, Robert and John were focusing quite intentionally on **emotion.** These days that's not a big surprise. But in the 1970s only a small number of psychologists actually took the observation of emotion seriously. Levenson and John were led by the man who really helped them understand emotion more than anyone else, Paul Ekman. Ekman (2013) showed that the face was not "a researcher's nightmare" as the highly influential and famous Jerome Bruner had previously suggested. Paul showed us how to study people's faces, and to see small anatomical facial muscle movements that conveyed reliable emotional information.

Nowadays, thanks mostly to Susan Johnson, we have emotionally focused couples therapy (EFT), so we know how important emotion is for clinical work. EFT has made a huge impact on the way most of us go about the business of doing couples therapy. But back in the 1970s not many of us were actually observing emotions. So, John and Robert thought maybe this balance gets regulated to be a mostly positive balance in a functional couple. Or, this balance also gets regulated to be a mostly negative balance in a dysfunctional couple. In either case it's regulated, that is, there is a homeostatic set point. But in one case that set point makes people happy, while in the other case it makes people miserable.

Well, is that the mysterious missing homeostatic set point in social systems? Not a bad idea.

But wait a minute. What are we really saying? Is that even possible? Does it even make sense? In unhappily married couples, for example, compared to happily married couples, they would be doing things more frequently that they themselves rated as more negative? Isn't that illogical?

Why would people do things that make them feel bad? Yes, it is totally illogical. It's crazy. Why would they actually do things that have negative payoff? Yet that turned out to be true. Levenson and John found that unhappily married couples were objectively doing more negative affect exchanges (yes, we were also *observing* their emotions), and they were also rating these very exchanges more negatively than happily married couples.

Another way to say that is that their PERCEPTION OF AFFECT fit what objective observers saw. The objective observers said, yes, you unhappily married couples are doing much more negative affect exchanges than happily married couples, and the couples agreed, yes we are. No wonder you're unhappy, we thought. Yes, they agreed, no wonder.

We had to collect data and also observe and code actual emotional behavior. Once we did, we found that the actual ratio of observed positive-to-negative behaviors among happily married couples during a conflict discussion averaged 5.0, whereas the ratio of positive-to-negative behaviors among unhappily married couples during a conflict discussion averaged 0.8. These set points aren't even close!

These ratios have gotten a lot of press. Recently John was leaving a Starbucks in Seattle and a guy drove by in his truck, rolled down his window, and gave John the thumbs-up sign yelling, "Five to one, right?" John returned the thumbs-up sign with a smile. So the word is getting out.

Finally in this research we had a valid homeostatic variable that was totally out of whack for couples who were miserable in their marriages, and "in whack" for happily married couples. That homeostatic set point needs to be 5 to 1 even during conflict, and it fits emotional behavior as well as the couple's perception of emotion.

> **FAMILY HOMEOSTASIS:** *There is a set point at which positive and negative affect are in balance for happy, stable relationships. It is 5 to 1. There is another set point of the balance between positive and negative affect for unhappily married couples. It is 0.8 to 1.*

COERCIVE FAMILY PROCESS: BALANCE IS TOWARD NEGATIVE AFFECT ESCALATION

This idea that there can be a family system that is regulated but with a very negative affect set point, has been highlighted in the past 50 years of truly beautiful research at the Oregon Social Learning Center (OSLC) under the amazing leadership of the late Gerald Patterson and his colleagues Marion Forgatch, Patty Chamberlain, and John Reid. Using observational methods, these researchers identified a cycle of parent-child interaction that has been shown to lead to the development of antisocial behavior in adolescents. This pattern is called **the coercive cycle.** In the coercive cycle the child misbehaves, maybe to get attention, and the parent tries to set limits. But in response to the limits, the child only escalates their negative affect. This pattern of the child escalating in response to the parent's limit-setting continues until the parent finally gives in, which reinforces the whole chain of escalation by the child. The OSLC group said that the family is actually training the child to be aggressive and to rapidly escalate negativity, including with peers as well as the family. Patterson coined the technical term for these kids: "little monsters." Patterson (1982) also noted that these families don't seem to show much affection or to experience much positive affect together. So clearly the coercive cycle of escalating negative affect carries over into other aspects of family life. This observed pattern in families led to decades of productive research and also to a highly effective parent-training therapy that was extended to families with oppositional toddlers by Carolyn Webster-Stratton (1992), one of John's colleagues at the University of Washington.

THIS HOMEOSTASIS CONCEPT SUGGESTS NEW GOALS FOR THERAPY

From this idea of affect balance theory of homeostasis we can derive new goals for therapy. They are really very simple.

1. GOAL: Change the perceived balance of positive and negative affect during conflict so that it is FAR more positive than negative (five times as positive as it is negative). We can do this by:
   a. Decreasing the amount of negative affect during conflict, and stopping the ESCALATION of negative affect into (what we will eventually call) the Four Horsemen of the Apocalypse (criticism, defensiveness, contempt, and stonewalling), and
   b. Increasing the amount of positive affect during conflict, particularly humor and affection.

2. GOAL: Increase the amount of positive affect during non-conflict interactions.

When we look at outcome research, what is so interesting about these new goals is that most therapies are not too bad at reducing negative affect during conflict.

What most therapies are not good at, however, is increasing positive affect, either in conflict or in non-conflict contexts. The reason for this, it seems, is that we need a better theory about positive affect itself, which, as you will see, is all about the couple's friendship and intimacy, and their shared meaning system. These goals will lead us to have to understand how couples build trust and commitment, rather than mistrust and betrayal. We begin by defining trust, so that we can actually measure it in any couple's interaction.

Indeed there have only been two dismantling studies of couples therapy, one conducted by Neil Jacobson (1984) on his behavioral couples therapy, and one conducted by us on our Art and Science of Love workshop (Babcock, Gottman, Ryan, & Gottman, 2013). Both studies have found that **for an intervention to be effective it needs to change both conflict and friendship/intimacy.** That's a very important result. Make sure you memorize that fact, because it will guide your therapy with couples. These changes in goals primarily involve the positive affect systems, and we currently know the least about these systems in relationships and families.

SUMMARY, SO FAR

1. We claim that we desperately need a 4SD family systems therapy. Maybe we can get there if we revise and complete general systems theory. So, let's collect some data. What did we discover?

2. CONCEPT #1. Homeostasis in families is the balance between (perceived *and* observed) positive and negative affect.

3. In therapy we need to DECREASE the amount of NEGATIVE AFFECT during conflict.

4. In therapy we need to INCREASE the amount of POSITIVE AFFECT during conflict.

5. In therapy we need to INCREASE the amount of POSITIVE AFFECT during non-conflict interactions by improving FRIENDSHIP and INTIMACY.

6. *The Coercive Cycle* is behavior escalating toward the unbalanced negative.

CHAPTER 3

What Is Trust?

CONCEPT #2: The trust metric

Just what is trust? A trait? Is trust a belief? A value? Does trust equal morality?

Social capital research never defined it. And if you can't define it, you can't change it. Let's try to build up our definition of trust brick by brick, one interaction at a time. What are couples actually most concerned about when it comes to deciding whether or not to marry? When we interviewed both dating and newlywed couples about their major concerns about marriage, their number one concern was TRUST, and their number one fear was BETRAYAL. Furthermore, almost all the newlywed conflict discussions were directly or indirectly about trust. Can I trust you to remain sexually faithful to me? Am I more important than your friends, than your mother? What if . . . ? On and on, it was all about trust. Those couples who wound up trusting one another had very different kinds of conflict discussions and were very different in our apartment "love lab" than couples who failed to develop trust.

Now we have one more important thing to tell you. We can turn to Game theory to understand trust. Game theory can be used to predict the outcome of a couple's interaction. Originally, Game theory was created by mathematicians to help predict economic outcomes. Later, two psychologists named Thibaut and Kelley used game theory to examine outcomes of human behavior. Game theory can also help us to analyze couples' behavior. When two people interact in a given way, which interaction will work best to benefit each one of them? In Game theory, that's called an *individual payoff*. And which interaction will predict the highest payoff for both of them? We call that the *couple payoff*. Game theory helps us figure out behavior exchanges that produce either the highest individual payoff or the highest couple payoff.

As we noted earlier, individual partners will rate some interactions as positive and some as negative. Using math, we can calculate at what point they are in balance. Game theory helps us do that. But game theory isn't just about positivity or negativity and its balance. By translating *payoffs* into numbers, we can calculate which combination of individual payoffs will produce the highest payoff for the couple. We can sort this out by creating a Game theory chart called a matrix. A matrix is simply a table, so common an idea that you can insert a table in any Word document. So you're probably already familiar with matrices, without even knowing it.

Why is that cool? Good question, so let's look at an example of a matrix and see how it helps us to predict the payoffs or effects of a behavior exchange for a couple. This is a table that comes from a study done by Harold Kelley, the guy who brought Game theory to psychology. Kelley asked 100 couples to rate how they felt about the behavior of doing housework, either alone, together, having their partner do it all alone, or just neglecting housework altogether. The scale Kelley's couples used to rate their feelings about the housework dilemma was 0 = VERY NEGATIVE to 10 = VERY POSITIVE, kind of like the video recall rating dial we had couples use to measure their feelings about their interactions in our lab. Below is a sample table John made up for a fictional couple after he read Kelley's study. Let's call them Al and Jenny. Now take a look at the numbers in the matrices below. Four possible combinations of behavior are rated by Al and Jenny in terms of payoffs for each partner. They are all about the plan for doing housework. Each number in the first two rows and the first two columns, left to right, represents how one partner will feel if their partner cleans or doesn't clean, combined with whether or not they, themselves clean. The first table comes from Jenny rating her own payoffs, given different conditions. The second table represents Al's payoff ratings.

JENNY'S PAYOFFS

	Jenny cleans	Jenny doesn't	
Al cleans	10	4	14
Al doesn't	5	0	5
	15	4	

AL'S PAYOFFS

	Jenny cleans	Jenny doesn't	
Al cleans	7	4	11
Al doesn't	3	0	3
	10	4	

In reading this game theory matrix, we see that Jenny doing all the cleaning alone without Al gets rated a 5 by her, while in the matrix below, Al's doing all the cleaning alone without Jenny gets rated a 4 by him. He's not as happy with cleaning all alone as Jenny is.

SOLVING THE GAME THEORY MATRIX: FINDING EQUILIBRIUM POINTS

Now let's introduce another concept. There is a solution to some game theory matrices. Notice the Game theory matrix is not the same for Jenny as it is for Al, even though both Al and Jenny hate the idea that nobody cleans the apartment. But to see the potential conflict here, let's look at the totals shown in the margins: the *marginal totals*. (Don't worry. This math is just arithmetic.)

FOR JUST AL'S PAYOFFS (second table):

Jenny not cleaning (regardless of what Al does) gets a *column* total of only 4. Her cleaning (regardless of what he does) gets a column total of 10. So his payoff goes from 4 to 10 by getting her to clean (regardless of what he does). That's a big win for Al. So, the bottom line message for Al is that HE REALLY NEEDS TO GET JENNY TO CLEAN.

FOR JUST JENNY'S PAYOFFS (first table):

Al's cleaning (regardless of what she does) gives her a *row* total of 14. Al's not cleaning (regardless of what she does) gives her a row total of only 5. So she goes from 5 to 14 by getting Al to clean (regardless of what she does). That's a big win for Jenny. So, her bottom line is that SHE REALLY NEEDS TO GET AL TO CLEAN.

So if we use *a self-interest metric* (in which each person's goal is to maximize only their own payoff), logically we have deduced that AL MUST GET JENNY TO CLEAN, and JENNY MUST GET AL TO CLEAN. Do you now see the basis for a knock-down-drag-out fight in store for this couple? They'll have one if their payoff metric is based on thinking only of their own self-interest.

THERE ARE TWO EQUILIBRIUM SOLUTIONS TO A GAME THEORY MATRIX: THE VON NEUMANN EQUILIBRIUM AND THE NASH EQUILIBRIUM

Von Neumann thought the way to solve any Game theory matrix was to look at the worst possible outcomes and pick *the best of the worst*. It's a *cut your losses* solution. That is called **The von Neumann equilibrium.**

What's that for Jenny? Well, her worst payoffs are 0 and 4, so she picks 4, which is JENNY DOESN'T CLEAN and AL DOES CLEAN.

What's that for Al? Well, his worst payoffs are 0 and 3, so he picks 3, which is JENNY CLEANS and AL DOESN'T CLEAN.

So logically, according to the von Neumann Equilibrium solution, they are going to have one whale of an argument about which one cleans while the other doesn't clean.

But there's another way to look at their tables. Notice that their highest-rated option, for both, is cleaning together. With any individual change in option, neither of them can do any better than the clean together option. This is called **The Nash Equilibrium**. John Nash won a Nobel Prize in economics for suggesting this kind of a solution. Instead of the best of the worst, it's the solution where no one can make a unilateral move (independent of what the other does) that increases their payoff. Remember the hit movie *A Beautiful Mind* starring Russell Crowe, Jennifer Connelly, and Ed Harris? That was all about John Nash and his demons. If we look back at Al and Jenny's individual tables, the same truth emerges. Neither of them, through any unilateral move, can do any better than BOTH CLEANING. For if Jenny decided not to clean she'd move from 10 to 4. And if Al didn't clean, he'd move from a 7 to a 3. So it's a no-brainer. Pick the Nash equilibrium, the choice that maximizes both their payoffs.

Here's a further thought: What if we combined Al and Jenny's payoffs into one table by adding together their scores for each box, then looking at this mutual payoff metric, and maximizing that metric, the sum payoff metric? We'd get:

THE COUPLE'S PAYOFFS

	Jenny cleans	Jenny doesn't	
Al cleans	17	8	25
Al doesn't	8	0	8
	25	8	

Again, the solution is obvious: with 17 the highest rating here, they can't do any better than both of them cleaning! Just like Nash suggested. John reasoned that by maximizing the sum of both people's payoffs, we could actually measure the trust in a relationship. He called it *The Trust Metric*. He included this concept in his book, *The Science of Trust*. Trust can be measured in any interaction by how both partners act to maximize the sum of BOTH THEIR PAYOFFS, not just one of their payoffs. That is, both people have in mind their partner's best interests (as well as their own) in their actions. Specifically,

> *Trust exists when the behavior exchanges that are most likely in the system are those that maximize the sum of both people's payoffs. Each partner has their partner's back.*

When we look for a solution to Jenny and Al's matrix, with the von Neumann solution, Jenny and Al fight, but when we look at the Nash solution, both Jenny and Al collaborate.

TO SUMMARIZE

A game theory matrix or table has two solutions:

The von Neumann Equilibrium. The solution or payoff metric is based on maximizing your own payoff and minimizing your partner's payoff. Then you WIN. With this equilibrium solution, you cut your losses. You assume your partner is an adversary who is just as smart as you are and just as selfish. With this solution you get the best of the bad options. The result in our example? Jenny and Al fight tooth and nail, but they cut their losses. They pick the least of two potentially bad outcomes.

The Nash Equilibrium. The solution or payoff metric is to maximize BOTH partners' benefits. The equilibrium solution assumes that no one person can do any better with a unilateral shift in behavior. Instead, they should get the best for both. The result for Al and Jenny? They do best and create the most trust when they clean together.

By the way, why did von Neumann and Nash come up with such different equilibrium solutions? Von Neumann was a very untrusting guy. He was the author of a first nuclear strike strategy toward the Soviet Union. He did not trust the USSR at all, and he based his reasoning on determining what would be the best of the worst outcomes in foreign relations during the Cold War. The worst outcome was all-out thermonuclear war. But the best of the worst outcomes was for us to hit them before they hit us. A no-brainer for von Neumann. So he advocated this policy. He was a very influential man with the U.S. government and the military. Also, von Neumann was actually the real person who inspired the scientist character in a wheelchair that Peter Sellers played in Stanley Kubrick's 1964 film, *Dr. Strangelove, or: How I Learned to Stop Worrying and Love the Bomb*. Von Neumann was also in a wheelchair in his last few years, probably a result of exposure to nuclear radiation in the early A-bomb tests for the Manhattan Project.

Now let's go back to our research, and how we have used Game theory to understand and measure trust. First we needed to define and validate what a payoff actually looks like for couples, a payoff that could be used for any interaction. None existed before the Levenson-Gottman video recall rating dial was tested with demonstrated validity. The rating dial discriminates happy from unhappy couples, and predicts which relationships will get more happy or less happy over a three-year period. It predicts divorce or stability as well. So, what does this have to do with trust?

OUR TRUST METRIC

First, let us ask, what is the bottom line about trust? Here is the answer:

It is absolutely necessary to have trust in a relationship for the relationship to have a homeostatic balance where positive affect predominates over negative affect.

IMPLICATIONS FOR THERAPY

In Chapter 2 we saw that in couples therapy we have to greatly increase the balance toward positive affect, and greatly down-regulate the couple's negative affect, both in conflict and on non-conflict contexts. That's fine to say, but how do we accomplish these goals? First, let's officially state this goal.

POSITIVE AFFECT BALANCE HOMEOSTASIS IS IMPOSSIBLE WITH A LOW TRUST METRIC

In therapy we have to do a lot more than get people to be nicer to one another. We have to also help people to express their emotions with one another and to validate each other's emotions. In other words, we have to do a lot more than negotiate contracts for change.

Knowing that a family or couple's homeostatic balance toward negativity characterizes their interaction system means that the couple has a problem with their trust metric. So, changing the couple's balance toward negativity so that it balances instead toward positivity means that we have to help couples to change their trust metric.

In other words,

To create the balance toward positive affect we have to build TRUST.

It turns out that we can rebuild trust by resetting the homeostatic balance of both behavior and perception (often called the outsider and the insider views of affect). Here's why that matters so much. If you don't know these facts about trust and homeostasis in families, you might design exactly the wrong couples therapy, which is precisely what happened in the history of couples therapy.

GAME THEORY SHOWS THAT EARLY BEHAVIORAL MARITAL THERAPY IN THE 1970S MADE A BIG MISTAKE

Behavioral marital therapy started off quite innocently, with the best of intentions. In the 1970s, Azrin, Naster, and Jones (1973) created and wrote about a form of therapy called Reciprocal Contingency Contracting. This therapy was inspired by a book written by a general family systems therapist, Don Jackson (with William Lederer), called *The Mirages of Marriage* (Lederer & Jackson, 1968). What a great title!

In their therapy the therapist helped the couple negotiate a contract so they could each get what they wanted from one another. No kidding—one of the contracts they mentioned included his taking out the garbage Friday morning in exchange for fellatio Friday night. These therapists acted as if they believed that it was possible to build an effective therapy by creating contracts, with both partners working from a metric of pure self-interest.

As Game theory proves, that doesn't work, and these contracts will probably get sabotaged. Why? Because the couple will then always apply the von Neumann solution, which is based on a "cut your losses" metric. The early behavioral marital therapy assumption was wrong. A couple needs to have a high trust metric, which is that each cares about the partner's payoffs as well as their own payoffs. Then they could get to the Nash equilibrium solution.

SO, TRUST MUST ALWAYS BE BUILT IN COUPLES THERAPY

We think that is a rather cool conclusion that comes just from Game theory. Trust is actually a theorem of Game theory, a *provable* necessity.

Many therapists intuitively knew that a "give to get" way of thinking just seemed antithetical to a true love relationship. However, it took Bernard Murstein (1999) to prove it. With brilliant research he studied the effects of "exchange orientation" (or "E") in which people are, in effect, emotional accountants who keep track of the balance sheet of the good things each person has done for the other. He found that E is actually characteristic of : (1) both ailing marriages and friendships, and (2) impeded progress for new couples in courtship. So Murstein showed that a perfectly reasonable give-to-get hypothesis—the famous Lederer and Jackson QUID PRO QUO—was, in fact, 180 degrees wrong, not to mention counterproductive. Furthermore, what our trust analysis has shown is that the problem isn't that one must simply stop this emotional record keeping, or stop being a Murstein "E person." Partners must do the opposite. Both partners must work for the other's benefit in order to build the trust metric. The answer is not give to get, it's just give to give.

This idea can be illustrated by a dual-career couple with young children that John did therapy with. He was their sixth couples therapist. After a few sessions the husband came into a session and announced that they would be quitting therapy. Because they had paid for this session, John asked them if they would agree to stay for his usual 90-minute session. He said this would be a favor to him, so he could understand why his therapy had failed so badly for them. They agreed and, as usual, John began by asking them about their week. The husband said that they had had a big fight that week. They had gone to a party. The husband said that he was having a very good time speaking to a woman he had just met there when his wife came by and asked to leave because she was exhausted. On the drive home, the husband said that he resented having to leave. In fact, he told his wife that he was quite attracted to this woman, and he was having a better conversation with her than he had had with his wife in years. Then they had a huge argument. John asked him what he was thinking at that point, and he said that he lamented because he thought he could do better in another relationship than in his current marriage. John asked the wife what she was thinking during that fight, and she answered that she wished she had married a more mature man. She added, here he was a new father, and he still was chasing skirts. John thanked them and said they could go now, because he understood why his therapy had failed. They asked him to explain. John said, "Well, the problem with your relationship is that you have a betrayal metric.

Neither of you have established trust, nor have you ever made a real commitment to this relationship." They protested, saying, of course they were committed. They had a house and children together, after all. John said, no, trust is about negotiating and making decisions always thinking about BOTH people's welfare. Instead they had both negotiated the best deal for themselves and ignored the best interests of their partner. Also, commitment was about cherishing what they had and nurturing gratitude for their partner's positive qualities. Instead, they had made negative comparisons when things got negative, thinking they could do better elsewhere. They left. When John checked with them two months later, they were seeing their seventh therapist, and talking a lot about building trust and commitment.

CAN ONE BUILD TRUST JUST BY BEING NICE TO ONE ANOTHER?

Another way that we might assume that couples build trust, or a safe haven, is by simply being kind, considerate, generous, loving, and nice to one another. Makes sense that you might trust more those people who were nice to you. This reveals another mistake that early behavior therapy made, which was in the area of friendship and intimacy. There was an untested assumption and another problem with quid pro quo positive reciprocity: What if there was nothing positive to reciprocate? In other words, it might not be enough to get people to meet a positive with a positive if there were very few positives to reciprocate in the first place. So these early therapists invented the idea of *love days*. The therapist would help people select positive things they were going to do for their partner during the love day. Sometimes the therapist would ask them to keep their positive a surprise and ask the other person to guess, or be on the lookout for that love act.

However, surprisingly, the basis for this intervention also turned out to be totally wrong. Not just a little wrong. Two researchers, Robinson and Price (1980) did a study in which they placed observers in a couple's home for a night, who noted positive things each partner did for the other. What was remarkable about their study was that they also had the couple note positive things done for each other. Beforehand, both observers and couples were trained to code reliably with the same coding system. The researchers discovered that the difference between happily and unhappily married couples lay not in how positive they actually were, but in how much positivity they noticed. When observer counts were compared to couples' counts, it turned out that unhappily married couples missed 50% of their partner's positivity!

So therapists did not need to work at all on getting their clients to be more positive. Instead, they had to work on getting their clients to notice the positivity that was already there. Isn't that amazing? Think about it. If you didn't know this, you'd be working in therapy to get a couple to become nicer to one another when all you had to do was to get them to NOTICE the nice things they were already doing for one another. We think that's mind blowing!

So, if being nice doesn't build trust, what does?

SOCIAL CAPITAL RESEARCH

Trust is actually an issue at every level of society. Sociologists typically use a survey question, "Do you think that, in general, people can be trusted?" This is known as social capital research. Believe it or not, there are varying U.S. low- and high-trust regions. For example, very a low-trust region in the United States is Nevada; a high-trust region is Minnesota. If we were to map trust regions in the United States, we would find that, in general, trust decreases as we move south. Okay, we know that trust varies, but does trust matter? Let's just look at one variable, violent deaths per 100,000 people by region. As we move geographically from high- to low-trust regions in North America, the rate of homicide increases. But is this true of only one societal-level variable? No.

IT TURNS OUT THAT THERE ARE VAST UNIVERSAL CONSEQUENCES OF LOW TRUST.

In low-trust regions, there is:

- Less voting, social participation
- Less philanthropy
- More crime
- Lower longevity
- Much poorer health
- Lower child achievement and lower scores on other child outcomes
- Less effective interventions in schools
- Large income gaps between rich and poor
- More political corruption
- Poorer economic prognosis for the future

These kinds of results have now been generalized across countries (e.g., Brazil is at 2% versus Norway at 65%. Norway is in much better shape than Brazil)

Want to read more about social capital research? Read *Bowling Alone*, by Robert Putnam (2000).

WHAT IS A SAFE HAVEN?

Sue Johnson's EFT has emphasized the importance of creating a safe haven in the relationship. That seems to make a lot of sense, at first blush. But what is that? What does a "safe haven" mean? Perhaps it's all about building trust, which is a central key variable in social capital research.

But we are still left with the key question, what the heck is trust? Game theory has the answer: As we noted, we can create a metric for trust. And, as it turns out, we can also create a metric for betrayal. And that leads us to a precise definition of commitment, one based on Caryl

Rusbult's work. Game theory can be a math tool to precisely define trust and commitment. How?

Having a high trust metric means that both partners are doing precisely those behavior exchanges that maximize the sum of both of their payoffs.

BACK TO OUR TRUST METRIC

Just as with Al and Jenny, our trust metric is derived by the principle, maximize the sum of both partners' payoffs. Maximizing summed payoffs of *both partners* yields the Nash equilibrium. No trust yields the von Neumann equilibrium, the best of the worst.

Later we'll define a "betrayal metric" as both partners working to maximize their own payoff and minimize partner payoff, which is a win-lose mentality von Neumann would have liked. As we mentioned, he was not a very trusting guy. Also, his own relationships with women really sucked. One story about him is that after living in his home for more than 10 years, he had to ask his wife where in the kitchen he could get a glass for a guest's drink. We imagine that if he knew his own kitchen so little, guess who did all the kitchen work, always by herself with no companionship from her husband? Not a very cozy relationship.

As we have noted, a centerpiece of Sue Johnson's EFT is building a safe haven in the relationship. She is speaking from an attachment theory perspective, extending John Bowlby's idea that a mom can be the safe haven from which a crawling baby can explore the world. Indeed, the brilliant developmental psychologist Joe Campos found that a crawling baby will explore a new environment, and keep crawling back or looking back to mother if baby is scared (Boccia & Campos, 1989). This is called social referencing. Campos built a visual cliff in his lab, which was a real cliff where the space beyond the edge was topped with transparent glass so that the baby could go over the cliff edge without getting hurt. A baby would approach the cliff, stop, look down, and then look back at mom.

If Campos asked mom to look scared, the baby wouldn't go off the cliff; the baby would stop, and maybe cry, and maybe return to mom, the safe haven. But if Campos had mom look relaxed and smile at the baby as it was approaching the cliff, the baby would go right over the cliff (safely onto the glass). Later researchers actually removed the glass and put the baby in a harness so the baby was totally safe. Now the baby could actually go over the cliff edge and into the air rather than onto glass. Sure enough, the baby would go right off the cliff and into thin air if the mom's look told the baby that mom was relaxed and happy. The photos of the baby going over the cliff show a happy baby sailing through the air. That's real trust (Burnay & Cordovil, 2016).

But what do we mean by a relationship being a safe haven for us grown-ups? We suggest that one essential ingredient of what might be considered a safe haven for adults in a relationship is a high trust metric. In John's apartment lab, all the arguments the 130 newlywed couples had, below the surface, were about trust. The issue was always, in some form, "Can I count on you?" or "Will you be there for me?" or "Am I more important than your mother?" or "Will you be faithful to me?"

Trust as an issue opens up with many sub-segments like a big fan. Trust is built in many ways, by keeping promises, being transparent, being honest, showing our partner that he or she comes first, and by listening well when one's partner is upset.

A lot of conflict in a new relationship is about TRUST: "Will you be there for me?"

For example,

- Will you be there for me . . . .
- When I'm sad?
- When you have hurt me?
- When I'm angry with you?
- When the world has hurt me?
- When I'm stressed out?

- When I'm disappointed?
- When I'm horny?
- When I'm upset?
- When I'm lonely?
- When I'm feeling trapped?
- When I'm bored?
- Just how important am I to you?

When examining the arguments these couples had, we discovered three things:

1. First of all, if you have a high trust metric, your conflict discussions balance toward positive affect. If the trust metric is high, the balance is where it ought to be (5 to 1 during conflict). It balances toward a healthy behavior homeostatic set point.
2. Second, if you have a high trust metric, your conflict discussions balance toward a maximum positive payoff sum for both partners. So the balance is toward a healthy Nash equilibrium payoff homeostatic set point.
3. Third is a contribution made by John's former student, Dan Yoshimoto (2005) in his doctoral thesis. Dan interviewed partners separately to determine if they could talk to one another calmly when they were sad or angry. He discovered that a couples had a high trust metric when they showed the ability to have discussions that were calm and emotionally accepting, that is, conversations that included calm acceptance of their partner's anger and sadness (even if it was about the relationship).

WE CALL THIS ATTUNEMENT.

THE PRECISE MEANING OF "ATTUNEMENT"

The word is used loosely by many people, but we mean something very specific in our use of the term. Attunement refers to a very different kind of listening. It is not listening in order to frame a rebuttal, or even listening neutrally. It is listening with compassion about one's partner's pain. It has a lot of interest in it, which means it includes a lot of open-ended questions asked by the listener. It's also nondefensive, self-disclosing, accepting, and nonjudgmental. It is also empathetic. It is stress reducing. In attunement people are willing to see things for a moment from the partner's perspective with empathy just so their partner will not feel so alone. Not that they are giving up on their own perceptions. They are **not** being compliant; it's just that they are acting like they believe that, as our friend Dan Siegel says, there is no immaculate perception in a conflict, just two highly flawed perceptions. Siegel has explained how mindfulness plays a huge role in tuning into our bodies so that we can be present and attuned to one another in real time, as partners and as parents.

The acronym ATTUNE was designed by us to stand for:

A = Awareness of partner's emotions
T = Tolerance that there are always two valid perceptions
T = Turning toward partner's negative emotions
U = Understanding partner's negative emotions
N = Non-defensively listening, and
E = Empathy expressed

Dan Yoshimoto discovered that Attunement was also correlated with more constructive conflict discussions (as scored by objective observers), a much more positive Oral History Interview (as coded by objective observers), greater marital satisfaction, and fewer thoughts of divorce and separation. Our Oral History Interview coding was a very good predictor of the future of a relationship (Buehlman, Gottman, & Katz, 1992). Very cool. So,

How do couples build a high trust metric? They ATTUNE.

But why are they attuning to one another? The answer is that they are attuning to one another BECAUSE they are each showing that they care about one another's feelings. They are demonstrating that "how you fare in this world is as important to me as how I fare in this world. I've got your back." They are attuning to build their trust metric.

IMPLICATIONS FOR THERAPY ·

At this point the reader might be asking these questions: "Okay, so I can see what's important here. But how do I use this in therapy?" That's a good question. You may also be asking, "How do I get people to have that 5-to-1 positive-to-negative affect balance during conflict?" Here is the answer—you have to help them build trust. Fine, you might say, "Now how do I get people to build the trust metric? How do I get people to attune?"

We have developed and empirically tested methods that can be used effectively in couples therapy to reach these goals (Babcock et al., 2012). Some of the specific materials for accomplishing these goals have already been described in our book *Ten Principles for Doing Effective Couples Therapy* (Gottman & Gottman, 2015). A complete description of all our tools can be found at our Gottman Institute website (https://www.Gottman.com) and in our clinical trainings. Here is a brief guide that outlines what we do.

1. How do I get people to have that 5-to-1 positive-to-negative affect balance during conflict?

   Answer: We have three conflict blueprints that couples can use in therapy sessions that make this goal achievable, with the therapist's help: (1) For current issues we use the Gottman-Rapoport Conflict Blueprint that includes the Two-Oval Compromise method; (2) for past emotional injuries, we use the Aftermath of a Fight or Regrettable Incident format; and (3) for gridlocked conflict, which has an existential basis, we have people use the Dreams Within Conflict method.

2. How do I build that trust metric? How do I get people to attune on a calm, everyday basis?
   Answer: We use our "Guide to Great Listening" booklet and help them build rituals for attunement. (See our website https://www.Gottman.com). It's cheap, and we hand it out to our clients.

3. How do I get people to build the trust metric throughout the relationship?
   Answer: The trust metric is built by partners being there for one another, which means listening to negative affect. Accomplishing this in therapy usually involves teaching people: (a) how to listen to anger by realizing that anger is usually about a goal that is being blocked. A great question to ask an angry partner is, "Help me understand . . . What are your concerns?"; (b) How to listen to sadness. Sadness usually involves a loss, so it is productive to ask, "What is missing in your life right now?"; (c) How to listen to fear. Fear is usually about feeling unsafe, so it is productive to explore how to help make the partner's world safer; (d) How to listen to stresses by teaching the skills of the "Stress-Reducing Conversation"; and (4) How to process past emotional wounds, using our Aftermath of a Fight or Regrettable Incident. Throughout therapy, our therapists also use the Dan Wile intervention, which involves speaking for a partner who is not getting his or her leading-edge feelings across, and helping move that person from an attack-defend mode into a self-disclosure mode. See Wile's (1993) book, *After the Fight*.

4. How do I get started getting these skills?
   If you are a couples therapist, the *Ten Principles. . .* book we mentioned earlier describes each step of our form of couples therapy and how its use can accomplish these goals. Later we will summarize some of these methods in this book.

CHAPTER 4

What Is Commitment? What Is Betrayal?

CONCEPT #3: Betrayal and commitment metrics and building the safe haven

Let's get back to Sue Johnson's great attachment theory concept that there needs to be a safe haven in a relationship, one of the goals of EFT. We are now going to suggest that a high trust metric is a start, but still not enough to create a safe haven. Yes, that's really what we are saying. Trust is great but still not enough. Our data suggest to us that couples also need a HIGH COMMITMENT METRIC. What the heck is that? And for that matter, what do we mean by "commitment"? In this chapter we use Game theory to make this central concept precise and useful for therapy. To do that, we will start with the opposite of commitment: betrayal.

OUR BETRAYAL METRIC

Here's some surprising news. Betrayal is not the same as low trust. It's true that a low trust metric is a self-centered metric, but betrayal requires one additional quality, a win- lose mentality. It's not just about looking after number one, it's also about making sure that one partner wins and the other partner loses. As we mentioned, John was able to create and validate a betrayal metric. This metric might surprise you. We defined betrayal as any conversation in which the couple's rating dials were negatively correlated (over time). Why? Because in this case the relationship is not just low in trust, it is like a zero-sum game, that is, the partners' rating dials are negatively correlated, which means that one partner's gain is the other's loss and vice versa. So their rating dials basically sum to a constant. That's what "zero-sum" means. Here's an actual example from a couple who happened to be discussing his financial betrayals throughout the marriage. In Figure 4.1, the dark dots in the figure are the wife's rating dial and the light dots in the figure are the husband's rating dial. This may seem dire when you just look at these graphs, but the actual thoughts of each partner here are far more innocent and benign. She is thinking, "This is good. I know it's painful, but we are finally getting this all out so we can face it," so her ratings are increasingly more positive. On the other hand, he is feeling blamed as if she's thinking that everything is all his fault, so his ratings are increasingly more negative. Not the end of the world. Nonetheless, they have the character of a zero-sum game metric. Now let's move on to more dire circumstances.

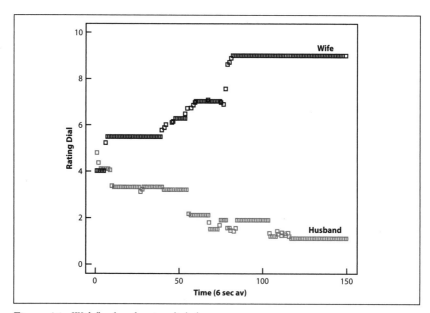

Figure 4.1. Wife/husband rating dial chart

THE OPPOSITE OF BETRAYAL: COMMITMENT AND LOYALTY

About 15 books have been written on how to treat infidelity, and yet none of them is based on an understanding about how couples actually create fidelity in the first place. We need to know how couples build loyalty, trust, and commitment, what betrayal actually is, and how betrayal emerges. We did not have an adequate clinical picture of the dynamics of betrayal until the clinical work and research of Shirley Glass and her masterpiece, the book, *Not Just Friends* (Glass & Staeheli, 2004).

The late Shirley Glass taught us that in affairs, the usual "walls and windows" in a relationship get reversed. Normally, committed partners build a wall around their relationship that keeps others outside their relationship, and inside that wall, they keep a window open between them. But when there is an affair, one partner replaces the window with a wall between themselves and the other partner, while opening up a window to someone else outside the relationship. In other words, with infidelity, the couple's walls and windows have been reversed.

PREDICTING SEXUAL INFIDELITY: WHAT THE AMAZING CARYL RUSBULT TAUGHT US

We now understand that the opposite of betrayal is loyalty and commitment. To better understand what those are, we turn to Caryl Rusbult, who created her amazing, well-researched *Investment Model Of Commitment.* We are really delighted to tell you about her brilliant work.

CARYL RUSBULT'S 30 YEARS OF RESEARCH ON COMMITMENT: THE INVESTMENT MODEL

The late Caryl Rusbult is, unfortunately, not very well known to couples therapists, but she ought to be. She was a remarkable social psychologist.

In a very systematic series of studies over a 30-year period, she developed an *Investment Model* of marriage that helped us understand what commitment is in a relationship. Unfortunately, in 2010 Caryl died at age 51 of cancer. We're sorry that we never got to meet her. Rusbult showed us that in committed relationships people invest emotionally, and that 100% emotional investment leads the partners to:

1. Emphasize what is positive in their partner and in the relationship.
2. Cherish their partner and the relationship in their minds.
3. Sacrifice for the relationship.
4. Care about how things are for their partner, not just for themselves.
5. Maximize their partner's positive qualities, and minimize their partner's negative qualities. This leads to what Rusbult called couples' "pro-relationship cognitions," or what we call, "Tooting their own horn."
6. Nurture gratitude for what is there, instead of nurturing resentment for what is missing.
7. Feel lucky to be in this relationship and to have this partner. Begin to think that *no one in the world can compare with this partner.* The partner is seen as irreplaceable. This is highly personal romance.

In contrast, the critical variable that starts the cascade toward betrayal is when people start making negative comparisons in which they rate their partner as less desirable or valuable than some other real or imagined alternative partner. Caryl Rusbult demonstrated that making negative comparisons of one's relationship to some other potential relationship leads eventually to actual BETRAYAL. This is the key variable, which we abbreviate as a "NEGATIVE COMP."

When Negative Comps have been made, it turns out that people have emotionally invested only partly in the relationship, and that partial investment leads them to eventually emphasize what is bad about their partner and the relationship, and to eventually TRASH their partner and the relationship in their minds. After a fight, or a disappointment, they find it easy to nurse a grudge. They don't make sacrifices as readily for the relationship. When negotiating with their partner, they try to get the best deal for *themselves*, regardless of how things wind up for their partners.

In contrast, in the Positive Comps case, after a fight or a disappointment people find it hard to nurse a grudge. They may try, but a voice enters their mind that says, "Remember, she took real good care of you when you were sick last month," and thoughts like that make it impossible to nurse a grudge.

Surprisingly, that means that betrayal goes along with minimizing one's partner's positive qualities and maximizing one's partner's negative qualities. Most of the issues in the relationship have become WIN-LOSE battles. In turn, this leads partners to form what Rusbult called "anti-relationship cognitions." And here comes contempt. People start nurturing resentment for what is missing; they feel unlucky to be in this relationship, and to have this partner. They feel sorry for themselves. They begin to think that many other people in the world would be better companions for them than this partner. Then the partner is thus seen as highly replaceable and others are seen as more desirable.

RUSBULT'S IS THE ONLY RESEARCH TO ACTUALLY *PREDICT* SEXUAL INFIDELITY

Here is Rusbult's very important finding: People begin the cascade toward betrayal by making negative comparisons of their partner with other real or imagined alternative partners. She also discovered that while partners make these negative comparisons, they also invest less and less in the relationship, they nurture resentment for what is missing in their partner, and they actively begin to look for substitute providers for what's missing. On the other hand, when people cherish their partner's positive qualities and make positive comparisons between their partners and other alternatives, they build commitment and loyalty. These people invest more and more in the relationship, they sacrifice for the common good of the relationship, and they nurture gratitude for what *is* there in the partner, rather than resenting what is missing. We think that they are really making a decision to stay in love.

Negative comparisons are the thought, "I could do better elsewhere."

In sum, Rusbult discovered that negative comparisons are the beginning of the cascade toward infidelity. Now, that's really interesting!

So, we thought, a person who is moving down the cascade of betrayal and who is making negative comparisons must also be relating to their partner with a zero-sum game mentality. In that case one partner's gain is the other partner's loss, so . . . each person negotiates for the best deal they can get, regardless of costs to the other person . . . so . . . they are thinking in a way that will erode their trust metric. A while back, John had the good fortune to do a study on lower-income couples' decision-making in which he combined Rusbult's measures with his own observational measures. He discovered that negative comparisons are indeed connected with a high betrayal metric.

HOW DO COUPLES BUILD BETRAYAL?

A high betrayal metric means that the relationship IS a zero-sum game, a win-lose power struggle. When partners negotiate any agreement, each of them wants to be the winner and get the very best deal for themselves. Period. The other person's benefits are to be minimized. This coincides with minimizing the partner's positive traits and maximizing the partner's negative traits. It builds resentment for what is missing, instead of nurturing gratitude for what is there.

In contrast,

LOYALTY and COMMITMENT are built by CHERISHING what one has and nurturing gratitude.

Rusbult's Investment Model means that when people are making negative comps, they aren't ALL IN the relationship. They invest less emotionally. They won't sacrifice as much for their partner. They have a kind of negotiation mind-set, trying to always get the best deal for themselves, regardless of the costs to their partner. It's a win-lose game theory metric. They will not nurture thoughts that this is a great relationship and they are lucky to be in it. Instead they will nurture thoughts of their partner's limited and flawed character and most importantly, they can do better. Every time something goes wrong (like when they disagree, have a fight, or are disappointed), they will fantasize about someone else better for them, a real or imagined other relationship. Their fantasies will grow over time, until they feel so lonely that they feel justified in actually crossing boundaries.

On the contrary, when people are making positive comparisons (positive comps), they are ALL IN the relationship. They invest emotionally. They sacrifice for their partner. They have a kind of *us* mind set in which they consider their partner's benefits as well as their own. It's a cooperative game theory metric. They will often think that this is a great relationship and they are lucky to be in it. They will reflect on their partner's wonderful character. Every time something goes right they will feel appreciative toward their partner. If something goes wrong, they will talk it over with their partner so that they can get their needs met in this relationship, not some other one. And foremost, they will build strong boundaries between themselves and potential romantic others.

THE COST OF A HIGH BETRAYAL METRIC IS A SHORTER LIFE SPAN

When Tara Madhyastha and John examined the data from John and Robert Levenson's 20-year longitudinal study (Gottman, 2011), they found that husbands in couples with a high betrayal metric lived significantly fewer years, compared to couples with a strong commitment metric (uncorrelated or positively correlated rating dials). So, consistent with the data from social epidemiology, the betrayal metric predicted lower longevity while the commitment metric predicted greater longevity. In a separate study in John's lab, Tara and John found that this betrayal metric was related to chronically faster baseline blood velocity, meaning at each beat of the heart their hearts were contracting harder. This is regulated by beta-adrenergic sympathetic neurons, so these men's sympathetic nervous systems were much more active chronically than men in relationships with a high commitment metric. Although these results are just correlational and very tentative, they suggest that we might be on the right track in understanding commitment and betrayal. And maybe why some men don't live as long as some women.

Here is our hypothesized (not yet proven) cascade of steps that moves couples toward infidelity. It is consistent with Rusbult's Investment Model and what Shirley Glass also wrote about in her book *Not Just Friends* about infidelity. Mind you, this cascade can be glacially slow, sometimes taking years to reach its dismal end.

THE GOTTMAN-GLASS-RUSBULT HYPOTHESIZED CASCADE TOWARD BETRAYAL

1. Partners start turning away from bids for attention by dismissing their partner's negative affects, or turning against their partner when the partner expresses negative emotions. There are very few attunements. Partners negotiate the best deal for themselves and try to win in conflicts, regardless of the costs to their partner. They feel justified in doing this.

2. Negative Comps accompany these events of turning away/against.

3. "My partner is not there for me" becomes a prevalent thought. They turn toward their partner's bids, on average, about 33%

of the time. (Couples not on the cascade turn toward bids an average of 86% of the time).

4. Flooding or physiological arousal occurs whenever a partner's negative affect is expressed. Hypervigilance begins. "I scan her face for negativity, and when I see it, I leave," said one client of John's.

5. Conflict becomes hard to exit. The probability of entry into negativity is greater than the probability of exit. This creates the "Roach Motel model of negativity"—they check in, but they don't check out. Repair does not work. (This is called the negative absorbing Markov state of affect.)

6. The couple starts avoiding their issues and conflicts. They suppress negative affect, but that doesn't work very well, so they have occasional big blowups (that are not processed).

7. The couple starts avoiding self-disclosure. They don't want to bring things up for fear of a blowup. So they start keeping secrets from their partner. An innocent, self-sacrificing kind of deception begins.

8. Bidding for attunement declines.

9. They start investing less and less in the relationship. Loneliness builds.

10. They try to become less dependent on the relationship to get their needs met. They may start confiding their disappointment to others, but not to their partner.

11. Less sacrificing for the relationship begins, and the partner begins looking for others to satisfy their needs. (We call this "substituting.)"

12. They begin maximizing their partner's negative traits in their mind. Defensiveness begins. During conflicts they declare their own innocence. Blaming begins.

13. They start minimizing the partner's positive traits in their mind. Criticism begins. They start taking no responsibility for their mutual problems.

14. Trashing versus cherishing begins. They start becoming contemptuous toward their partner. The couple's Shared Meaning System erodes, especially their discussions of mutual goals, future dreams and plans, and rituals of connection.

15. They start trashing their partner to others. Contempt builds even more. Deception builds. Their "Story of Us" starts to go negative in that they reshape the story of their history into a negative one. More me-ness than we-ness starts (When they describe their relationship, they use more I-me-mine words than we-us-our words).

16. They build resentment versus gratitude, and see their partner as selfish. They trust their PARTNER less. Stonewalling begins.

17. Loneliness in the relationship builds, and vulnerability to having other relationships starts. They start seeing this relationship as dying or dead. They yearn to feel more alive.

18. They or the partner refuse sex more often, and saying no to sex becomes punishing. They begin having very little sex, romance, affection, fun, play, adventure, and courtship. Low sexual desire follows. Individual porn use and masturbation may increase.

19. They have fewer pro-relationship cognitions, and more anti-relationship cognitions.

20. They no longer denigrate alternative relationships. They start new secret liaisons that, at first, are innocent. They don't tell their partner about these, just to avoid conflict and to minimize the partner's suspicion.

21. They begin to reverse their "walls" and "windows" (as Shirley Glass puts it). They thin the wall between themselves and others and open up potential windows to others.

22. They keep more and more dangerous secrets from their partner. Deception increases about minor transgressions, like a stolen kiss.

23. They begin actively turning toward others for needs, seeking what's not in the relationship elsewhere.

24. They begin giving themselves permission to cross boundaries into infidelity. Real betrayal unfolds. Deception becomes a way of life. They take more and more risks that feel justified by their intense loneliness and emptiness in the marriage.

It's a long, slow cascade. We know that many affairs do not follow the slow cascade we are proposing. Some betrayals are merely a matter of opportunity, poor impulse control, and immorality, for instance, the classic one-night stand. However, Gigy and Kelly (1992) in the California Divorce Mediation Project discovered that most affairs are not about sex at all. They are about finding someone who genuinely likes you within the context of loneliness in a devitalized marriage. So, in hypothesizing this very long 24-step cascade we are suggesting that the process of actual betrayal can be, and mostly is, glacially slow. It can also occur out of the couple's awareness. This hypothesized cascade also has important implications for what needs to be reversed in treating infidelity among couples that opt to stay together. Current estimates are that a very low percentage of affairs ever become relationships (3–11%), and of those there is a very high divorce rate (75% in a 10-year period). So building relationship number two is no easy matter. We now are conducting a randomized clinical trial for treating infidelity.

Now that we've outlined what leads to betrayal and infidelity, let's come up for air, return to happier climes, and talk about commitment.

THE POWER OF COMMITMENT IN SHUTTING DOWN THE FEAR SYSTEM IN THE BRAIN

Jim Coan's research at the University of Virginia demonstrates the power of commitment (Coan, Schaeffer, & Davidson, 2006). Coan puts a person in a functional MRI tube, which measures activity (via glucose metabolism) in various parts of the brain. Coan induces fear by attaching a shock electrode to the big toe of the person in the tube. The person in the tube sees either a blue circle, meaning no shock is coming, or a red cross, meaning that there is a 25% chance that a shock will occur.

Meanwhile, someone is holding that person's hand. It can be a stranger or the person's lover. For heterosexual individuals, if a stranger, or no one, holds that person's hand, the fear system of the brain (mostly the amygdalas) will light up, showing the brain activation of the fear system. That person is feeling fear. However, if the person in the tube is happily married and is holding the spouse's hand, the entire fear system of the brain will shut down. The person is not feeling fear. Isn't that cool?

Coan also did this research with gay and lesbian couples, before they were permitted to marry in Virginia (and before the landmark Supreme Court decision allowing same-sex couples to marry throughout the United States). He found that the fear system of gays or lesbians will shut down if they are holding their lover's hand, but only when they considered themselves to be married. Interestingly enough, the fear system will shut down in gay and lesbian uncommitted couples when they are holding a stranger's hand. For these people, this means that a stranger is better than a non-committed lover at reducing fear.

Jim showed with these studies that commitment physiologically builds the safe haven that attachment couples therapists are trying to create. John helped Jim Coan and Sue Johnson to collaborate, and they discovered that, at the beginning of couples therapy with EFT, when couples are presumably unhappy, holding a spouse's hand will arouse the fear system, but, after EFT, hand holding shuts down the fear system.

WHAT TO EXPECT IN A LIFETIME OF LOVE

What can one actually expect in love? Many writers have suggested that love fails because people have expectations that are too high. What does research tell us that we ought to expect in love? Should we get smart and lower our expectations? The answer, as we will see (based on a decade of research by Donald Baucom), is no, don't lower your expectations. Isn't that a surprise?

Our research has informed us that there are three phases of love in a lifetime of love. Here's what you can expect from love:

- **PHASE 1: Falling in love:** "limerence"
- **PHASE 2: Trust:** Are you there for me?
- **PHASE 3: Commitment:** loyalty versus betrayal

Each phase of love is highly selective.

Phase 1 of Love: Limerence

Let's start with Phase 1, falling in love, which Dorothy Tenov called "limerence." We know a great deal about this phase of love. We know that a cascade of hormones and neurotransmitters flows like a wild river through the body of a person who is *in love*. Each of these hormones or neurotransmitters is like one facet of the sparkling diamond that limerence creates.

- **DHEA (dehydroepiandrosterone)** is a natural amphetamine, creating a wonderful high just by itself, which spells a readiness for sex; the mind is going very fast.
- **Pheromones consist of sex scents,** creating just the right combination of smells and tastes, and generating a powerful attraction, almost an intoxication. We know from the research of Claus Wedekind (Wedekind et al, 1995) and his T-shirt study that only those people whose immune genetics (called the "major histocompatibility complex") are most different from one's own genetics smell attractive; these pheromones draw us magnetically.
- **Oxytocin** is the amazing cuddle hormone. Women have to secrete oxytocin to make milk flow when they breast-feed. Oxytocin speeds birth. Men and women secrete oxytocin after orgasm. It binds us and calms the fear system in the brain; oxytocin is stimulated by touch, by hugging, by cuddling, by

comfort; it means that the other feels just right to hold. It is the hormone of trust and bonding, but it also reduces fear and good judgment (read *The Moral Molecule,* and *The Trust Factor,* by Paul Zak [2013, 2017]).

- **PEA (phenylethylamine)** spikes at ovulation. It regulates approach and romance. It is the hormone of love at first sight and explains the magnetic pull of limerence.
- **Estrogen,** which both men and women secrete, is the hormone of a soft receptivity; we are receptive to this person's approach.
- **Testosterone** creates an aggressive, lustful sexual desire, and causes us to seek novel sex with the person we are in love with.
- **Serotonin** creates emotional sensitivity and keeps our irritability low.
- **Dopamine** is the neurotransmitter of the pleasure center in the brain, so in limerence it creates joy, high excitement, extreme pleasure, and risk taking. It produces the anticipation of reward; it crafts the feeling that something wonderful is about to happen.
- **Progesterone** is sedating and calming, and during limerence it needs to be inhibited.
- **Prolactin** reduces aggression and increases a desire by both genders to become supportive and nurturant.
- **Vasopressin,** like oxytocin, is the monogamy molecule in males, and it also creates an aggressive possessiveness in males.

Each of these neurotransmitters or hormones fosters a facet of this wonderful jewel we call falling in love. Only the right person can set off this amazing biochemical cascade. He or she has to smell just right, taste just right, feel just right in our arms, and be easy to be with and talk to. Like Tom Hanks said in *Sleepless in Seattle,* they make you feel like "coming home," but perhaps to a home you have never known before.

In her studies of this state of being in love, the terrific researcher, Helen Fisher (2016) puts people in a functional MRI tube. When they see a photograph of the person they are in love with, the whole septal area of the brain, the pleasure center, lights up, as compared to seeing a picture of a stranger. Recall from your intro psych class that Olds and Milner (1954) discovered this pleasure center in the rat brain. Put an electrode in it and rats will press a bar that stimulates the pleasure center. They will keep pressing that bar, not even stopping to eat when they are hungry. It's the center of most of our brain's dopamine production, which is so central to understanding both pleasure and addiction.

How long can this phase of limerence last, this sense of being in love? Many have suggested that it has a shelf life of at most 18 months. However, Fisher has found that there appears to be no limit to how long we can be in love with our partner. Even after 21 years that pleasure center still lights up for some couples. So we think (also based on our own experience) that being in love can last a lifetime. By the way, Fisher's (2016) book *The Anatomy of Love* is really worth reading. She points out that even in arranged marriages, most people still go into limerence. Isn't that fascinating?

Phase 2 of Love: Building Trust

There is a second phase of love that begins after some important move into commitment has occurred (like a wedding). A kind of buyer's remorse sets in, and the reduced-fear state that oxytocin had produced fades somewhat. People then start seeing the red flags that spell danger, the ones they were blind to when they were in heightened limerence. This explains why when couples are first ostensibly committed, they fight the most. People are mostly fighting about issues involving trust. All the arguments of the 130 newlyweds John saw in his lab were about issues related to trust.

If the couple does succeed in establishing mutual trust, meaning they now have a high trust metric (both of them know that their partner is thinking of maximizing their benefits and they don't think of their partner as selfish), then their sense of we-ness builds, and their me-ness diminishes. When we conduct their Oral History Interview, their language contains more "us, we, our" words and fewer "I, me, mine" words. They will often move into a new level of commitment and investment in the relationship. For example, they may decide to become pregnant. Then they move on to Phase 3 of love.

Phase 3 of Love: Building Commitment and Loyalty

The third phase is all about investing everything in this relationship. An ancient phrase used at weddings used to be, "I plight thee my troth." "Plight" meant to braid into oneself, and "troth" meant trust and truth. The wedding vow meant we now braid ourselves together in trust and truth. The meaning also implied, "I give you everything I have to give. There's nothing left over for anyone else. Everything, material and emotional, that I have to give, plus my whole truth, is braided into *this* love. Neither of us has anything left over to offer anyone else. If things aren't going well, each of us will talk to one another about it, because we are all we have." It is the full statement of, "I am my beloved's and my beloved is mine." Our research indicates that only now is the relationship a safe haven. A safe haven requires both a high trust metric and a high commitment metric.

What It Means to Have High Trust and Commitment Metrics

A high trust and commitment metric are all about romance and passion in the relationship. Being in love can last a lifetime. High trust and commitment are all about saying to yourself and to your partner that no one else on the planet will do but this person. This love is not just about having great sex. It is also about making love with this person. No one else will do. It is very personal. Both partners are all about cherishing what each of them has, nurturing gratitude for it, and minimizing the partner's negative qualities. This implies the following:

- Our relationship is indeed a safe haven.
- We are a "we," we're a great team.
- We are each 100% invested in this relationship.

- We each think: There's no one else who can take your place.
- We are there for each other.
- We cherish what we have, and nurture our gratitude.
- Even when we are apart, we each think of and savor our partner's positive qualities, and minimize the importance of our partner's shortcomings.
- We put a high fence between ourselves and alternative relationships.
- We denigrate potential alternative relationships.
- We feel proud of our relationship.
- When things don't go well in our relationship, we give voice to our needs rather than withdrawing, or building resentment, or complaining to others.
- We are loyal to one another.
- We construct a very positive story of us, and of our partner's character.
- We sacrifice for one another and the relationship even when there aren't clear benefits to ourselves.
- We resist temptations.
- We stay in love for a lifetime.

Back to expectations. What about this old idea that one should lower one's expectations in order to have a great relationship? As we mentioned, psychologist Donald Baucom actually spent a decade studying this complex idea, and he discovered that it was false (Baucom, Epstein, Rankin, & Burnett, 1996). To have a great relationship one should expect to be treated well. People who expect to be treated well by their partners usually do get treated well. People who lower their expectations actually get treated less well. We think this is also a great lesson for parents. When parents treat their children well, this builds the child's expectation that he or she SHOULD be treated well. So it's a safeguard against the child getting abused in the future.

CASE OF A COUPLE DEALING WITH INFIDELITY

A couple came into our lab as part of a Canadian TV show and went through John's lab procedures. The following is a greatly reduced version of the interview John had with this couple (TH = therapist, H = husband, W = wife). We offer this case just to illustrate some of the issues involved in dealing with infidelity in a couple that has decided to stay together. This couple needs to rebuild trust and commitment, and to also heal from the betrayal.

TH: So, this has been quite an experience, going through the lab. What's it been like?

H: Everyone has been very nice.

W: Yes, it has been very good so far.

TH: Okay, so I had a chance to look over your tapes, and the questionnaires you filled out. There are some real strengths in your relationship, even though you are facing a huge crisis in trust right now.

W: We are trying to move on beyond that.

TH: Tell me what your own understanding is right now about the affair, why it happened, and where you are now in your relationship.

H: Well, we have seen several therapists, so far. We're working on it.

W: No. We have just seen two ministers. That's all.

OUR COMMENT: *Clearly, she isn't quite as sanguine as he is.*

TH: And what did you take from them about all this?

H: They advised us to put all this behind us and move on.

W: In our faith, and that's what we're trying to do. We are both very devout Christians.

TH: I know that.

H: The affair is over. I have come back to my family. So I am moving forward.

TH: And do you understand his decision to come back to you?

W: Not really. No.

OUR COMMENT: *Once again, she hasn't had a chance to ask him some very basic questions.*

TH: Do you want to try to tell her why you're back?

H: Okay, I'll try again to tell you. I love your family, and our children, and I really value the kind of person you are. I have a lot of respect for you, as a mother. And as a wife.

TH: And how does that sound to you?

W: Really how it sounds to me is that it sounds hollow and empty to me.

TH: Can you tell him that in your own words?

W: I don't believe you. I don't really know why you're back. I don't know what you saw in her either.

OUR COMMENT: *They really need to talk about some very basic questions that they have been avoiding.*

TH: Can you tell her how you're reacting to what she just said?

H: You know, she was someone from work. We had that in common. We could talk about work easily.

W: I don't see why you couldn't talk to *me* about your work. I always wanted you to. I kept asking you to talk to me. But you were always so quiet.

H: There wasn't much to say about it. It was stressful. That's it. You had enough to worry about.

W: But I kept asking you about your work. I know it's been very hard for you these past few years. I wanted to know what you were thinking. But you talked to her instead of me.

OUR COMMENT: *He seems quite resistant to telling her what he feels.*

TH: There have been some real financial setbacks, I understand.

H: Yes, it's been very hard changing locations at work, being reassigned, moving, not being able to sell the old house, buying a new one that's not what we want really, deciding to remodel it, moving the whole family, starting all over again.

W: It's been hard on me too. But we've done it together, haven't we? I handled the whole remodel myself, didn't I.

H: You've been great. I know you have been amazing. You always have been amazing.

W: So why did you go to her?

OUR COMMENT: *Now they are getting to this phase of our therapy with affairs we call atonement.*

TH: You don't really know why the affair happened.

W: No, I don't. I saw her picture, and I'm much more attractive than she is. I don't get it. If she were beautiful maybe I could see it.

H: No, she's not as beautiful as you are.

W: So, why then? Why did you cheat on me? What did you see in her that I don't have?

H: She was very insistent. She was aggressive with me. Sexually aggressive.

W: So? Was she better in bed than I am?

TH: Maybe you could explain what the experience was for you, what you saw in her.

H: The ministers told us not to talk about it, not to dwell on it.

OUR COMMENT: *This is a common piece of therapeutic advice, not to dwell on the affair, but to move past it.*

TH: But it leaves her not understanding why you left, or why you're back, so it might be better to try to explain some of what happened to you.

H: She was very needy. She really needed me.

W: And we don't need you?

OUR COMMENT: *Suddenly she has shifted to "we," an attempt to include the children and to get him to express remorse.*

H: I know you do. But you're very self-sufficient. You handle everything yourself. You do everything so well. And I don't. I don't make enough money. I haven't done that well at work.

W: I'm self-sufficient because I had to be. You were always at work. I backed off because you were so stressed these past years. I didn't want to add to your burdens. And I didn't. And I hated being so alone.

OUR COMMENT: *We are condensing several phases of our therapy here per what the television producer wanted. Normally, in our therapy to help couples recover from an affair, we start with atonement and purposely do not examine the reasons for the affair. Understanding those reasons doesn't start until after atonement has been completed. Then the second phase of therapy, called attunement, can commence.*

TH: I recall from your Oral History Interview that a style of you both backing off was characteristic of your relationship. Even back when you graduated from college, and you couldn't decide if you wanted to get married at all.

W: Yes, we backed off then and gave each other lots of space, until it seemed right. Then it was right, and we married.

H: That's always been our style. We never fight. We never argue things out.

W: I always thought that you wanted that.

H: I did. I hate yelling and arguing. I didn't grow up with that kind of family.

OUR COMMENT: *Conflict avoidance is a very common accompaniment to an affair, as is avoiding disclosing one's needs.*

TH: Your conflict discussion was about you not wanting to be seen as badgering him.

H: Yes, she has been badgering me, since this all broke open.

TH: About what? What has she been badgering you about?

H: This affair. All the details. I haven't wanted to add to her pain. The ministers also said not to dwell on it. It's over.

TH: [to her] I think the problem is that you haven't badgered him enough. You have both avoided conflict and your scores show that you are both at 100% in loneliness. Does that seem right?

W: It is for me. That loneliness is still true for me.

H: Me too. Really, that high on loneliness?

OUR COMMENT: *Avoiding self-disclosure usually goes along with conflict avoidance in affair couples.*

TH: Yes. Let me ask you something. The affair partner needed you, and she was insistent on you responding to her, right?

H: That's true. She was very aggressive.

TH: Was there anything attractive about that? About being needed by her so desperately?

H: Yes, I think there definitely was.

TH: Can you say more? Tell her what you mean by that. Because she doesn't get it.

W: Right, I don't get it.

OUR COMMENT: *We are prodding him to explain what drew him to the affair partner, because this is part of the unspoken anguish of the hurt partner.*

H: A lot of times I feel like just a paycheck with a pulse to you. You don't need me for anything. You're self-sufficient with the kids. I don't feel essential. A lot of times I don't even want to come home from work.

W: I didn't ever know you felt that way.

H: I do, sometimes.

TH: But the other woman, she wouldn't back off and give you space. She wouldn't let you withdraw. Is that right?

H: That's right. She held on to me.

TH: And you rose to the occasion (bad pun, sorry). You were there for her.

H: Yes I was. I felt she needed me.

TH: She wouldn't let you withdraw, and you came through for her.

H: She had so many problems. She really needed me.

TH: And you were there for her.

H: Yes, I was.

W: I needed you too. But you always got so mad when I asked you to talk to me about how you felt, about your work.

TH: You were silent. And you were being strong in the face of all the stresses.

H: My whole family growing up, everyone was silent. It was so quiet. We never had anyone in. Like for dinner. Or friends in. All I recall was that everyone was so quiet. And I suppose that was fine, everything was okay. There was no yelling like in some families. So I am like that. Very, very quiet.

W: Unlike in my family, you mean. We are much more expressive.

H: I always liked your family. Except for the yelling.

W: They love you.

H: And I love them too.

TH: But in your own marriage, you were quiet, like in your family growing up.

H: She had enough on her hands without me complaining.

W: But I knew you were stressed. I just couldn't get through to you.

TH: So you both coped with enormous hardships, but you did so quietly, and alone.

W: Yes.

OUR COMMENT: *Here is a reason for the affair, and that could give the therapist something to work on.*

TH: So avoiding talking about how alone you both felt left you both vulnerable. To loneliness. And left him feeling like you didn't need him. That was the huge attractiveness of the other woman.

W: But I was giving you so much.

H: I know you were. But I guess that was a lot of it. She needed ME. For me. For what I was to her. She didn't need me for what I could do for her financially. She's a lot more successful at work than I am.

W: I do need you. I really did need you also.

H: I don't really believe that.

W: I know you don't. Now I know that.

TH: So, I'd say that your marriage is still in a crisis. Would you agree?

W: I would.

H: I would also.

TH: See I think those ministers were totally wrong. Research has shown that after an affair, people need to talk about it. Desperately. They need to talk about it, they need to understand it. They need to build a new relationship. And you don't do that without a lot of pain.

W: I am in a lot of pain right now. I don't know what to do to make it better.

H: I don't know either.

TH: There's a PTSD response to betrayal. The betrayed person keeps trying to figure out what went wrong, what was true, what was a lie. You can't stop thinking about how your whole world came crashing down. And he is dealing with a great loss as well.

W: That's true. I can't sleep. I can't stop thinking about you and her together. About why. I can't put it all out of my mind.

TH: You have to keep talking about it. And the loneliness and conflict avoidance has to change. But you can't do it on your own. You need a competent couples therapist, not these ministers who keep advising you to avoid talking to one another. Does that make sense?

W: It does to me. Now.

H: To me as well.

CHAPTER 5

A Good Theory Needs Data

We think that part of the problem for the old general systems theorists was that they never collected much data. **Any good theory we develop needs to be disconfirmable.** There has to be the possibility of showing that one's ideas are wrong, or the theory will not grow and change over time as new results are discovered. The great thing about doing research is that Mother Nature gets to speak to us and inform us so that our intuitions will become smarter over time. Again, as Einstein once said, if we knew what we were doing, it wouldn't be called research.

In graduate school many of us learned that it's a bad idea to do research without a hypothesis. We disagree. First we have to observe. Then we have to detect a phenomenon, a pattern in the data. Then we can frame a hypothesis.

Next we can see if these patterns replicate. Finally, we can try to build theory to explain why these patterns occur. Make sense?

So John and Robert Levenson decided to observe couples.

OBSERVING INTERACTIVE EMOTIONAL BEHAVIOR, PHYSIOLOGY, AND SELF-REPORT: COLLECTING LOTS OF DATA

Beginning in the 1970s, way before the age of personal computers, John and Robert Levenson created a lab at Indiana University for seeing couples. Every university then had at most one computer. Faculty brought heavy boxes of IBM punch cards to a window, and they would come back hours later for the results of the data analysis they had ordered. John and Robert's lab got really lucky; they got to house their own computer, a PDP-11, which was about the size of two refrigerators. All that computer did was sync the physiology data they collected as people talked, with the video time code. Couples came into the lab after being apart for at least 8 hours. Then they were videotaped as they talked for 15 minutes about the events of their day, were interviewed about their areas of conflict, tried to resolve their top conflict, and talked about a positive topic.

After these interactions, they operated our video recall dial, turning it as they independently watched their videos to indicate what they were feeling during the interactions. Then the couple went home. Later, John and Robert coded the videotapes moment by moment to describe the couple's behavior. After John moved to the University of Washington, he built an apartment lab in which 130 newlywed couples spent 24 hours interacting without being given any specific instructions. John also developed and validated interviews he could quantify, like our Oral History Interview.

FIRST DESCRIBE, THEN FIND
PATTERNS, THEN HYPOTHESIZE

In the 1970s psychology was at somewhat of an impasse. Walter Mischel (1968) had written a powerful book in which he pointed out that psychology hadn't done very well at predicting and understanding human behavior. The best personality measures accounted for no more than 9% of the variation in human behavior. A full 91% was attributable to error. Scientists call this "accounting for variance." That means that we can identify the variables that affect the variation in some important outcome, like homicide, suicide, or divorce. If we can account for a chunk of that variation, we know we're on to understanding how the system works.

When Robert and John followed up their first 30 couples three years later, they found that they could account for almost 80% of the variation in changes in marital satisfaction, even controlling for various initial levels of marital satisfaction. They kept doing this same basic research, following couples for as long as 20 years, studying couples across the entire life course, including studies of gay and lesbian couples for a dozen years, and studies of the couple's children as they developed, from infancy to age 15. Their initial findings replicated and were extended as they continued to do this basic research. The fundamental idea of this research was that DESCRIPTION MUST PRECEDE THE CONSTRUCTION OF THEORY.

They first made some basic assumptions: (1) that unhappy relationships were somehow similar to one another, (2) that happy relationships were somehow similar to one another, (3) that happily and unhappily married couples were reliably different from one another. These are big assumptions. Leo Tolstoy, in *Anna Karenina*, wrote that all happy families are similar, but every unhappy family is unhappy in their own style of misery. Tolstoy was wrong, because over the next 40 years of research done in both their labs, all three of John and Robert's assumptions turned out to be true. There are indeed masters and disasters of relationships, and masters resemble each other, disasters resemble each other, and masters and disasters are very different from each another.

Twenty years ago John teamed up with his wife, Julie, and the two of us began applying basic research toward helping couples and families. Here are the final assumptions: We can use the basic information to prevent relationship disasters, and we can turn a relationship disaster into a relationship master. So far, our research has confirmed these two additional assumptions. But this is still a work in progress. We continue to ask both basic and applied questions about relationships and families. And there are still more assumptions to test. We are studying couples with more and more of the common comorbidities that accompany relationship distress to see if our methods, when tweaked in certain ways, can help these couples, too.

As we've mentioned, John and Robert started with no theory but with a lot of curiosity. They believed that what general systems therapy lacked the most was data. So they gathered mountains of it: Multimethod data.

Levenson-Gottman Lab: Three Measurement Domains

In their lab, Robert and John sampled from three separate domains. Here's how the data were measured in each domain:

1. *EMOTIONAL BEHAVIOR: Using videotape, then computer-assisted coding, and weighting the emotion coding data.*
2. *PERCEPTION: Using video recall procedure and rating dial.*
3. *PHYSIOLOGY: Data over time.*

We can display some of these data as time series, like the familiar Dow Jones industrial average (Figure 5.1).

Now you know what data we collect from couples. Next, we can use the data to ask a very fundamental question. . . .

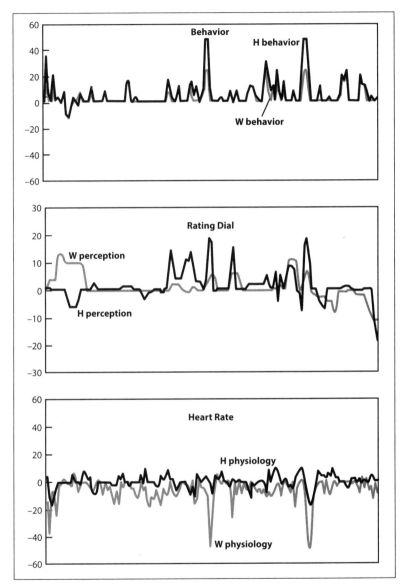

Figure 5.1. Behavior, Rating Dial, and Heart Rate Chart

CHAPTER 6

So, What's a Relationship?

WHAT IS A RELATIONSHIP?

This may seem like a ridiculous question, particularly as here we are on Chapter 6. However, when we are doing individual therapy, it's obvious who the client is, but when we're doing couples therapy, who is the client? The husband? The wife? Both? Neither? Is there always an identified patient? You might answer, the relationship is the client, of course. Duh!

Okay, so what's "the relationship"? How do you define it? What are its limits? Does it exist in some way independent of the two people in it? Could we derive its qualities by knowing each partner's personality profile? Is the WHOLE really greater than THE SUM OF ITS PARTS? That was a major contention of general systems theory. But what does that even mean? What the heck is "the whole"?

THE TEMPORAL FORM IDEA: TO DESCRIBE RELATIONSHIPS, LOOK FOR SEQUENCES

The idea here is that a relationship equals the collection of temporal forms, or reliable patterns of interaction over time, patterns that two people build when they interact. It's a very ephemeral thing. After meeting one another, these temporal forms get built rapidly, and then move toward a unique set of *fixed* patterns for any two people, and these patterns become stable over time. In part they consist of either intentional or unintentional "rituals of connection" (see William Doherty's [1997] book, *The Intentional Family*). Levenson and John found 80% stability in these interaction patterns over time, regardless of whether the couple got any therapy at all. Eighty percent is a lot of stability. What does that stability look like? It means that it's possible to actually edit these videos of couples together even though they are years apart, and most of the time it looks like one big long conversation. Yes, they have changed their clothes and grown older, but most couples are still mostly arguing with one another in the same way over time.

When two people first meet they may be very tentative about how they interact. Does one of them ask all the questions? Do they each talk equally? Are they having fun? Does one person dominate? Eventually, their patterns of interaction become familiar, and they start counting on how things will be, for example, how they will relate first thing in the morning, upon reunion at the end of the day, when they travel together, and so on.

Here's an interesting example: There are two couples new to kayaking, both paddling in double kayaks, and we notice both of their kayaks are going around in circles. Neither couple is very good at kayaking in a straight line. However, in one kayak Harry is yelling at Jane because she does not know how to do a J-stroke, but he does. Harry is impatiently trying to instruct her. He is angry, and Jane is crying. Harry tells her to stop crying and "just paddle right." In another kayak, Jody and Phil are also going around in a circle, both convulsed by their own wit and laughter. They're laughing at themselves and how ridiculously bad they are at kayaking. They start splashing one another. Both of these couples are building TEMPORAL PATTERNS as they interact.

Why do all this description and all this analysis of a couple's sequences of interaction? Well, the thought is that once we can nail down what are dysfunctional versus functional *patterns* of interaction, we can hopefully get useful interventions for couples therapy.

To help us identify temporal patterns of interaction, we will use another math tool invented by Claude Shannon, who was a student of Norbert Wiener. The tool that Shannon invented is called **INFORMA-TION THEORY.** Game theory was Math Tool #1. This is Math Tool #2. Stay tuned because Shannon's information theory will lead us to a very important new idea: the Repair Concept.

HOW DOES ONE DETECT PATTERNS IN A COUPLE'S INTERACTION?

"Information" implies that some kind of pattern exists. Events occurring over time are not predictable if they are just random white noise. "Information" implies there is at least some predictability in a series or sequence of events. But what does that mean? The basic element of temporal form is a sequence. This is what we look for. Let's take an example.

Suppose we are doing therapy with Harry and Jane. Harry claims that Jane is a very angry woman, and that he is afraid of Jane's temper. We are examining a videotape of our session, and we are trying to predict when Jane gets angry. First we look for:

1. AN UNCONDITIONAL PROBABILITY: We notice that overall on the tape, Jane gets angry toward Harry about 10% of the time. That's not very often, so why does Harry complain about hating Jane's anger? So far we have estimated the "unconditional" probability of Jane's anger (without any conditions) = .10. But then we also compute:

2. CONDITIONAL PROBABILITIES: We notice on this tape that right after Harry is contemptuous of her, Jane does get angry 50% of those times. Therefore, we can estimate the CONDITIONAL probability of Jane's anger (given Harry's prior contempt) = .50.

3. Here's where information theory comes in. IF THE CON-DITIONAL PROBABILITY OF JANE'S ANGER ≠ THE

UNCONDITIONAL PROBABILITY OF JANE'S ANGER, then we have reduced our uncertainty in predicting Jane's anger. Her anger is more likely if we know Harry's prior behavior. (We actually use a statistics test to test for this inequality.)

4. Now we've seen that there is a sequence: HARRY'S CONTEMPT → JANE'S ANGER.

5. So now we have something significant to tell this couple. "Harry, you're right, Jane does get angry a lot, but only after you say something contemptuous to her." So Harry has a choice. If he really hates Jane's anger so much, he can try the experiment of eliminating his contempt.

Longer sequences. Jim Sackett is a brilliant primatologist who is a professor at the University of Washington, a colleague of John's. Sackett realized that, by increasing the time lag between events, we can empirically discover longer and longer sequences. This idea was further developed statistically by John's friend Roger Bakeman (Bakeman & Gottman, 1986). In the world of research, these were breakthrough BRILLIANT IDEAS! Because now we could search for repeating patterns in couples' interactions.

THE SEARCH FOR PATTERNS IN MARITAL INTERACTION

Let's review a little history. How did people study marriages early on? Sociologists were the first to measure marital satisfaction with high reliability and validity. In 1938, Louis Terman published the first scientific study of marriage. He was the same guy who invented one of the first intelligence tests while at Stanford and also studied gifted children. (Terman believed that there would turn out to be something like emotional intelligence in kids – and he was right!). After decades of work and lots of studies, the field eventually settled on the use of one major measure of relationship satisfaction, the Locke-Wallace (Locke & Wallace, 1959) Marital Adjustment Test. That's the one we have also used for the past 45 years.

Beginning in the 1970s, psychologists started to incorporate OBSER-VATIONAL DATA into their study of marriages. Harold Raush was the real pioneer who first used information theory to discover sequences in marriages. While at the National Institutes of Mental Health he conducted an observational study of couples who were having their first baby. His 1974 book that followed was a major breakthrough. Just after that book came out, John had the opportunity to host Raush at Indiana University. Raush only had one copy of the book with him. Raush let him borrow it but he needed it returned the next day. John stayed up all night reading it, then got to ask Raush questions the next morning at breakfast. Later, Raush and John collaborated at recoding his tapes with John's new observational coding system.

Many of us followed Raush's example. We were all still asking the Louis Terman question: How are happily married and unhappily married couples different? But now we had videotapes. Those of us who were trained in observational methods loved this question, and worked to answer it. Later on, that included scientists all over the world.

Math Sidebar: Information Theory

All this math is really very new, vintage World War II. As we mentioned, Claude Shannon—a student of Norbert Wiener—was the father of information theory. If there is pattern, it implies that things aren't random, that there is some kind of predictable structure in the flow of interaction. To test for that structure, we compared the unconditional probability of a behavior to the CONDITIONAL probability of that behavior, with other behaviors as antecedents. There are statistical tests for this comparison. Basically, what we have done is we have reduced uncertainty in predicting one behavior by knowing another prior behavior of the partner's. To detect longer sequences, as we have mentioned, we used the brilliant lagged sequence idea suggested by primatologist Jim Sackett, one of John's colleagues at the University of Washington, and further developed by Roger Bakeman (see Bakeman & Gottman, 1986).

How We Got Into Studying Emotion

We all focused initially on cognitive problem solving during conflict before we figured out that the place we should really look was EMOTION. Here's how we got there. In John's lab they noticed that overall AGREEMENT (AG) and DISAGREEMENT (DG) types of codes were most effective at discriminating happily married from unhappily married couples. The **ratios** of AG/DG were even better at discriminating happy from unhappy couples. While conversing, the distribution of AGs was very liberal in happy couples, meaning there were lots of **AGs** throughout the course of the conversation, while in unhappy couples, the distribution of **DGs** was very liberal (especially YES-BUTs). The unhappy couples sounded just like the Monty Python Argument Clinic.

The Monty Python Argument Clinic

In the Monty Python argument clinic a man (our hero) goes up to a receptionist and says, "I'd like to have an argument." He's in a special clinic for arguing. The receptionist directs him down the hall. At first he enters the wrong room in which a man behind a desk berates and insults him mercilessly. Our hero whimpers in reply, "I came in here for an argument," and the guy behind the desk says, "Oh, I'm sorry, this is abuse. You want room 12A." As our hero leaves, the man behind the desk mutters to himself, under his breath, "Stupid git." Our hero opens the door to room 12A and says, "Is this the right room for an argument?" The new guy behind the desk says, "I've told you once . . ." Our hero says, "No you haven't." The reply is, "Yes, I have," and then they are off and running, mercilessly contradicting one another.

Here's what John's lab noticed—if you added the ABUSE room of Monty Python to the Yes-But room (a low AG/DG ratio), then you'd get the typical unhappy marriage with rebutting or gainsaying whatever the other person says, rebutting everything, with defensiveness ("I'm innocent—this all your fault), counterattack, escalation, exasperation, sarcasm, mockery, plus some insults and other forms of contempt thrown in. Also, some couples also stonewalled, especially the men.

WHY AGREEMENT AND DISAGREEMENT ARE NONTRIVIAL

The Masters of Relationship

Imagine a salt shaker filled with all the ways one can say "YES," including verbal and nonverbal acceptance of influence. A kind of "YES AND" mentality. Imagine conflict that is constructive and leads to greater understanding, empathy, true meeting of the minds discussion, and eventual compromise. And it's punctuated by lots of mutual laughter and silliness too. That's the masters.

The Disasters of Relationship

Now imagine a pepper shaker filled with all the ways one can say "NO," "YES, BUT," and DISAGREEMENT SPRINKLED THROUGHOUT INTERACTION. This spills out to the whole relationship (even the events of the day conversation), and at home these people tend to avoid one another. They stop having sex.

When agreement-to-disagreement ratio is high, WE ALSO SAW FOUR THINGS.

1. **Gentle start-up.** START-UP DETERMINES HOW A CONVERSATION WILL GO 96% OF THE TIME. This gentle start-up by the masters included reassurances that said, "We're okay" and "You're okay." It included taking responsibility even for part of the problem. It focused on the speaker describing his or her feelings and needs rather than criticizing the partner. In heterosexual couples the major male complaint is "It's always my fault." So it turned out to be like manna from heaven if a

woman began the conflict discussion by saying something like, "This isn't all your fault. I play a role in this conflict as well." We discovered that this was the #1 EFFECTIVE REPAIR, after spending seven years studying repair. Gentle start-up included nondefensive listening, with occasional validation and empathy, some of the time. What was powerful was listening, not listening to rebut, but listening to tolerate a different perception. Good listening to achieve understanding is not the same as compliance or saying, "Yes, dear."

2. **Calm and neutral affect.** When partners talked about their disagreements in a neutral manner, conflicts did not seem to escalate as much. People used to think a great relationship needed to be electric, exciting, harmonious resonance, full of sparks. However, neutral affect and gentleness, especially during conflict, turned out to be a hallmark of a strong relationship. It was also accompanied by:

3. **Physiological calm.** This was one of our best predictors of relationship happiness increasing over time.

4. **Shared humor.** Shared humor was used primarily by couples who could sense their partner's upset and engage the partner in humor, which reduced physiological arousal. It turned out to be one of the greatest repair tactics during conflict.

So, this little AG/DG ratio pointed us to the whole world of emotional communication.

Part of the reason Robert Levenson and John teamed up was because he was already trained as a psychophysiologist (a relatively new field in the 1970s), and they both thought that physiology would be an important component of emotion. It led to one of their first major findings. They discovered, after recontacting their first group of 30 couples three years later, that, independent of initial marital satisfaction, the more physiologically calm the couples had been during their interactions, the more their marriages improved over the three-year period. And these statistical relationships weren't small, they were huge!

TURNS OUT, there is only one stable dysfunctional pattern: The Negative Absorbing Markov State.

We think it is very cool that we can now conclude with some certainty that there is only one basic form of unhappy relationships. Our conclusion is that THE DYSFUNCTIONAL TEMPORAL MARITAL PATTERN IS: The Negative Absorbing Markov State of Unhappy Couples. HERE'S WHAT WE MEAN BY THAT (see Figure 6.1).

In this diagram there are two circles. The circle on the right represents neutral or positive affect. The circle on the left represents negative affect. What the diagram shows is that in an unhappy relationship, *negative affect is easy to enter and hard to exit*. We call this diagram the NEGATIVE ABSORBING MARKOV STATE.

The word MARKOV in the absorbing state is named after a very famous Russian mathematician, Andrey Markov (19th century). Another name John and Nan Silver gave this DYSFUNCTIONAL PATTERN was the Roach Hotel Model of negativity. Like the advertisement for the trap for this pest, unhappily married couples check in, but they don't check out. When things go that negative, it's as if they have stepped into a bog of quicksand. No matter how much they wriggle, they just sink deeper into negativity. It is quite probable they will ENTER into negativity. Furthermore, it is quite improbable that they will EXIT from negativity. We can compute the ratio of EXIT FROM negativity compared to ENTRANCE INTO negativity, and, for unhappily married couples, unfortunately that ratio will be low. **As a new goal of therapy,** we really want it to be hard to enter negativity, and easy to exit from negativity. Make sense?

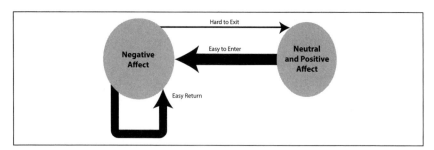

Figure 6.1. The Negative Markov Absorbing State

In fact, the couples you will see in your practice will fall into one of two interactive patterns. In one pattern their friendship has deteriorated so much that no matter what they try to talk about, or do together, they always wind up in the NEGATIVE ABSORBING MARKOV STATE. Negativity has then *spilled over* into all of their interactions. In the other pattern you will see in your practice, this NEGATIVE ABSORBING MARKOV STATE only happens during conflict discussions. That's a very good sign, and it makes your job a lot easier.

WHY? Why does the Negative Absorbing Markov State exist?

CONCEPT #4: Repair

The answer is, they are in the Negative Absorbing Markov State due to the failure of repair.

Most couples during conflict try repeatedly to repair a conversation that has started to go negative. In the NEGATIVE ABSORBING MARKOV STATE, these repair attempts tend to fail.

In most of our social interactions, we will at some point inevitably fail to connect. In fact, what John discovered was that most conflicts are a result of the failure to connect emotionally. When reporters ask us what couples mostly argue about, we answer, "Absolutely nothing!" They generally don't pick a topic and have a conflict discussion about it. We can get them to do that in the lab, but it isn't very natural. Instead, in everyday living a couple at times tries to connect with one another, and these attempts sometimes fail. That's the source of the typical argument. For example, they decide to watch TV, and he's got the remote. He is channel surfing, and she says, "Leave it on that channel," and he replies, "I will. I just want to see what else is on." She says, "No, leave it." He replies, "FINE!" She then says, "The way you just said 'fine' hurt my feelings. Why are you suddenly so angry?" He says, "I'm NOT ANGRY! It's just that you always get your way." She then says, "I don't even want to watch TV with you anymore." He says, "FINE!" and leaves. What were they arguing about? Not a topic. They were arguing because a bid for connection failed. The anatomy of that argument is that a bid to connect didn't work, and that failure to understand one another's need led to a sudden spike in negative affect (anger, disappointment, hurt, or panic that the connection has been severed). And they didn't process the regrettable incident.

Repair is always the sine qua non (essential piece) of a great relationship. John's friend Edward Tronick discovered that even in mother-infant interaction with a 3-month-old baby, moms and babies were miscoordinated a whopping 70% of the time. The moms who repaired had securely attached babies, while the moms who didn't repair had insecurely attached infants when the babies were 12 months old. In fact, Tronick went on to stage breaks in mother-baby interaction using what he called "the still face." In that break in interaction, the mom has an expressionless face and becomes nonresponsive to the baby. What happens then is fascinating. Most babies will try to repair the interaction, even when they are just 3 months old. Tronick believes that successful repairs that happen normally in everyday mother-baby interaction get the relationship to grow to new levels of meaning, something that needs to happen as children grow up and relationships grow and deepen (Gianino & Tronick, 1988).

The same is true of couples. One of the most important things that we do in couples therapy is to help couples repair prior emotional injuries, which are usually about failed emotional connections. Sometimes these failures feel like betrayals. Sue Johnson calls these "attachment injuries," and she has found—by studying treatment failures—that they need to be repaired for the couples therapy to be effective.

Negative Affect Increases in Newlywed Conflict Discussions OVER TIME

The curves in Figures 6.2 and 6.3 speak for themselves. The more our newlywed couples talked about an area of disagreement, the more negative they became. This tends to happen for all couples, except those couples who repair, and repair early.

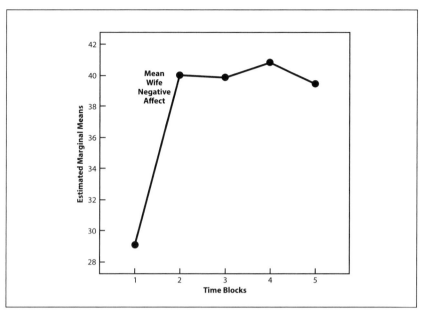

Figure 6.2. Mean Wife Negative Affect

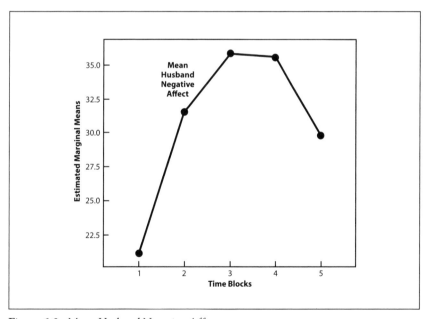

Figure 6.3. Mean Husband Negative Affect

WHY WE NEED THE CONCEPT OF *REPAIR*

There is a story about a woman who is married to a computer programmer. She says to him, "Honey, will you please go to the store and get a loaf of bread and if they have eggs get six?" He comes back with six loaves of bread. She asks, "Why did you buy six loaves of bread?" He replies, "Because they had eggs." Great communication and connection are less likely than continued connection just because we have two different brains in any relationship.

This is easy to prove. If we estimate generously that the probability of one person being totally emotionally available and a great listener when with the partner is 50%, then (assuming independence) the probability that *both* partners are emotionally available at the same time is $.5 \times .5 = .25$. So, even with this generous estimate, 75% of the time is ripe ground for miscommunication; either one person is emotionally available and the other person isn't, or nobody is home. So we need repair. Expecting communication to be easy is like expecting to hit a hole in one every time we play golf. Effective repair also potentially creates new meanings, new understandings of one another, so we grow together over time. We learn how to love one another better the longer we are together, BUT ONLY if we repair effectively.

Agreement: a 180 degree turnaround by a partner;	Repair question — asks a question to get to partner's feelings
Affection: compliments, caring;	Softening: I or we statements, without blame
Compromise: finding a middle ground;	Request for direction: trying to gain information
Defining the conflict, summarizing both points of view	Taking responsibility, own part of conflict
Guarding — a warning to back off	Self disclosure — revealing personal thoughts as reasons for negative behavior
Humor	Topic change: ending topic or changing subject
Making promises to change	Understanding, positive mind reading, empathy, showing they are grasping what other is saying
Monitoring discussion — keeping in track, addressing negativity in interaction	We're okay — compliments relationship or teamwork
	Damaged repairs: Repairs that start of well, but then continue a "yes–but" ending that damages the intended repair. They need editing.

Figure 6.4. The Couples' Repair Coding Categories

So, How Do Couples Repair Effectively?

In a project, John's former graduate students, Janice Driver and Amber Tabares, developed a coding system (the Repair Coding System) to study the conflict conversations of 130 newlywed couples and see how they repaired effectively, or failed at it. These were the categories of repair that they observed. Their project took them seven years to complete (Gottman, Driver, & Tabares, 2015).

What Does Effective Repair Look Like?

1. **The START-UP AFFECT was gentle.** Effective repair needs to happen early in the conflict conversation, before negative affect has escalated too much. Setting the stage by being warm and reassuring so that the couple *started* with positive affect was very important.
2. Cognitive repairs were more likely to fail than emotional repairs. So, getting the conversation back on track, suggesting solutions, appealing to logic, were all ineffective repairs. Repair in a love relationship isn't like repair in a business meeting. Talking or asking about feelings mattered most.
3. **The best repairs:** Taking some responsibility was the ultimate best repair; topic changes were okay; shared humor was great; self-disclosure was great ("this is how I am feeling right now"); expressing agreements, validations, empathy were all effective repairs; saying something like "We're okay" at the end was effective; and so was tooting our own horn. We're A GREAT TEAM ("tooting our own horn"); compliments to the partner; summarizing both; questioning of partner's feelings; softening anger; self-deprecating humor; understanding the partner's emotions; positive mind reading (e.g., "You seem kind of disappointed, right?") were all great repairs.
4. **The worst repairs:** Driver and Tabares discovered the "damaged repair" (which needed an editor—for example, "That

was a great suggestion you just made, but here's your fatal flaw"); cognitive repairs (appeals to logic); warnings to back off; promises to change; trying to keep discussion on track; defensiveness that justifies or excuses oneself; and defensiveness that justifies one's right to complain or express a need by bringing up past hurts, or things the partner has done wrong.

IMPLICATIONS FOR THE GOALS OF COUPLES THERAPY

Knowing that the balance between positivity and negativity is what gets regulated in family systems is useful in the assessment phase of couples' therapy. Specifically, we will look for three possibilities.

1. **THE NEGATIVE ABSORBING MARKOV STATE.** We need to assess in a couple the extent to which negative affect has become the ABSORBING STATE just during conflict in this relationship. Remember, an absorbing state is one for which negative affect characterizes every conflict discussion a couple ever has. In that case, almost every problem-solving conversation they try to have will devolve into blaming, accusing, and defending oneself, or the Four Horsemen of the Apocalypse (criticism, defensiveness, contempt, and stonewalling). That will also be true for any CONFLICT intervention you try. You'll get swamped by their negativity, and so will they. Yikes!

2. **SPILLOVER OF THE NEGATIVE ABSORBING MARKOV STATE.** We ALSO need to assess the extent to which negative affect has become the ABSORBING STATE during conflict in this relationship, but has also **spilled over** into every aspect of their lives. In that case almost every conversation they try to have will devolve into blaming, accusing, and defending self. That will also be true for any NONCON-

FLICT intervention you try. You'll get swamped by their negativity no matter *what* intervention you try. Double yikes!

3. **ESCALATION, not reciprocity.** The initial assumption researchers made in the 1980s about dysfunctional couples interaction was that there would be chains of similar, *reciprocated* negative affect (Hahlweg & Jacobson, 1986). Anger would be followed by anger, sadness by sadness, disappointment followed by reciprocated disappointment, and so on. This was called the "reciprocity of negative affect." It made a lot of sense. However, it was wrong. A more detailed coding of affect in our labs revealed that it was ESCALATION, not RECIPROCATION-in-kind, that discriminated happy from unhappy marriages. So, as clinicians, we will need to assess the extent to which the couple meets any complaint, or even any attempt to state a need, with an *escalation* to the Four Horsemen of the Apocalypse. Here they aren't just bickering, or nattering, they are ESCALATING. Now why would they do that? Why do people escalate? The answer we discovered is that they escalate because they can't get their negative affects heard at all in a calm manner. As you'll see, it's because they aren't ATTUNING emotionally when there's no conflict. As you will also see, the interventions you will select are different in these three cases.

We Now Have Some New Goals for Therapy

1. *Get Couples Out of the Negative Absorbing Markov State.* We want to help make it harder to enter negativity and easier to exit, which characterizes happy love relationships. To accomplish this goal, we use the GOTTMAN-RAPOPORT CONFLICT BLUEPRINT. That blueprint is very different from active listening in three ways: (1) there are responsibilities for BOTH the speaker and the listener; (2) the listener must summarize the ENTIRE POSITION of the speaker; and (3)

the rule is that the couple postpones persuasion and problem solving until both people can state their partner's position to their partner's satisfaction. That is step 1; the second step is problem solving and compromise, using our two-oval method, which is usually about 5% of the work.

2. *Eliminate Spillover.* The negative absorbing Markov state may have spilled over into all other interactions, like the events-of-the-day discussion. To accomplish this goal, we teach the skill of ATTUNEMENT. Attunement requires a very different form of listening, not listening for rebuttal, but listening to understand and empathize, without judgment, recognizing that there are always two very different perceptions in any interaction, and there is no immaculate perception. We use our booklet called *How to Be a Great Listener.*

3. *Help Make Repair Effective.* The therapist will want to facilitate effective repair during a conflict. We discovered that the most effective repairs are: (1) repairs that are done early, before negative affect escalates; (2) focused on either self-disclosure of emotions or exploring a partner's emotions by asking questions; (3) taking responsibility for even a part of the problem. We use our Repair Checklist.

CHAPTER 7

Flooding and Physiological Calm

This idea is so important we gave it a separate chapter. It was the real reason that John and Robert started collaborating. Nonetheless, they were totally amazed that physiology turned out to be *so important* in relationships. In their first study they found that during conflict, the faster people's heart rates, the faster their blood was flowing, the more they were sweating, the more they moved around, THE MORE THEIR RELATIONSHIPS DETERIORATED OVER THE NEXT THREE YEARS. The calm couples had relationships that improved over time. That was a big surprise, and it replicated in the next six longitudinal studies we did. It was true across the life course, and it was true for gay and lesbian couples as well. This is Concept #5 in our new general systems theory: The importance of physiological calm.

CONCEPT #5: THE IMPORTANCE OF PHYSIOLOGICAL CALM

After Bob and John's predictive research, Janice Kiecolt-Glaser and her husband, Ron Glaser (an immunologist), teamed up with Bill Malarkey (an endocrinologist) and they did a study in which they took small drops of blood from newlyweds as these couples discussed an area of conflict (Kiecolt-Glaser, Bane, Glaser, & Malarkey, 2003). From measuring the amount of adrenaline and cortisol these couples secreted they could predict the fate of their relationships 10 years later! In the endocrinology they also found a mechanism for the wide-spectrum decline in immune functioning when marital conflict contained criticism and contempt (coded from videotapes of the conflict).

WHY IS PHYSIOLOGICAL CALM SO IMPORTANT? A BIT OF STRESS BIOLOGY

Research has discovered that active listening—invented by Bernard Guerney (1965, 1991), and popularized by Harville Hendrix (1988) as "mirroring"—cannot work on its own. In the superbly designed Munich marital therapy study, investigator Kurt Hahlweg (Hahlweg & Jacobson, 1986) discovered that the active listening intervention was totally ineffective. Even for those few couples that made significant gains in marital satisfaction, at 8-month follow up most of them had relapsed.

John and Bob discovered that a speaker in attack-defend mode, *even in a great relationship*, can expect to usually get attack-defend right back or, more commonly, an escalation to one of the Four Horsemen. Therefore, the burden for good communication *cannot* rest entirely on the listener. Guerney thought he could just generalize Carl Rogers's (1961) empathic listening technique to couples. However, the client in individual therapy is usually complaining about someone other than the therapist. Empathy is easier when one is NOT the target. This is not the case in marital conflict discussions. Even in individual therapy, when the client complains about the therapist, this is usually labeled "resistance." It's hard for anyone to take someone complaining ABOUT YOU. We have seen His Holiness the Dalai Lama respond to a hostile questioner with compassion. But he's not married, and he meditates three hours a day, so it doesn't count. The rest of us have trouble with hostility or defensiveness directed at us.

Therefore, to make Guerney's active listening work, we claim that the therapist must also help **downregulate the speaker**, as well as try to get the partner to be a great listener. Dan Wile (1988) calls this moving a speaker from attack-defend mode to self-disclosure mode.

If you've ever tried doing couples therapy, you probably know that sometimes the therapist may require some soothing as well as the couple (see our *Ten Principles for Doing Effective Couples Therapy* book; Gottman & Gottman, 2015).

WHAT ROLE SHOULD THE THERAPIST PLAY IN PHYSIOLOGICAL SOOTHING?

We suggest that the therapist should *not* do the soothing, but instead help a couple to build their self-soothing skill and teach the couple an awareness of their own FLOODING and its consequences, all USING PULSE OXIMETERS. They are now cheap (around $15 each at the time of this writing) and available online. Make sure the two you get (one for each partner) are FDA approved and have an alarm you can set. Most of your clients can even buy two. We suggest that the therapist teach the couple to take effective breaks, increase their "vagal tone" (we'll explain that term later, and how to use Heart Math's emwave device and mindful meditation), and teach partners to read one another our scripted relaxation instructions. This puts calming into the couple system. It helps make the therapist less central. By using the pulse oximeter, they can learn how to create a safe haven when they desperately need one. It goes on the index finger; press the on button and it reads out a measurement of heart rate and the percentage of oxygen in the blood, just using a cool laser light. There's no chance of getting electrical shock. Set the heart rate alarm so it goes off when the heart rate exceeds 100 beats per minute (bpm) and the oxygen level goes below 95%. It's simple. Just follow the instructions.

It is impossible to tell when a person's heart rate has exceeded 100 beats a minute just by looking at the person. Research has even shown that it's hard for the person to tell what his or her own heart rate is (Eichler & Kartkin, 1994). When you use a pulse oximeter, then you can tell.

In one therapy session with a policeman and his wife, one of our therapists reported that the husband's heart rate reached 140 beats a minute, and yet he appeared outwardly very calm. The therapist showed the couple the pulse oximeter data he was collecting on his computer along-side the video of their conflict discussion. Seeing that opened up a much more open and emotional discussion of how completely overwhelmed he felt about his wife discussing selling their house and moving.

It is usually not only informative but quite a relief for a couple to learn that one or both of them is physiologically flooded, and that defensiveness, counterattack, anger, and withdrawal are all natural responses to being physiologically flooded. A couple that John recently worked with kept their pulse oximeters on in every session. When one partner's oximeter beeped, John guided that person in deep breathing and relaxation until that person could take in information again. The wife at one point said, "I had no idea that his withdrawal was due to his heart being so upset that he just could not listen anymore." The husband at one point said that when he was calmer, he could feel her pain and not hear her anger as just her attacking him.

VERY IMPORTANT IN THERAPY: DEALING WITH THIS FLOODING

THE FACTS: Our research over the past four decades on couples and relationships has shown us that one thing every couple needs to deal with is elevated and diffused physiological arousal, which we call flooding, which is not just physiological, but can be cognitive and emotional as well. It's called diffuse because a lot of physiological systems become active at once.

Here's information about the physical part of flooding. YOUR BODY HAS TWO STRESS AXES, one that is involved with the secretion of adrenaline and the other with the secretion of cortisol. Both stress axes are part of the sympathetic nervous system, which is our body's *accelerator* for speeding up metabolism and getting us ready to act in the face of perceived danger. Stresses are known to increase adrenal responses through either the sympathetic nervous system, which gives rise to increased secretions of the catecholamines (dopamine, norepinephrine, and epinephrine) or the hypothalamic-pituitary-adrenocortical axis, which gives rise to increases in cortisol (see Gunnar, Connors, Isensee, & Wall, 1988; Larson, Gunnar, & Hertsgaard, 1991); also, the adrenal medulla and adrenal cortex are known to interact (Axelrod & Reisine, 1984). The catecholamines (adrenaline is one) are secreted by the adrenal medulla in response to direct stimulation from preganglionic sympathetic neurons; cortisol is secreted by the adrenal cortex in response to pituitary-hypothalamic secretions, as well as by feedback from the adrenal medulla. To summarize, these are our two accelerator sympathetic stress hormones: cortisol and adrenaline. When your body becomes physiologically aroused (we'll call it becoming FLOODED for short), there are HUGE psychological effects that will change the nature of your interaction with your lover. Here's a summary of these effects.

Psychological Effects of Flooding

- You cannot take in, or process, new information.
- Everything your partner says or shows on his or her face feels like an attack, no matter what it is.
- You tend to shut down.
- You tend to stonewall, avoid eye contact, avoid facial expressions, and avoid all other signals that you are listening.
- You wish your partner might suddenly vanish.
- You totally suck as a listener.
- If you're talking, you tend to repeat yourself.
- If you're male, when you are repeating yourself you think your partner might suddenly get it, feel close to you, and suddenly want to have sex with you.
- If you're trying to listen, you find you lose your concentration.
- You mistakenly believe that repeating yourself louder will make your partner more agreeable.
- You have little access to recent learning.
- You lose total access to your sense of humor.
- It is harder for you to think logically.

- It is harder for you to be a creative problem solver.
- It is harder for you to see things from your partner's perspective.
- It is harder for you to empathize with your partner.
- It is harder for you to be polite.
- It is hard to recall why you're with this person at all.

FLOODING AND TAKING BREAKS

After just a 20–30 minute break, access to these skills more or less returns. We know because we've done the experiment in our lab. We've *interrupted* marital conflict, and for 20 minutes had people just read magazines and not talk to one another. After that break, when they started talking again, it was like they'd had a brain transplant. Suddenly they had a sense of humor again, could listen, and could even empathize.

As we mentioned, our bodies have two stress axes, one that results in us secreting CORTISOL (from the cortex of our adrenal glands), and the other that results in us secreting ADRENALINE (from the medulla of our adrenal glands). Both of these hormones speed up the SYMPATHETIC part of our autonomic nervous system, which is designed to get the body ready to act in the face of life-threatening danger. It is part of our evolutionary heritage. This is usually a very adaptive response. However, when it occurs during a conflict discussion, it makes us unable to listen, unable to process new information, and more likely to be defensive or aggressive. Not good.

How can we tell if one of our clients is flooded and how can we know that that's why that person can't empathize? The answer comes from the pioneering research of Loring Rowell (1986), the world's expert on how the cardiovascular system responds to all kinds of stressors. John got to take a seminar from Rowell at the University of Washington. Rowell found that this flooding all tends to happen *when our heart rates exceed around 100 bpm*. For Olympic rowing athletes, Katona, McClean, Dighton, and Guz (1982) discovered that it happens at around 80 bpm. That's when we start secreting those two stress hormones. This point is called the heart's "intrinsic rhythm," the pacemaker rate. The vagus nerve (in the right atrium) is a brake on this intrinsic rhythm, so that when the vagal brake is released, the heart's rate can rapidly jump to 100 bpm, within one heartbeat.

This vagal brake points to another part of our peripheral nervous system, thankfully, the part that mostly slows all this physiological arousal down. It's called the parasympathetic branch. If we can engage that parasympathetic branch, we'll calm down, and all those creative, logical, good listening, empathetic, and humor-filled processes will return to us again. We can hear pain instead of just attack. What we discovered is that in a structured break we can actually help clients engage these parasympathetic (also called cholinergic) processes. We don't directly calm the sympathetic (also called adrenergic) branch; we actually engage the parasympathetic branch. That surprised us.

We've learned through research that people cannot tell that they are physiologically flooded, and you as a therapist can't tell either, unless you're using a PULSE OXIMETER. For example, we've had young people step up and down a block and get their heart rates up to 170 bpm. Then we ask them to sit down and raise their hand once they feel they are back to baseline. They raise their hand at an average of 125 bpm, hardly close to the usual baselines of 80 bpm for women and 75 bpm for men. Therefore, we say:

HERE IS THE BOTTOM LINE: THEY CANNOT TELL THAT THEY ARE FLOODED

AND

NEITHER CAN YOU, UNLESS YOU USE A PULSE OXIMETER.

But you can help them get better at it, by building in that break. YOU, AND THEY, NEED A WAY TO ACTUALLY MEASURE HEART

RATE TO KNOW IF THEY ARE FLOODED. The most sensitive therapist in the world cannot tell if a client is flooded just by looking.

WHAT'S HAPPENING IN THE MIND DURING FLOODING?

How can our clients become more sensitive to their bodies? Because of Pavlovian conditioning, flooding is *also* a state of *mind*. Often it is JUST a state of mind. We can get our clients to ask themselves the following questions:

- Do you feel like you'd rather be anywhere on the planet than in this room talking to this person?
- Do you feel overwhelmed and disorganized by all this negativity?
- Does this feel like it's all come out of nowhere?
- Do you want to leave?
- Do you feel unappreciated?
- Do you feel blamed?
- Do you feel picked on?
- Do you feel powerless in convincing your partner of anything?
- Does this all feel totally unfair?
- Are you repeating yourself?
- Do you feel like right now your partner doesn't even like you?
- Do you hate the way your body feels right now?

THEN YOU ARE PROBABLY FLOODED.

Sometimes physiological arousal does accompany flooding. When it doesn't, what is probably happening is that prior conditioning has taken over. The client's **state of mind** is therefore the most important clue to flooding. If physiological arousal accompanies flooding, then we also know that if our heart rate is above about 100 bpm—or, if you're in great shape make that 80 bpm—you are probably in a state we call diffuse

physiological arousal (DPA), which only sometimes accompanies physiological flooding. Lots of physiological subsystems are activated during
physiological flooding, so that's why we say "diffuse." For example, our
heart is beating harder and our arteries are constricted, so our blood pressure goes up. We also start sweating more from our palms and the soles of
our feet, where the eccrine glands are.

Above 100 bpm our body has started secreting adrenaline, and lots
of systems are firing (for example, the heart is pumping more rapidly, contracting harder, and arteries are constricting). Your clients may experience a thing psychologists call tunnel vision, so that they cannot process
information very well. They actually cannot hear as well; their peripheral
vision is compromised; they lose their sense of humor; they lose phil-
osophical perspective; they can't be creative problem solvers; they can't
empathize; and they will want to withdraw or become more aggressive,
to shut down all that friggin' negativity. That means they can't listen
very well TO YOU EITHER when they are flooded. They will want to
withdraw, or you'll see them get mean. They have exceeded their carrying
capacity for negative affect. So it's best if they don't keep talking when
they are flooded!

A SURE SIGN OF FLOODING: REPEATING ONESELF.
When people become flooded they often repeat themselves, which we
call THE SUMMARIZING YOURSELF SYNDROME. This is the only
behavioral indicator we have ever found of physiological flooding. If you
find yourself doing this in your own relationship, you will find yourself
actually thinking something like, "I just know that if I repeat my point
of view my partner will probably say something like, 'Oh, now I get what
you're saying. I now totally agree with you, and feel so close to you. How
can I have been so blind? Now let's have sex.'" Or maybe that latter
thought is just a guy thing.

This is just like a couple John was once working with. The wife
said to her husband, "I don't feel you're listening to me." John could tell
the husband was flooded because of what he said next: "Okay then, let
me repeat my position." John said, "Okay, you're flooded." He replied,
"No, I'm not. I'm totally calm." John said, "I can tell you are flooded

because what you just said was illogical, and you're usually a very logical person." The husband thought for a moment, and then said, "Oh, I should ask HER to repeat HER position!" John said, "Right! So now breathe."

HAVE YOUR CLIENTS LEARN TO SAY, "I'M FLOODED. I NEED A BREAK"

As we mentioned, in our lab, if a couple takes a 20-minute break without talking, just reading magazines, when they again start talking about the conflict issue they become much more positive, calmer, do not escalate, and are far better listeners. At home they need to stop immediately, without either person finishing what they were going to say. During an actual break it becomes most effective if people can engage in PACED BREATHING at 6 to 10 breaths a minute. They just count slowly to 6 when they inhale, and they count slowly to 6 when they exhale. After a break that is really self-soothing, when people start talking again, they are very different. Before they take a break, it is very important that they have an appointment to check in again with one another right after the break. If either is still flooded, they can take another break. A break should not last more than 24 hours, at least in our experience, to avoid leaving either person feeling abandoned. Research shows that people can learn to become more sensitive to their bodily cues of becoming flooded (Katkin & Murraby, 1968).

If the therapist asks flooded clients to summarize what their partner is saying and then validate it, THEY CANNOT DO THIS VERY EASILY WHEN THEY ARE FLOODED! It's not that they don't love their partner enough. It's not that they are narcissists (although that's still a possibility). If they are flooded their BODY WON'T LET THEM BE EMPATHIC! Their body is saying "DANGER! DANGER! LET'S GET OUT OF HERE!" Or, "IT'S TIME TO FIGHT NOW!"

HOW YOU CAN HELP IN A SESSION

For most people, if you get them to slow their breathing, their heart rate will also slow down. So, if their pulse oximeter alarm is going off, you can say, "Let's try an experiment right now." Have them exhale while they *slowly* count to six, and then inhale as they also *slowly* count to six. They will be breathing from 6 to 10 times a minute. Their heart rate should then slow down a little, after a while. You can also help them use progressive muscle relaxation to calm down. We have a booklet available for clinicians with these instructions. Sometimes, a great idea is to have one partner read the instructions out loud to the other partner so the reading partner's voice gets paired with soothing for the other partner.

You can help your flooded clients BUILD their vagal tone, and then they will be better able to self-soothe. That alone has a big effect on relationships. If you would like to read more about this physiology, and also about mindful meditation, we suggest B. Grace Bullock's (2016) book, *Mindful Relationships*. Mindful meditation can change the way our brain processes information. Richard Davidson (Davidson & Begley, 2012) discovered – in studying people's brain waves – that people are either relatively or left frontal lobe dominant. Davidson asked people to imagine a typical day for them. If they were right frontal lobe dominant, they tended to see even neutral events as if they needed to withdraw from the world. They tended to feel either fear, disgust, or sadness, emotions that get us to withdraw from the world. So they saw their typical day as very negative. If they were left frontal lobe dominant, they tended to see even neutral events as if they needed to approach the world. They tended to feel either curiosity, interest, excitement, joy, or anger, all emotions that get us to approach the world. Yes, folks, anger is an approach emotion. So they saw their typical day as very positive. With mindful meditation training people shifted from right to left frontal dominant. Mindful meditation had very fundamentally changed their brains. That's a powerful intervention.

CHAPTER 8

Change

_____

FORCES THAT MOVE COUPLES TO CHANGE: A NEW FIELD THEORY

Psychotherapy is all about creating the right conditions for CHANGE. So, let's ask the questions, "What is change?," "What forces create change?," and "What parameters can the therapist use to facilitate change?" Aren't these great questions? They are really *the stuff* of psychotherapy.

Every therapist, every day, is thinking about their clients' needs, how they could be happier, more satisfied, or more effective. "Perhaps if he were more receptive, I wonder how their relationship would be different." Or maybe, "If she weren't so sure that the world was against her?" What to change, how to change it, these are all the everyday concerns of all of us therapists in our clinical offices. Change is what we try to work with and what we try to understand. Change is the everyday stuff of psychotherapy.

Most of the time in the "old days" when the old general systems theorists talked about CHANGE and the forces that created change, they were speaking metaphorically. For example, in their charming book *Change*, Paul Watzlawick, John Weakland, and Richard Fisch (1974/2011) talked about how illogical and paradoxical change can be. To clear up the concept of change, they said one needs to talk about *two kinds of change*: first-order and second-order change. Okay, sounds smart, sounds interesting, but what did they mean by these two concepts of change? In first-order change they claimed that individual parameters might change in a continuous manner, but the structure of the system does not change. In second-order change the structure of the system changes. Hmmm . . . let's ponder that. What were they talking about?

It was very difficult to understand exactly what they meant, what precisely they meant by "parameters," or "the structure of the system," or the "parameters of the system," but not parameters of "the structure" of the system. It was also unclear how a therapist might accomplish first-order changes (which they deemed were not as good, and were actually fairly trivial) versus second-order changes (which were the ideal). Also, their ideas about what forces might impel couples to undergo change remained at the level of metaphor. Interesting reading, but it was hardly science. Since 1974 it hasn't become any clearer.

Okay, so what do we do about this confusion? We certainly want to understand change, since that's the stuff we deal with as therapists. Well, in this book we will be precise about change. In this chapter we will also actually meet the concept of the couple's interactive FORCE FIELD. That's right, we said FORCE FIELD. We're not kidding. We used the math of calculus, because that math was actually designed 400 years ago to deal precisely with CHANGE ITSELF.

In presenting a purely visual graphical analysis of a relationship's force field, we will help you think VISUALLY about their relationship, the forces that keep it stable, or stuck, and the forces that impel it to change. The actual mathematics are not important for the clinician to understand (they are in Appendix 2 in case the reader is interested). We hope therapists will take this presentation in the spirit of fun and understanding of couple dynamics. We think we will shine a light on CHANGE, so it's not at all confusing.

In a later chapter we will extend these very same ideas to families with a new baby. What we are tackling in this chapter is an understanding of CHANGE itself, and an understanding that is precise, measurable, and clear. These concepts can be used for DEFINING NEW CHANGE GOALS OF COUPLES THERAPY, for KNOWING HOW TO CRE-

ATE THESE CHANGES, and for TRACKING how effective our therapy is in helping the relationship to change. We are going to be talking of creating our RELATIONSHIP BUILDER.

Here's how we are thinking about change. You are a couples therapist and you are just meeting your clients for the first time. Of course, you're observing them, wondering about what their relationship is like. Perhaps you watch her trying to get closer to him in your session, but she does it in a kind of attacking way, and you notice him getting very defensive. So you start thinking, "I wonder what would happen if, instead of getting defensive, I could get him to just listen to her, and be understanding, and validating." Then you think, "Well, maybe she ought to be gentler with him as well, leave off the attack. What would happen then?" Maybe you're wondering what their relationship would be like if you could help them to just make these small changes.

That's the kind of thinking all of us do in therapy every day in our offices. We are imagining CHANGE, and we are wondering what changes would be enough. We're wondering how we will accomplish these changes in treatment. That is how very concrete our thoughts are about change. In this chapter we will show you how you might use SIMULATIONS to actually test predictions like these. First we will need to be able to think about our theory of how people influence one another in love relationships. Then we can actually use mathematics to IMAGINE CHANGE.

SUMMARY, SO FAR

We've completed much of the unfinished work that von Bertalanffy started in 1968, 50 years ago. We have discovered that systems do indeed have a homeostatic set point (sometimes even more than one), and that set point is about the BALANCE between positive and negative affect. We have seen that dysfunctional systems don't REPAIR; they get stuck in a negative absorbing Markov state. These systems also erode TRUST and COMMITMENT and can even become BETRAYAL zero-sum games. Okay, so now we know how things in couple relationships can go wrong.

LET'S MEET HENRI POINCARÉ

Now, how do we change these dysfunctional systems? Part of our answer is that we have to identify the right **parameters** to change. We will see that there are six of these parameters for each partner. Getting to our discussion of these parameters requires the math that Henri Poincaré thought up, as applied by us in conjunction with the mathematician James Murray (2002) and his students. John and James Murray worked together for 15 years on the "love equations" (Gottman, Murray, Swanson, Tyson, & Swanson, 2002; Gottman, 2015).

Our hero, von Bertalanffy, also thought that mathematics would have to be involved in a full understanding of systems theory. He created a set of **differential equations,** but they were very vague. Unfortunately, Bateson and those guys never picked up on von Bertalanffy's math. Too bad, we think. We totally agree with von Bertalanffy about the need for these equations (we will call them "love equations"). Von Bertalanffy thought that these equations would have to be **linear.** If he had known about Henri Poincaré's 19th-century math work, it would have been a breakthrough for him. So, okay, who was Henri Poincaré? John started life as a mathematician, so he knew about Henri Poincaré.

Poincaré was a great French mathematician and physicist who worked on *nonlinear* systems. He was actually the real father of chaos theory. He invented this new field of mathematics when he tried to solve the "three-body problem" in the 19th century. Three centuries prior to Henri, Sir Isaac Newton, the great British physicist, developed his whole theory of gravitation considering only two bodies, the Sun and another planet like ours, making the assumption that the effects of the other planets (and our moon) were negligible. He just hoped that adding a third body or more to the gravitational equations would be just a minor fix to his grand theory. But the actual math for including a third body like the moon remained unsolved for centuries. Solving that math would lead to a revolutionary breakthrough in how we understand the universe.

As a young man Poincaré entered a contest to solve the three-body problem, and to do so he invented a whole new branch of math. A lot of money was at stake in that contest. He won the prize, and got lots of congratulations, but not before he himself discovered a big mistake he'd made. Yikes! He frantically bought up all the printed books that contained his mistake and corrected it. Then it was republished. He paid for all of that. There went the prize money. Yet what he'd discovered was totally revolutionary.

He actually realized that the system involving three planetary bodies can *appear* periodic and stable, just like the planets going around the sun, but—and this was uncanny—the system can still be totally unstable. Figure 8.1 is just one example of the kinds of potentially chaotic orbits created by gravitational forces acting on a system with two suns and with a much smaller third body right in the system. The third planetary object (even if it's tiny) can go into wild orbits. These wild orbits come precisely from Newton's famous gravitation law (the inverse square law). The system LOOKS really stable. But it's not.

With the right perturbations, even with just three bodies, these planetary motions *can* get really wild. In fact, there is good *evidence* suggesting that our solar system is, in fact, a chaotic system (Peterson [1993] proved it). Under the right perturbations, planetary motion IN OUR SOLAR SYSTEM can become disrupted and chaotic. Hopefully that will never happen to our solar system, but it *can* happen. Shocking, isn't it? Well, just think of what happens to a couple when a baby arrives. Yes, that's our equivalent of the three-body problem (see our 2008 book, *And Baby Makes Three*).

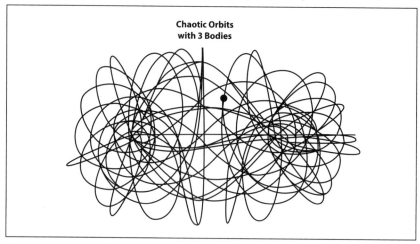

Figure 8.1. Chaotic Orbits With 3 Bodies

As we will see in Chapter 14 the mother-father-baby system will prove to be as *potentially* chaotic as Figure 8.1. As Poincaré moved from two to three bodies, a whole new world opened up to him. That will also be the case when we add the baby to the couple.

The beautiful **nonlinear** math that Poincaré developed languished for more than half a century until the development of electronic computing. Then, in the 1950s, Edward Lorenz—a meteorologist—rediscovered Poincaré's discovery of "sensitivity to initial conditions," which is one characteristic of nonlinear chaotic systems. That sensitivity means that small perturbations can get magnified over time. This became famous when Lorenz discovered his renowned butterfly effect. It's called the butterfly effect because meteorologist Lorenz suggested that even a butterfly moving its wings in South America could potentially trigger a hurricane in Florida. Small disturbances in a chaotic system can get amplified in an unpredictable way, with possibly catastrophic consequences.

Most nonlinear systems usually are NOT chaotic, though. In fact they tend to be stable, and very orderly, and to have very nice regulatory feedback processes. It's especially true that very few *biological* systems are actually chaotic. Most are amazingly regulated, but they are also nonlinear. Poincaré showed us how to study these systems, and how to *use graphics* to understand these nonlinear regulated systems. The graphics mean we can VISUALIZE the solutions. Very cool. We don't need to go over the math; we can just present the diagrams, and these diagrams are very intuitive.

MATH TOOL #3: WHAT THE *NONLINEAR* MATH ACCOMPLISHES

First of all, Poincaré's math permits stable solutions that represent homeostasis. Linear equations don't accomplish this, because they tend to be unstable. So, linear models are terrible models for describing regulated systems. The nonlinear math also includes the possibility for FEEDBACK. So, nonlinear differential equations can fully describe a couple's or family's interactive system, and it can include *feedback* into the system.

That was essential to von Bertalanffy's fundamental diagram, which we showed the reader in Chapter 1. As you will see, the feedback takes the form of *repair* for modifying negative affect, and *turning toward or away* (positive or negative damping) for modifying positive affect. More about that feedback part later. It's very relevant for therapy.

But first, what are the data for these nonlinear equations? The specific emotion coding that John developed can create a kind of **Dow Jones** of any couple's conversation. That affective behavior, physiology, and the rating dial will be our basic data.

For example, three graphs are shown in Figures 8.2–8.4. Each one represents a different couple and their cumulative positive MINUS negative affect over time during their conversation. If the graph goes up over time, then positive affect exceeded negative affect. So, as they talk we are scoring their conversation. This isn't a new idea. In fact, there was once a *Saturday Night Live* skit about Olympic judges scoring a couple for how effective they were at ruining their relationship. In their skit, the husband came in to breakfast and sat down, pouring his own coffee. Then the wife came in and sat down, pouring her own coffee. The judges said something like, "They get 6 points for ignoring one another and not pouring

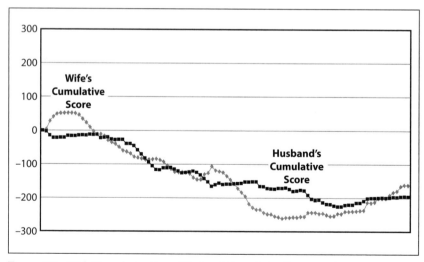

Figure 8.2. Wife Cumulative Score/Husband Cumulative Score graph

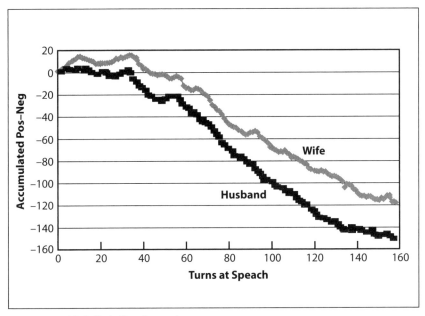

Figure 8.3. High Risk Couple graph

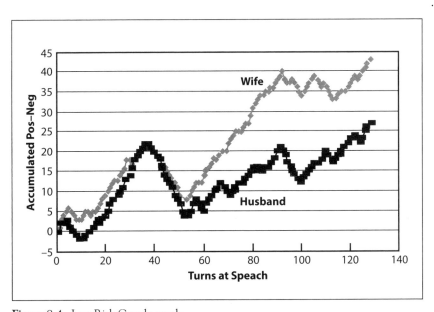

Figure 8.4. Low Risk Couple graph

103

the coffee for their partner." Then he opened the newspaper, blocking her out visually, and the judges said, "He gets a 10 for that move. He has completely shut her out! Well done." That's kind of what we did, scoring affect as positive and negative. Except we were able to weight those positive codes more heavily if they were predictive of happiness or stability, and weight those negative codes (like the Four Horsemen) if they were predictive of unhappiness or instability. So we had a slight advantage over the Saturday Night Live judges.

If the cumulative POSITIVE-MINUS-NEGATIVE went down, then negative affect exceeded positive affect. If the cumulative POSITIVE-MINUS-NEGATIVE went up, then positive affect exceeded negative affect. Figure 8.2 shows an actual example of a couple's SPAFF Dow Jones curve of a conflict conversation for an unhappy couple.

What John and Robert's lab discovered was that there was indeed a low-risk and a high-risk pattern to these Dow Jones kinds of cumulative curves (Figures 8.3 and 8.4). Not a very complicated finding, but quite lovely (we think). We are mapping the flow of emotions between people, and that flow will eventually lead us to be able to discuss the emotion force field that governs stability and change in the couple's system.

Nothing really new here. This is precisely **the balance theory of affect** that we talked about when we discussed homeostasis. Remember the 5 to 1 ratio? Fine, so what do we gain by using the time series and coupling them with the equations?

What we gain is really quite amazing, even spectacular, and it comes from the math Poincaré invented and the equations our colleague, the mathematician James Murray, and his students developed with us. We will talk about just the behavior coding part of what goes into these love equations, but it's important to recognize that the data could just as well be the video recall rating dial, and also physiological data. One day, we are hoping, getting these data will be easy to do in a clinician's office as part of the assessment of a couple's relationship.

To begin with, the math added a very simple idea: **HUSBAND-WIFE PHASE SPACE.** That sounds highfalutin', but it's just a graph. By the way, this idea also works for same-sex couples, but the language

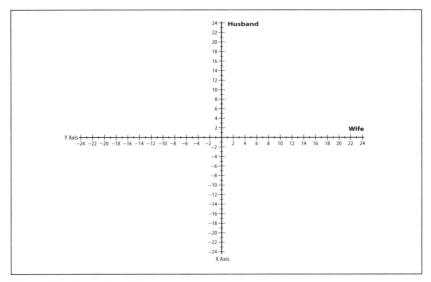

Figure 8.5. Phase Space Chart

is easier using "husband" and "wife." We'll talk about same-sex couples soon. All we will do to create PHASE SPACE is to plot the husband as the y-axis and the wife as the x-axis (as in Figure 8.5).

Now let's think about the four quadrants of this husband-wife phase space. We are going to talk about the COUPLE'S PHASE SPACE POR-TRAIT (Figure 8.6).

In the upper-right quadrant everyone is positive, THEY ARE BOTH SMILING. Both people are just like two happy bunnies nibbling on a huge carrot (Figure 8.7). Life can't get any better than this for our two bunnies. As we will eventually see, some couples are drawn to this positive-positive quadrant because there's AN ATTRACTOR in the positive-positive quadrant forcing them to move there. However, if the data are drawn toward an attractor in the lower left, the negative-negative quadrant, it is like two very unhappy bunnies, bunnies caught in a terri-ble thunderstorm. Both bunnies are frowning, looking sad.

That's as complex as you have to get to understand the math of these phase space diagrams. Our ailing couples we see in therapy are just like the two bunnies in a storm. So, what's our therapeutic goal? Help them to be

Figure 8.6. Phase Space Chart with photo quadrants

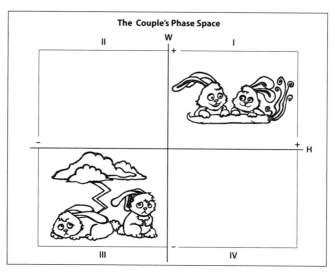

Figure 8.7. Bunnies in Phase Space. Illustrations © Julia Eppes.

like two bunnies happily ensconced in carrot land. **THAT'S AS MUCH MATH AS YOU NEED TO KNOW.** (If the reader would like to know more about the math, see Appendix 2, or read John's book *Principia Amoris* [Gottman, 2015], or *The Mathematics of Marriage* [Gottman et al., 2002].)

The real therapy question is how do we get our two bunnies to carrot land? So that's all there is to phase space. Just asking that question takes us a long way toward understanding what **change** is all about.

THE FORCES THAT CREATE STABILITY AND CHANGE

So, here's some news. We can't actually talk about CHANGE without also talking about STABILITY. Does that make sense? If we don't know the ways in which the couple's system is stable, we can't know how to create change. To understand stability, we need to introduce the idea of a couple's "phase space portrait."

What is the couple's PHASE SPACE PORTRAIT? Well, to describe CHANGE, the couple's phase space portrait has to depict their FLOW LINES OF CHANGE. It is graphically depicting the flow of emotions between people. It has to describe how people *move* through an interaction, how they change over time, and it has to describe the places to which they are drawn. Change is now redefined to be all about FLOW lines on our graph in phase space.

To get this phase space portrait and the associated flow lines, we had to view a couple's interaction as a process in which each person tries to influence the emotions of the other, to get that other person to move away from that person's perspective and closer to the partner's perspective. So interaction can be viewed in terms of SOCIAL INFLUENCE. Well, how do people in a relationship mostly move one another? They do so with EMOTION, a word that also has the word MOTION in it.

Therefore, to compute force fields and flow lines of emotional change, we need to have a SOCIAL INFLUENCE THEORY for fitting curves in phase space that also map where the system is stable. To compute those stable curves (called "null clines"), we needed a theory of social influence. After four years of thought, John realized that our basic social influence theory could come from the fact that in John's data NEGATIVE AFFECT had much more power to do harm than POSITIVE AFFECT had power to do good. Our best predictions arose when negative affect was high. We knew this because in discriminating the masters from the disasters of relationships and trying to predict stability or divorce, we found that during conflict discussions, couples needed that famous 5-to-1 ratio of positive to negative to predict future stability and happiness. To keep things good over time, it took five positives during the conversation to offset the power of just one negative. Negative affect was very powerful, in fact, five times as powerful as positive affect. So negative affect was a much better predictor than positive affect.

That's precisely where the NONLINEARITY comes into our nonlinear LOVE EQUATIONS, because the effects of negativity are more powerful than the effects of positivity. That can be described in an influence function with two straight lines for influencing the partner, one line for positive affect and another line for negative affect. Two lines, so we call it bi-linear.

In our **bi-linear** social influence theory we assumed that positive affect has a positive effect on partner and negative affect has a negative

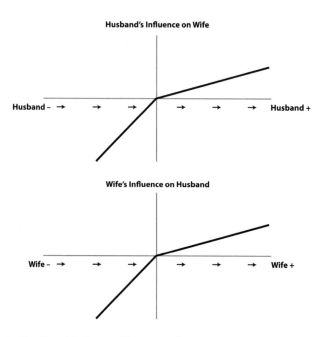

Figure 8.8. Our Social Influence Theory graph

effect. BUT we also assumed that negative affect is more powerful than positive affect, and zero influence comes from no affect.

We can actually plot these influence functions (Figure 8.8).

Take a close look at these graphs, because we will be seeing more of them. Let's take a little time and explain them. Along the horizontal line, the x-axis, one partner ranges from positive affect (on the right) through negative affect (on the left). The vertical axis (the y-axis) tells us how us how one partner's affect influences the other partner. At the zero origin, we assume there is no affect, so there is no influence. As a person starts becoming more positive (moving to the right of the origin), the line goes up, so positive affect is assumed to have a positive influence on the partner. As a person starts becoming more negative (moving to the left of the origin), the line goes down, so negative affect is assumed to have a negative influence on the partner. Here's the kicker: Negative affect is assumed to have a more powerful negative result on the partner than positive affect has a positive result. The slope is steeper in the negative affect ranges than in the positive affect ranges. That's the basic assumption of our equations.

ADDING FEEDBACK TO SOCIAL INFLUENCE

Next we decided to add FEEDBACK in the couple's system, including repair and damping. What are these?

> **Repair:** *After a threshold of negativity, we assumed that maybe people could REPAIR the interaction, making it more positive, thus downregulating negativity. We also needed to know when repair kicked in, so we needed a THRESHOLD FOR REPAIR. Repair can fail, either by being too late or by being a failed repair, which makes interaction even more negative.*

> **Damping, turning toward:** *After a threshold of positivity it's possible to amplify positivity by the partner TURNING TOWARD (like using shared humor), or to downregulate the influence of positivity*

by the partner TURNING AWAY from or AGAINST the other partner. Also, the threshold of modifying positive influence can come early or late.

Here, in Figure 8.9, is a picture of our *full* influence function, with POSITIVE and NEGATIVE slopes, and FEEDBACK parts that include REPAIR and DAMPING. Notice also that there are two parts to repair and damping, a threshold at which each begins, and the size or effectiveness of repair or damping. There are some big surprises about repair and damping that emerge from the math. One is that happy-stable couples repair early. That confirms what we discovered by actually coding REPAIR attempts by newlyweds, but here it is corroborated by the math (Gottman, Driver, and Tabares, 2015). Also, the math shows that if a partner repairs early, the repair doesn't have to be very big. If one repairs late, the repair had better be large; unfortunately, large repairs also have the potential to be destabilizing. Damping can also have some interesting properties. As we showed in our book *The Mathematics of Marriage* (Gottman et al., 2002), for some couples strong early damping can create a positive attractor where there might have been none. For other couples, late and weak damping can allow positive affect to build.

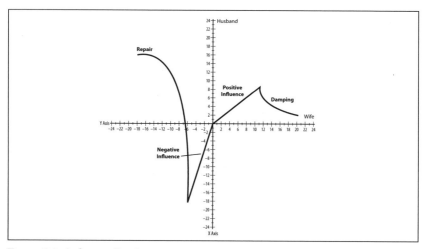

Figure 8.9. Influence Graph

WE ACTUALLY GET INTERACTIVE *FORCE FIELDS*

The math also gives us a very cool phase space portrait. *It is a vector emotional force and emotional energy field around every attractor, or an emotion flow diagram* in which a vector has direction, not just magnitude. Therefore, our new general systems theory (love equations) also determined *a vector force that has energy and flow lines, and arrows that show how things will flow AND CHANGE in the relationship terrain (PHASE SPACE).* The arrows and lines define the FLOW in phase space. This FLOW in phase space is very much like the flow of a river. The force that moves the couple along their emotional flow lines in their phase space portrait is the natural flow of their emotions from one person to the other. Emotional interactions create the force field that impels the couple toward their attractors. The attractors are the points of stability of the system, so we define BOTH stability and change in the couple system.

We think that this is amazing! We are saying that when two people interact they create an emotional energy force field between them. Note that this is not a New Age woo woo concept, but an actual emotion force field. It's not made up; the math implies that there's a force field surrounding the flow of emotion from one person to another. We haven't actually detected it with measuring instruments (except for physiology), but it could be a portrait of something physically real. However, that is pure speculation.

Figure 8.10 shows an actual force field portrait for a whole group of really **HAPPY STABLE MARRIAGES** in one of our studies. This is A GROUP PHASE SPACE PORTRAIT. The darker lines are what mathematicians call "null clines." Null clines are where nothing changes for that partner, the stable curves. Remember, we are saying that we cannot understand what impels them toward change without a knowledge of their stabilities. That's a part of the math. In this diagram, two null clines meet and form a POSITIVE ATTRACTOR in the positive-positive quadrant. When we said that to understand CHANGE we needed to also understand STABILITY, we really ment these null clines are the stabilities of the system. The stable places on the phase space portrait are the attractors, where the null clines meet. The attractor draws the couple toward it, just as our planet draws objects toward it, like an apple falling from a tree.

The arrows move on *emotional force field flow lines*. They move the couple toward their attractor (a stable steady state). As we mentioned, the dotted lines in the figure are null clines. They are where either the husband or the wife stay constant, and they are determined by our influence functions. The point at which these two null cline curves intersect is a steady state of the system. It can be either a stable steady state (*an attractor*) or an unsteady stable state (*a repeller*). The repellor forces flow away from it.

That's a lot to take in, but that's the graphics our equations generate. These ATTRACTORS are the SOLUTIONS to our love equations. Figure 8.10 is a composite of the phase space portrait of happy, stable marriages. They have a positive stable attractor in the positive-positive quadrant. It turns out that happy, stable couples are INDEED JUST like two bunnies chewing on a huge carrot.

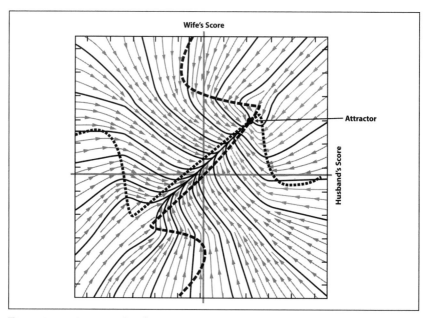

Figure 8.10. Attractor Graph

WHAT DOES IT MEAN TO HAVE A POSITIVE ATTRACTOR DURING CONFLICT?

It means that no matter where the couple starts their conflict conversation, they will eventually be drawn BY THE EMOTION FLOW LINES to their positive attractors, and the flow diagram represents how they move there. The dynamics are set up so that they will be okay. They can even have a negative start-up, and it won't matter. They'll be okay. If we have also computed their phase space diagram in their events-of-the-day conversation or their positive topic conversation, and they also have a positive attractor there, it means that their ability to connect emotionally during nonconflict times will also be okay. Everywhere they interact, they will eventually become those two bunnies chewing on a carrot again.

This would be a huge strength of our couple, revealed by their phase space force field portrait. On the other hand, suppose they had a positive attractor during the events-of-the-day conversation, but a negative attractor during the conflict conversation. That would suggest that their friendship was probably okay, but they really need an effective conflict blueprint. During conflict they typically wind up as two bunnies in a thunderstorm (no carrot). So the phase space portrait tells us what we need to work on in therapy. Can you see what we gain from an understanding of a couple's emotional phase space portrait?

WHAT DOES IT MEAN TO HAVE A POSITIVE ATTRACTOR IN PHYSIOLOGY?

We can also use the pulse oximeter heart rate and oxygen concentration data to get a phase space portrait. But what does that actually mean? Using their pulse oximeter data, a positive attractor would suggest that there is a physiologically CALM PLACE, a physiological safe haven in their relationship. They are able to create the biological component of this safe haven. That's pretty cool. The relationship is, to some extent, a port in a storm.

Here's what the math actually taught us:

1. Happily married couples **repair** at lower thresholds of negativity than unhappily married couples. They don't wait until the interaction gets too negative before repairing. That was a big surprise. There was an old maxim that a good marriage was created by the number of tongue bites a couple had, meaning that they waited, just enduring their partner's negative affect. Not so, said our love equations.

2. Happily married couples have less emotional inertia than unhappily married couples. Emotional inertia was one of the parameters of the influence functions. If one has a lot of emotional inertia, it makes one less open to the partner's influence. One is like a Mack truck, hard to get moving or to slow down.

3. People have more emotional inertia during negative affect than during positive affect.

4. Happily married couples have more positive start-up than unhappily married couples. They start more positively, even before social influence happens.

5. Happily married couples have more positively *influenced* steady states than unhappily married couples. Not only do they start more positively, they also get moved more each other toward even greater positivity.

6. The difference between uninfluenced and influenced steady states means that a person is somehow better in a good relationship, better than where that person started initially.

7. As you'll see later, mismatched influence functions pose a very special challenge for a relationship, and for the couple's therapist. They also EXPLAIN the famous demand-withdraw asymmetry in heterosexual couples (more about that in Chapter 9).

8. Feminist theory claims that there needs to be a fair balance of power in a relationship for women to feel respected. We can

now validate that assumption with our **fairness metric**, which examines how much power each partner has to influence the other, with either positive or negative affect. We feminists were right! When a relationship is balanced in power and influence, it tends to be a happier relationship.

9. Also, it's easier to build the trust metric when there is fairness (equal power across partners).

These love equation results were consistent with actual observational coding of REPAIR by the Driver-Tabares study of newlyweds. Those results were reported in a recent article by John, Janice Driver, and Amber Tabares (Gottman et al., 2015).

A CLINICAL CASE

In the phase space plot in Figure 8.11 we see an unhappily married couple. Using our coding of their interaction, we have fitted the equations to their conflict discussion. We've used their emotion data, coded with John's specific emotions coding system (abbreviated "SPAFF"). The heavier lines are parts of their null clines, and where they cross are the steady states (attractors). Notice that the arrows are all heading toward the negative-negative quadrant. The darker shades in the diagram are valleys, or minimum values. This couple has negative start-ups, high emotional inertias, and strong negative influence slopes; they repair late and damp early. Their force field will draw them strongly toward the negative-negative quadrant and their negative stable attractors.

There's a new thing in this diagram. We have used the math program called Mathematica to plot this diagram with SIMULATION SLIDING BUTTONS on the left. We can move these buttons away from the actual data to IMAGINE what their phase space portrait might be if the parameters of the math model were different.

In Figure 8.12 we see this same couple, but the data come from their events-of-the-day conversation. In that conversation, they have positive

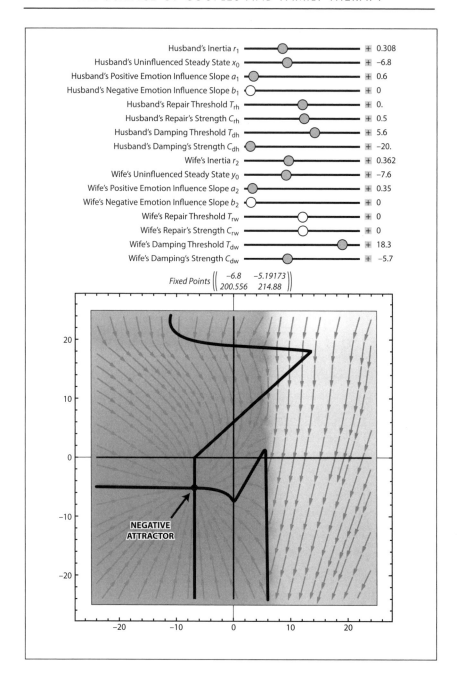

Figure 8.11. Negative Attractor Graph

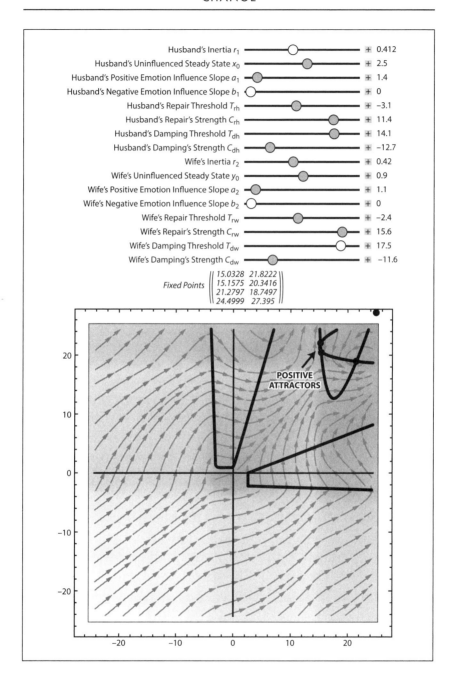

Figure 8.12. Positive Attractor Graph

start-ups, low emotional inertias, and strong positive influence slopes; they repair early and damp late. Their force field will draw them strongly toward attractors in the positive-positive quadrant. Notice that the force fields draw them to the positive-positive quadrant. Okay, so negative affect hasn't spilled over from conflict; it hasn't become pervasive for this couple. That's a strength in this relationship.

So they have a positive attractor but only when they are not in conflict. It means that they do not have pervasive negative states. They can be friends and wind up in a good place, so long as they don't conflict. We conclude that they really need ONLY a conflict blueprint. Isn't that informative? It doesn't mean the therapy will be a cakewalk, but it'll be easier than if their negative attractors were pervasive throughout their entire relationship and we have negative affect spillover.

SIMULATION: A QUANTITATIVE FANTASY

As we noted, to the left of the phase space diagram in Figures 8.11 and 8.12 there is a stacked set of sliding buttons. These buttons allow us to vary the math model parameters so we can SIMULATE what this couple's phase space portrait might look like under different conditions. It's like a *therapist's quantitative fantasy*. We would be using the buttons to see what might happen to this couple if we could figure out a way for him to start the conflict conversation being much nicer (for example), or accepting more influence. Have you ever thought, sitting in your office, "I wonder what their relationship would be like if I could get [HIM or HER] to be nicer"? Well, guess what, simulation can make those predictions. Your fantasy now can become quantitative. We can just use the sliding button for start-up and "make him [or her] nicer," and see how their phase space portrait would change. Then, and only then, if that looks good, we can think about how to accomplish that. That's what simulation is all about. It's about IMAGINING CHANGE. We can actually do this in our lab, and we are working on an app now that will make it possible for a therapist to do this in his or her office.

Implications for Therapy: Phase Space Portrait of a Couple

Using the phase space plots in therapy is still a dream for the future. The implications for therapy of the math model are HUGE. Once we do an assessment of the couple's phase space and look at the diagram, we can then SIMULATE the couple's behavior in conditions we haven't yet observed them in. Or we can just let the computer program do this. To do this simulation we change math model parameter values until we see what needs to happen for them to develop a strong positive attractor. That helps us select the appropriate interventions. Isn't that cool? We can use the math to suggest the best interventions! Of course, we aren't there yet. We still have to do small experiments, called proximal change experiments, to help with these simulations, but we now know how to do these experiments.

To our knowledge, this is a FIRST, something we could never even have thought of doing before in PSYCHOTHERAPY. Once we describe the SYSTEM, we can SIMULATE the system's behavior as we change the parameter values. That is, we can do THOUGHT EXPERIMENTS on the system, and see how it might act under conditions we never observed the system in. We can have a QUANTITATIVE FANTASY.

Simulations for Selecting Minimal Therapeutic Interventions

We already know that the worst possible state of the system is if it only has a negative attractor and no positive attractor. Then it's completely out of whack. So what can be done? We just fiddle with the love equation parameters.

We can greatly affect the presence of a positive attractor and its stability in a variety of ways. Also, we can look at COMBINATIONS of various model parameter changes, and they can be SIMULATED in phase space diagrams. Then we can **imagine this couple** in other situations.

What would they be like if the husband had a more positive start-up? How positive would he have to be to counteract the wife's negative start-up? We can actually attempt to COMPUTE the best set of therapeutic changes for this couple to have a strong positive attractor.

Well, you might ask, how do you know that these interventions actually work to change the parameters of the math model? The answer is we need to do PROXIMAL CHANGE EXPERIMENTS.

PROXIMAL CHANGES: INTERRUPTING MARITAL CONFLICT

What's a proximal change? These are small experiments in which we don't try to change the whole relationship. These experiments are very much like what we therapists do every day in our consuling offices. We just try to change the couple's interaction from one conversation to the next, but here we see what shows up in their new phase space portrait. We have been doing these brief experiments in our "love lab," in which we interrupt marital conflict to try to make a small change in the way they talk to each other during conflict. That's one way of BUILDING a therapy that could be a 4SD therapy.

In fact, Amber Tabares and John did that kind of experiment years ago (Gottman & Tabares, in press). They had a group of 60 couples have a conflict discussion for 15 minutes. Next the couples were randomly assigned to three proximal change experiments, each lasting 20 minutes. Then they resumed their conflict discussion. In one condition the couples just read magazines for 20 minutes, without talking to one another. In another condition called "express compliments," the partners selected three adjectives that described their partner from a list of 60 positive adjectives and told a story about when their partner exhibited that positive trait. In a third condition called "express concerns," the partners selected three adjectives that described their partner from a list of 60 negative adjectives and told a story about when their partner exhibited that negative trait. As a procedural check, Amber coded the videotapes to determine whether people actually followed the instructions.

The group that read magazines had a huge reduction in physiological activity, which greatly affected their start-ups in the second conversation. In the express concerns condition start-ups—if they followed the directions—the second conversation became much more negative, while in the express compliments condition—if they followed the directions—start-ups in the second conversation became much more positive. That's just one example of a proximal change experiment we can do in our love lab.

The Tabares dissertation showed us that a brief intervention in which people just read magazines for 20 minutes produced both a heart rate decrease and a behavior change in husbands during the next conflict discussion. It came as a big surprise that actually reducing people's heart rates had a major effect on the next conflict discussion.

We also included two control groups in that study to either maximize or minimize RUMINATIONS about the previous conflict discussion as they relaxed. The rumination relaxation control group didn't get the benefit of a main effect heart rate and behavior change.

Tabares also found that she could predict from the first conflict discussion which couples would turn either of the two brief interventions into an opportunity to criticize rather than compliment their partner (the predictive effect accounted for 25% of the variance, which is a hefty effect size, usually called "moderate").

What this means for therapy is that the therapist may need to monitor HOW couples do brief prescribed interventions, and not simply assign them as homework. Unfortunately, Tabares found that unhappily married couples will characteristically sabotage an intervention designed to increase positive affect. We therapists need to monitor our interventions to make sure that they do not get sabotaged. One way to do that is to talk about how our homework or brief interruption of conflict could be sabotaged.

Even earlier, Julie and John piloted this simulation method in a series of 10 brief interventions that were the basis for writing a monthly column in *Reader's Digest*. Every month we had a distressed couple come to the love lab for an assessment. We coded and analyzed their data, and, fit our love equations, and, based on the data, we selected a brief intervention to transform their marital interaction in the second conflict discussion. Then we followed the couples for two years. All the couples changed dramatically and remained changed two years later. We wrote a book about these brief interventions titled *Ten Lessons to Transform Your Marriage* (Gottman, Gottman, & DeClaire, 2006). That was a fun and an inspiring start for a research program of proximal change experiments. Therefore, we found that some brief experiments, which we can accomplish in just one day, can produce lasting second-order changes.

It's now possible for a therapist to do a series of proximal change experiments using a library of our interventions designed to change model parameters. Our guess is that one brief intervention will do very little, unless it is very carefully selected on the basis of our preinteraction data.

Why should a therapist do these proximal change experiments in the consulting room? Well, clearly it's to accomplish two things: (1) they might increase positive affect during conflict, and (2) they might increase positive affect when the couple is not conflicting. That is, they could work to change the couple's FRIENDSHIP/INTIMACY system.

By the way, our friend Paul Peluso at Florida Atlantic University is using a math model just like ours (with different influence functions) to model individual therapy, with an actual client and an actual therapist. He's trying to find the math model parameters that predict if a new client will come back or quit, and he's done pretty well so far (Peluso, Liebovitch, Gottman, Norman, & Su, 2012; Liebovitch, Peluso, Norman, & Su, 2011). He uses different influence functions, because influence is actually very different in a psychotherapy relationship from influence in a love relationship.

PARAMETER CHANGES TO HEAL A TROUBLED RELATIONSHIP: PROCESS GOALS

Okay, so we saw that the influence processes of interaction create an emotional force field, with emotional flow lines and attractors. It can help us diagnose a relationship; it can help us articulate the forces of change. Okay, that's great. But now how do we use this information as therapists to systematically plan and create change? The answer lies in UNDERSTANDING the PARAMETERS of the influence functions and the attractors. By varying THOSE PARAMETERS (just like in a simulation) we can CHANGE THE PHASE SPACE PORTRAIT of our client couple. While this tool has yet to be developed for therapists, we can still learn a lot by understanding our parameters of change.

The following six parameter changes can act alone or they can act together, and can be done for one or both partners in a simulation (so a total $6 \times 6 = 36$ changes are possible). Our interventions can therefore be organized in terms of accomplishing the following six *process goals*. For reasons we will talk about later when we discuss TYPES of couples, we are assuming that the positive and negative affect slopes are FIXED for a couple and do not change. To create positive changes for a couple, we could:

1. Increase the positivity of their start-ups.
2. Decrease emotional inertias, because they limit accepting influence from the partner.
3. Decrease the threshold of repair so it is closer to zero. This means that they start repairing early, before their interactions get too negative.
4. Increase the strength of repair (using our Repair Checklist or Repair Card Deck).
5. Increase the threshold of damping by turning toward (which permits more positive affect to flow into the system).
6. Increase or decrease the strength (or sign) of damping. No damping or slight damping late can be great if the system is open. But positive damping early may force the system to become more open to positive affects.

We can now put together all our interventions so that they might facilitate these changes, and then one day we can find the OPTIMAL SIM-

ULATION (changed configuration of the parameters), our quantitative fantasy that gives us the exact set of interventions that are optimal for this couple.

How to Change the Six Parameters

Okay, you might be thinking, these sound like worthy process goals. Now how do I make them happen in therapy? Great question. Here's how.

1. Process goal: Increase the start-up positivity. How do we do that in therapy? Five methods.

1. **Increase the fondness and admiration system.** We can dramatically change start-up so that it is positive by increasing the Fondness and Admiration system. We can have the couple simply do a 20-minute exercise using THE POSITIVE ADJECTIVES CHECKLIST. From a list of 60 positive adjectives, they each pick three complimentary traits of their partner and describe an example of when their partner manifested that positive trait. Tabares showed that it is easy for couples to sabotage this exercise if they aren't warned, and don't follow instructions. So, in our couples' workshop the two of us role play humorous ways of sabotaging our exercises. To get our list, visit our website, Gottman Institute (www.Gottman.com).

2. **Teach gentle start-up.** The therapist teaches couples to begin in self-disclosure mode instead of attack-defend mode, to (1) state their feelings as I-statements, (2) about a specific situation and (3) to express a POSITIVE need (what they *do need* instead of what they don't need). They are also told that a need requires no justification, and not to dip into the past to prove one deserves the need or that one is blameless. The therapist helps them to get very specific with the positive need so that it is a recipe for success with that person. For example, instead of "I need to feel important to you," the clients may

say, "I need you to turn your phone off at dinner and just ask me about my day, and be a great listener, very interested and supportive."

3. **Teach positive self-editing.** We use a training audiotape that teaches the skill of self-editing out negative affect.

4. **A seven-week program of fondness.** We have couples follow a seven-week program where every day they get in touch with their fondness and admiration for their partner and give it voice. We have a booklet available that helps with this program.

5. **Ritualize cuddling.** Research worldwide (Northrup, Schwartz, & Witte, 2014) shows that only 6% of noncuddlers have a satisfying sexual relationship. So help them set things up at home so that there is a place and a time for cuddling, like in front of the TV.

6. **Change from a negative to a positive habit of mind.** We help people move from a negative habit of mind in which they are scanning their social environment for other people's mistakes, and move to a habit of mind in which they are scanning their social environment for things to appreciate. Then we help them express genuine appreciation even for very small things, and teach them the importance of doing that often. They are learning to nurture gratitude for what they have instead of resentment for what is missing.

2. Process goal: Decrease the emotional inertias of both people.

A high emotional inertia means that it is easier to predict the future from the past of just that person, as it doesn't change much, so it sets a limit on how powerful the partner's influence can be. What creates high emotional inertia? Our answer is that flooding creates inertia. To increase the influence of the partner, decrease emotional inertia by teaching SELF-SOOTHING methods. Inertia is usually created by a partner's physiology that is easily at or approaches FLOODING level. We discussed these interventions in Chapter 7.

*3. Process goal: Decrease the threshold of repair so it is
closer to zero. How do we do that in therapy?*

Teach the couple how to use the Gottman Repair Checklist or Repair Card Deck (see our website). The Repair Checklist is a one-page handout that we give to a couple that lists brief things they can say during a conversation that may be going badly. There are six categories of statements: (1) I feel, (2) Sorry, (3) Getting to yes, (4) I need to calm down, (5) Stop action!, and (6) I appreciate. An example of a brief repair under "Getting to Yes" when one's partner is angry is, "What are your concerns?" The idea of the repair checklist is that once people start getting upset they may not naturally think of these repairs, or they may wait too long before trying them. We see them as potentiually building the repair habit.

4. Process goal: Increase the strength of repair.

Teach the couple how to do effective repairs: (a) repairing early— such as taking responsibility for even a part of the problem; (b) reassuring their partner before the discussion begins; (c) using emotional, not cognitive business-meeting types of repairs; (d) self-disclosing; (e) accepting, not judging, the partner's emotions; (f) eliminating failed repairs (yes-buts) so that the sign of repair will be positive rather than negative; (g) summarizing BOTH self and other, not just self; (h) validating the partner's perceptions, feelings, and needs; and (i) at some point communicating, "We're okay."

5. Process goal: Increase the threshold of damping.

This is about increasing *turning toward* our partner, seeing our partner's needs, being responsive, permitting positive resonance moments, expressing and **letting in** reassurances, compliments, "We're okay," tooting our own horn (for example, saying, "We can get through anything together"), shared humor, being convulsed by one's own wit, silliness, playfulness, positive comparisons with other relationships, cherishing. Also, helping people to respond to genuine interest, affection, compassion, soothing (letting one's self be soothed and reassured).

*6. Process goal: Increase, or decrease, the strength of damping, that
is change responsiveness toward the partner's positive affect.*

This is about becoming more responsive, and more emotionally resonant with a partner. It is about the up- or downregulation of positive affect. It is not something we usually think about. A "negative damping" can create positive attractors for conflict-avoiding couples. This process goal is about how well the partners are coupled with respect to positive affect, how much they enjoy their partner's interest, curiosity, excitement, affection, humor, joy, soothing, validation, compassion, and so on. The dimension here is reponsiveness. That one single dimension is so important that it has been shown—in a series of experiments—to kindle and keep passion alive in relationships by Israeli psychologist Gurit Birnbaum (Birnbaum et al., 2016). Feeling special and desirable was especially important to women in these studies. We recently had the amazing experience of seeing a pair of courting lions on a photo safari in South Africa. What was so amazing about this couple was how incredibly responsive the male lion was toward every movement of the lioness.

Here are other potential proximal change interventions you might think of doing.

Specific Proximal Change Interventions

The materials for all of these interventions are on our website, as well as information about clinical training in using them. Many of them are also described in our book *Ten Principles for Doing Effective Couples Therapy* (Gottman & Gottman, 2015), as mentioned earlier.

1. *Constructive conflict goal: To decrease negative affect, and increase repair.*
   a. The Gottman-Rapoport Conflict Exercise.
   b. The two-ovals compromise method.
   c. Replacing the Four Horsemen with their antidotes.
   d. The Dreams Within Conflict Exercise.
   e. The aftermath of a fight or regrettable incident.

f. Therapist doing the Dan Wile intervention—speaking for a client, expressing all that person's emotions, positive as well as negative, and ambivalence, checking it out with the client, then having that person say it in his or her own words.

g. Physiological soothing, and the relaxation exercise (we have a booklet with guided relaxation instructions that a partner can read to assist in soothing; the partner does the soothing, rather than the therapist).

h. Taking effective breaks when flooded.

i. Emwave biofeedback (Heart Math company makes this device).

Friendship/intimacy goal: To increase positive affect during conflict and in nonconflict contexts.

a. Build love maps—Love Map Card Deck (also available free for cell phone use) .

b. Open-Ended Questions Card Deck (also available free for cell phone use)

c. Attunement—four skills, emotional check-ins.

d. Focusing (Gendlin, 2007).

e. Expressing Needs Card Deck (also available free for cell phone use).

f. Giving Appreciations Card Deck (also available free for cell phone use).

g. Aftermath of a positive event—(designed by one of our master trainers, Robert Navarra).

h. Aftermath of failed bids.

i. Positive Adjective Checklist.

j. Turning toward bids in all seven Panksepp emotional command systems.

k. Turning toward in past appreciations expressed.

l. Cherishing exercise.

m. Nurturing gratitude exercise.

    n. Guide to great listening.

    o. Seven-week fondness and admiration booklet.

    p. Having Fun Card Deck (also available free for cell phone use).

    q. Sensate focus, nondemand pleasuring.

    r. GottSex exercises—seven exercises (what is sex?, erotic love maps, talking about sex, initiating sex, welcoming partner saying no instead of punishing it, talking during sex, three Salsa Card Decks, Emily Nagoski Dual Process Erotic Love Map Questions).

    s. The stress-reducing conversation exercise.

    t. Baker's dozen suggestions for a great sex life.

There is one study (Ditzen, Schaer, Gabriel, Bidenmann, & Ehlert, 2009) using oxytocin nasal spray, which is easy to get through the Internet. With 47 couples, these investigators discovered that oxytocin significantly increased positive affect behavior in relation to negative affect during a conflict discussion. They also found that it significantly reduced salivary cortisol levels after the conflict compared with a placebo. To read more about how oxytocin affects trust, read Zak's (2013) *The Moral Molecule*. In that book Paul Zak also discusses the trust game, which therapists might find very interesting. See also John's book, *The Science of Trust*. We haven't actually used oxytocin in couples therapy, but John has a spray bottle handy just in case he encounters a couple so hostile that nothing else will work.

Shared meaning goal: Create or nurture this system.

One way to do this is to make moving through time meaningful and intentional by building rituals of connection (Doherty, 1997), discussing shared goals, supporting roles, discussing symbols of meaning (e.g., what is a home? What does love mean? What is our spirituality?).

    a. Build rituals of connection (Rituals Card Deck Exercise)

    i. Weekly date

    ii. State of the union meeting

iii. Weekly emotional check-in using Expressing Needs Card Deck (also available free for cell phone use)

b. Shared goals exercise

That's our list of most of our interventions and exercises. We just need to see what they each do when we interrupt conflict, use them, and have the couple try again.

WHAT OUR GENERAL SYSTEMS COUPLES THERAPY LOOKS LIKE

In Chapter 10 we will give the reader a feeling for what our couples therapy looks and feels like. We just note here that our theory is in the therapist's head. The therapy sessions themselves are organic and experiential. The topics emerge from what *the couple* brings to each session. Their own emotions and thoughts are what drive the therapy. There is no session-by-session curriculum in this therapy. The communication tools are used by the therapist as a way to help the couple deal with issues as they arise naturally in sessions.

CHAPTER 9

The Demand-Withdraw Pattern

AN IMPORTANT ASYMMETRY THAT DESTROYS TRUST

It has been variously called the "pursuer-distancer" pattern by Virginia Satir (1978), and the "demand-withdraw" pattern by UCLA psychologist Andrew Christensen (Baucom, McFarland, & Christensen, 2010). It characterizes many unhappy relationships. Here is the pattern: One person demands changes. The other person withdraws. Christensen describes it as an asymmetry of power during conflict because the one who wants changes is less powerful than the one who refuses those changes. Satir thought one unhappy partner wants more intimacy than the other unhappy partner, who responds by increasing emotional distance. Both patterns essentially look the same. The pattern is that one partner wants to avoid closeness or avoid change, while the other partner wants more emotional intimacy or wants change.

This pattern has reliably been associated with unhappy marriages in many empirical studies that observed behavior. As we noted, among heterosexual couples the demand-withdraw pattern is usually the women demanding change (or intimacy) and the men withdrawing. However, Andrew Christensen also discovered that when it is the man's concern, this gender pattern can be reversed. John and Neil Jacobson (Jacobson and Gottman, 2007) also found a reversed gender pattern with domestically violent couples where the man is the violent perpetrator. In that case the men demand change or greater closeness, and the women withdraw.

As far as Christensen's finding that it depends on who is presenting the issue, we know that in most heterosexual couples the woman brings up the issue 80% of the time. So the usual pattern will be the woman demanding change or intimacy, and the man withdrawing.

Men's and women's ideas of intimacy may be mismatched. In Figures 9.1–9.3, we can see a pattern first described by anthropologist Helen Fisher. Female close friends are most comfortable face to face, while male close friends find intimacy in a shoulder-to-shoulder arrangement. Fisher noted that this could become a mismatch in a male-female relationship.

Figure 9.1. Women's idea of intimacy: Face to face interaction

Figure 9.2. Men's idea of intimacy: Shoulder to shoulder interaction

A SIMILAR GENDER DIFFERENCE
EXISTS IN CHILDHOOD

Let's get back to this demand-withdraw pattern, which is usually a male-female pattern, with the male withdrawing. The pattern mostly is about negative emotions. We know that even very young boys and girls seem to deal with negative emotions differently. Four-year-old boys are less likely to accept influence from four-year-old girls, but girls accept influence equally from both genders. Stanford psychologist Eleanor Maccoby (Maccoby, 1980) was the first to discover this effect. John and his student Jennifer Parkhurst (Parkhurst & Gottman, 1986) also noted it in their

Figure 9.3. The mismatch: Mismatch face to shoulder interaction

studies of young children's friendships (see also Gottman [1983], a monograph titled, *How Children Become Friends*).

In middle childhood, there are very different playground play patterns with respect to negative emotions. In one school, we observed that boys look for rapid solutions as they work to keep the ball or game in play. They keep the game moving, exciting and high energy. The friendship relationships and dealing with emotions are the background for the game for boys. For example, we observed boys playing a run-and-chase game called "Smear" in which a large group chased the kid with the ball. When an 8-year-old boy named Brian started to cry, Billy, the unappointed captain of the team, stopped the game and asked, "What's wrong, Brian?" Brian said, "I didn't get the ball." "Okay," said Billy. "Jeff, throw the ball to Brian. Okay, let's go!" They were done and the game went on. They rapidly dispensed with the negative emotional disruption to the game.

We also noticed that 8-year-old girls, on the other hand, tended to play lower-energy games, and they stayed closer to the school building. They also played in much smaller groups. Once negative emotions were expressed, the girls would stop the play and the emotions would get fully processed. For example, two girls were playing hopscotch. Brenda started getting upset, so her friend Becca asked her what the problem was. They stopped playing. Brenda replied, "You said you thought my barrette made me look like a baby. That hurt my feelings." Becca then said, "I'm sorry. You do not look like a baby. I just don't like barrettes." Then Brenda said, "Why did you say the baby thing then?" Becca then explained that she used to wear barrettes and then one day her mom said she should stop wearing them because she was a big girl now in second grade. Brenda said, "My mom likes to put them in my hair, but maybe I'll tell her to stop." Brenda then said, "Well, why did your mom tell you to stop wearing them?" Becca said, "I don't know. She's always in a hurry in the morning and maybe she doesn't like to help me fix my hair." Brenda then said, "Well, she needs to be more patient and help with your hair. My mom does." Becca said, "Yeah, I know. Why is my mom always in a rush?" They kept talking and talking, having totally abandoned hopscotch. For girls, it was as if the game was background for the friendship relationship. Just the reverse for boys.

To paraphrase Mark Twain, "There comes a time in the life of every boy when he knows he has to go hunt for buried treasure. Just such a moment overcame Tom Sawyer, and so he knew he had to go find his friend Huck Finn." Young best friendships can be based on a very powerful bond, sometimes even outlasting their parents' marriages. There are many accounts, even of two 10-month-old children deciding almost instantly that they are best friends and strongly nonverbally demanding that their parents make time for them to play with one another (research initially done by William Damon; see Damon, 2006).

John, with his graduate student Jennifer Parkhurst, spent many years studying how children form these friendships and understanding the best friendships of children using observational methods. His two books *How Children Become Friends* and *Conversations of Friends* summarize this research (Gottman, 1983; Gottman & Parker, 1986).

Eleanor Maccoby also discovered a pattern in kids' friendships that exists everywhere on the planet. It is called the "gender divide." Among 3- and 4-year-olds, about 35% of best friends are boy-girl pairs; the rest of best friendships are either two boys or two girls. However, it appears that by age 7, these boy-girl best friendships have vanished. How widespread is this gender divide?

The same pattern of very young males and very young females playing with one another has also been observed in nonhuman primates. The gender divide has been attributed to the fact that rough-and-tumble play eventually becomes much rougher among males. Maccoby believes that in humans, the gender divide is due to the fact that young males do not accept influence as much from young females as females do from both genders.

Another possibility that could explain the gender divide is that the play preferences of boys tend to ignore emotions in favor of high adventure, while the play preferences of girls tend to emphasize the emotions at the expense of high adventure and to focus on more domestic play themes (like playing house). John and Jennifer spent a year recording the play of a pair of 4-year-old best friends named Eric and Naomi. Naomi was Jennifer Parkurst's daughter. Eric and Naomi considered themselves engaged to be married, and they played a game they called the Marry Game. Once, in playing this game, they said:

Naomi: Let's play the Marry Game.
Eric: Okay.
Naomi: Okay, husband, how was your day?
Eric: Fine, wife. How was your day?
Naomi: I worried that you wouldn't find the repair man. Everything in the house is breaking.
Eric: I looked everywhere for the repair man. I looked under the cat, and I looked on the other side of the moon.
Naomi: And you couldn't find him?

Eric: No. No repair man anywhere.

Clearly these conversations reflected what these kids thought married people talked about. Eric and Naomi were very good at negotiating play and finding compromises that showed *accepting influence*, as in the following excerpt:

Naomi: Let's play house.

Eric: I want to play Superman.

Naomi: Well, I don't want to be the lady he rescues anymore.

Eric: I want to play Superman.

Naomi: I want to play house.

Eric: I want to play Superman.

Naomi: House, house, not Superman.

Eric: Hey, Naomi! What if we play this is Superman's house?

Naomi: Okay. Yes, that's fine.

Eric: What do you want to play?

Naomi: I want to play that this is our baby and we show him around to our friends.

Eric: Okay.

[They do this for a while, when Eric exclaims:]

Eric: Naomi, this baby is dead.

Naomi: Oh, no! What can we do?

Eric: I will fly us to the hospital and I will operate to save the baby's life.

Naomi: Okay. I want to be a doctor too.

Eric: No, you're the nurse.

Naomi: Girls can be doctors, too. My mom said.

Eric: Okay, Naomi. Let's drive in this ambulance very fast to the hospital. Get in. Hurry!

Naomi: Please slow down, Eric. You're driving too fast!

Eric: There, we're here at the hospital. Now I'm going to operate—no, no, we are going to operate, Doctor Naomi. Now the baby is saved. That's a relief! What shall we do now?

Naomi: Let's keep showing our baby to our friends.

Eric: [Disappointed sigh] Oh, okay . . .

The important dimension is accepting influence. Eric and Naomi were able to accept influence from one another and were able to keep having both domestic and high-adventure play themes.

The demand-withdraw pattern among adults occurs most with negative affect.

Typical Demand-Withdraw Pattern

This demand-withdraw depiction of marriage is rather ancient. One partner (usually the wife) demands change or greater intimacy, and the other partner (usually the husband) withdraws. It can even be seen in old cartoons in which the husband hides behind his newspaper while the wife yells at him. No question, this is an empirically validated pattern seen in unhappy relationships, and it's reversed in violent couples. That is VERY interesting.

BUT WHAT *EXPLAINS* THE DEMAND-WITHDRAW PATTERN?

CONCEPT #6: The carrying capacity for partner's negative affect

The concept here is that couples are regulated by their carrying capacities for negative affect. We suggest that every interacting SYSTEM has a carrying capacity for negative affect. The term "carrying capacity for negative affect" is related to flooding, the internal feeling of being overwhelmed and disorganized by one's partner's negative emotions. The concept of carrying capacity comes from the biological population ecology literature. In this literature the concept of the carrying capacity of an environment was designed to place a limit on the population of a species. The carrying capacity equation was a far better fit to the data than the ancient Malthus idea that a population would experience exponential growth (Murray, 2002).

The carrying capacity concept we suggest is that in a relationship one person's emotional expressions are like a species in an ecological system. It is as if there is a population of negative emotions emanating from each partner, whose size ebbs and flows over time. Each person serves as the environment for the partner's population of emotions, and each person may have a specific carrying capacity for the partner's negative emotions. This carrying capacity is not presumed to be a trait. It may change over time. However, when a person's carrying capacity for the partner's negative affect is low, we suggest that conflicts will escalate, with negative consequences for the relationship. On the other hand, when a person's carrying capacity for the partner's negative affect is high, we suggest that conflicts will not escalate, with positive consequences for the relationship. That's actually what our data suggest.

Each partner's carrying capacity for the partner's negative affect is assessed in our lab by our 51-item questionnaire. On this scale a *higher* total score is indicative of a *lower* carrying capacity for the partner's negative affect. Examples of items are, "My partner's negativity comes out of the blue," "When my partner gets angry I feel attacked," "I just don't understand why he/she has to get so upset," "After a fight I just want to keep away from him/her," and "My husband's/wife's feelings are too easily hurt."

It is clear from our clinical work that for some people a partner's expressions of negative affect feel like being attacked by a swarm of angry wasps, while for other people a partner's negative affect merely provides information that evokes curiosity and empathy. We found evidence that this carrying capacity for a partner's negative affect is potentially a key variable that determines the nature of the couple's conflict interaction dynamics, and ultimately affects the success or failure of the couple's relationship. When that carrying capacity for negative affect is low, or becomes low, that partner will be much more likely to engage in thoughts and behaviors that will eventually terminate the relationship by creating a negative "story of us."

THE STORY OF US

In our lab we tap this story of us in our Buehlman coding of our standard Oral History Interview, which has proven to be a strong predictor of relationship stability or demise (Buehlman et al., 1992). In that study the Buehlman coding of our Oral History Interview could predict divorce or stability in the next four years with 94% accuracy. A low carrying capacity for negative affect is strongly related to a negative story of us. With a low carrying capacity, a person is much more likely to see the partner as an enemy and not a friend. Whatever the partner says tends to be seen as adversarial. We discovered that people with a low carrying capacity for a partner's negative affect are more likely to: (1) escalate their own negative affect during conflict; (2) become more physiologically aroused during the conflict; (3) criticize their partner or withdraw, that is, stonewall during conflict; (4) report being unhappily married; (5) seriously consider separation and divorce; and (6) rate the interaction as negative in our video recall rating procedure.

We also need to introduce another concept that is aligned with carrying capacity: whether or not the couple is connecting emotionally.

CONCEPT #7: Everyday calm emotional attunement

The concept we introduce here relates to everyday maintenance of the couple's friendship. In many cases our subjects told us that conflict was a real problem and the Four Horsemen emerged in their relationship *because* they simply couldn't talk calmly to their partner about their own negative emotions without feeling judged, dismissed, or rejected.

To further explore each person's everyday ability to calmly resonate to their partner's negative affect when *not* in the conflict context, we designed what we call an emotional attunement interview to measure the perceived emotional availability of a spouse to attune to a partner's everyday negative affect. Specifically what we mean by emotional attunement is the extent to which each spouse said that they could listen calmly, nondefensively, and empathetically to their partner when the partner felt either anger or sadness toward them, or anger and sadness toward someone outside the relationship. We decided to focus on anger and sadness (either toward the partner, or not) because these are the affects that emerged from our clinical experience as central to emotional connection. This interview was designed to measure each person's perception of their ability to fully process everyday negative emotional events with their partner, which we refer to as calm emotional attunement. To create this interview, we extended previous work in our laboratory using our parental meta-emotion interview, in which people were asked about their experience and philosophy about emotional expression and experience, particularly with respect to anger and sadness and with respect to their children's emotions (Gottman, Katz, & Hooven, 1997). The word "ATTUNE" in the Yoshimoto observational coding system of the interview was intentionally selected to fit an acronym to represent the scales we coded in the interview:

A = AWARENESS of the partner's emotions
T = TOLERANCE that there are always two different perceptions
T = TURNING TOWARD the partner's emotions instead of dismissing
U = UNDERSTANDING is the goal of talking about feelings
N = NONDEFENSIVE LISTENING
E = EMPATHY

We coded these variables from videotapes of the Yoshimoto (2005) interview. We also added the dimension of a calm and regulated discussion of anger and sadness by subtracting the coding of responses about whether these discussions were calm or were perceived to go out of control. We created only one variable from the coding of this interview: The *everyday calm emotional attunement* variable for each partner was a sum of a person's score on these six scales, designed to measure the perception that there is a calm mechanism in the relationship for fully processing the negative emotional events of everyday anger and sadness, either toward the partner, or about events or persons outside the relationship.

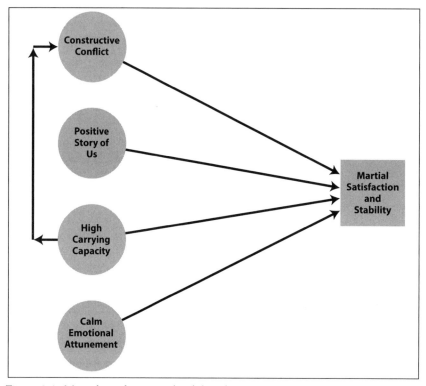

Figure 9.4. Marital satisfaction and stability chart

We summarize our findings in Figure 9.4. Don't take the arrows in this figure very seriously. We haven't yet established any cause-and-effect relationships, merely strong correlations.

What are we trying to say with this figure? We are suggesting that the demand-withdraw pattern is really an ARTIFACT OF processes that have to do with staying connected or disconnected emotionally. Specifically, we are claiming that the mismatch in the demand-withdraw pattern is actually a mismatch between spouses in the carrying capacity for a partner's negative emotions. When that mismatch occurs, we have discovered that people do not engage in calm everyday emotional attunement, and these dimensions are correlated with dysfunctional conflict (the negative absorbing Markov state), and also to a negative story of us.

Men have lower carrying capacity for negative affect than women: This EXPLAINS the demand-withdraw pattern, and we're done.

A consistent empirical finding in our lab is that men have a lower carrying capacity for negative affect than women. Men, we also know, are socialized differently than women with respect to negative emotions. Therefore, men are more likely than women to DISMISS their partner's negative affect than to ATTUNE to their partner's negative affect. There is a great deal of data to support the idea that men are much more easily flooded than women, although conclusions about the physiology of this gender difference are controversial (for a review of this research, see Chrisler & McCreary, 2010). Part of the complexity of this physiology is that women—for good evolutionary reasons, since they have typically mainly cared for and nurtured the young—are easier than men to fear-condition with Pavlovian pairing of an aversive unconditioned stimulus with a neutral unconditioned stimulus. However, in heterosexual love relationships, we consistently find more men have a lower carrying capacity for their partner's negative affect, and are more easily flooded than their women.

CHAPTER 10

Our Mighty Theory

The Sound Relationship House

Okay, so far we have identified what goes wrong and what goes right in couple relationships. We have even identified the interaction dynamics of what goes wrong and what goes right, and why. We know that we and others can predict the future of a relationship with remarkable accuracy. Great.

We have started talking about the dynamics of change, and the parameters that therapists can use to create change. Here's our story about our own journey in helping couples change their relationships. Twenty-one years ago the two of us decided to collaborate. We were out on a canoe on Puget Sound and John had just turned down a great job offer to be the research director for the Family Institute of Chicago, a place that conducted research and treatment. For years Julie had suggested that we bring our basic research findings into the therapeutic community. On our canoe trip, John was sad because he thought that could have happened in Chicago. (We were caring for John's mom at the time in Seattle, and Julie said she goes crazy if there are no mountains around her.) Julie suggested that we work together and make this all happen in Seattle. That's when our work together really started.

We started by trying to communicate our research findings to the general public and to therapists, and we quickly realized that we would need to build a theory and an assessment method that could be useful for practicing therapists. Julie led the way in this process because she had far more clinical experience than John, and also more experience working with difficult cases. This chapter describes what we came up with.

HOW TO DO A VALID SCIENTIFIC ASSESSMENT OF A COUPLE

Our assessment and treatment method is fully described in our book *Ten Principles for Doing Effective Couples Therapy* (Gottman & Gottman, 2015). We will assume that the couple has taken the validated and reliable Gottman Relationship Checkup questionnaires. In our clinical office, we begin with getting their narrative of why they are here at this time, and what they'd like to accomplish. We ask them to tell us the story of what brings them here at this time and what they would like to accomplish. The therapist then summarizes and validates.

The therapist then asks them to go back to the story of their relationship, how they met and what their first impressions were of one another. The therapist does an abbreviated form of our Oral History Interview of their relationship, and then observes them engaging in a brief 10-minute conflict discussion, using pulse oximeters as they interact.

Then the therapist schedules individual interviews, explaining that there are no secrets in couples therapy. In the individual interviews the therapist also gets a primary family history and asks about common comorbidities (such as addictions, violence, depression, anxiety, trauma, and affairs). After the individual interviews with both people, the therapist puts all the information together and gives the couple feedback. Then they all discuss the goals of treatment.

In this feedback we review the areas of our Sound Relationship House theory and talk about which areas are strengths in the relationship, and which areas need improvement. We assess their expectations and commitment to the therapy process, explain the therapeutic process, and give the couple some hope. For the questionnaires in the Gottman Relation-

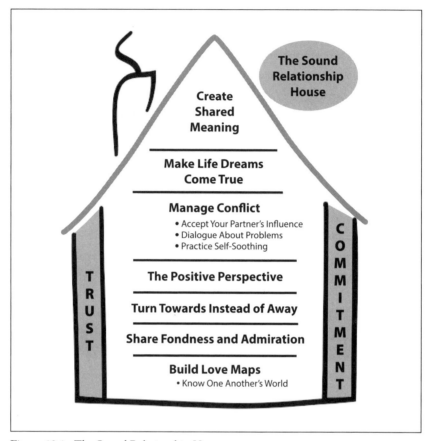

Figure 10.1. The Sound Relationship House

ship Checkup (https://checkup.gottman.com/) we also use the Sound Relationship House (SRH) theory. Figure 10.1 summarizes our theory.

OUR SOUND RELATIONSHIP HOUSE THEORY

The first three levels of the SRH theory (from the bottom up) describe friendship in relationships. Now here's part of the great thing about being a scientist. You can't just say, "Friendship is important in relationships" or

"Yes, congregation, let's now have a moment of silence for we all know how sacred is a golden friendship." That's okay for the clergy, or for Oprah or Dr. Phil. But as scientists we have to actually measure things reliably and validly, so we have to be able to DEFINE what we mean, and that automatically gives us a recipe for success. One advantage of the SRH theory is that **we can reliably and validly measure every construct in the theory**, which means that we know how couples either build or erode every level of the SRH. That means we know HOW TO BUILD EVERY PART OF OUR THEORY. So here's what we mean by "friendship" in the SRH. One needs to be able to do three things within the Friendship domain, as follows.

1. Build Love Maps

A love map is a road map one creates of one's partner's inner psychological world. It is the most basic level of friendship. It's about feeling known in the relationship. It's about feeling like your partner is interested in continuing to know you—and your partner feeling that you are interested in knowing her or him. What are your partner's worries and stresses at the moment? Do you know? What are some of your partner's hopes and aspirations; what are some of your partner's dreams, values, goals in life? What is your partner's mission statement in life? The fundamental process in making a love map involves asking questions, remembering the answers, and keeping them in working memory—open-ended questions that you want to know the answer to. Not closed-ended questions like, "Did the plumber come?" People rarely ask questions. When people ask open-ended questions, it's a kind of invitation as opposed to making a statement, which is like, "Take that." So three parts to love maps: (1) ask questions you're interested in, (2) remember the answers, and, (3) keep asking new open-ended questions.

2. Nurture Fondness and Admiration System

This is about building affection and respect in the relationship. People do this verbally and nonverbally. There are two parts to nurturing fondness and admiration. First, we need a habit of mind that scans our world for things to admire and be proud of in our partner and events to appreciate. That is the opposite of a critical habit of mind that scans for our partner's mistakes. Then the appreciation or admiration needs to come out of the mouth, or be expressed nonverbally; it can't stay hidden. The idea is to catch your partner doing something right and to say, "Thanks for doing that," "I noticed you did this and I really appreciated that," "I enjoyed the conversation at dinner," or "You look really hot this morning. I am having all these lewd thoughts about you." This is actively building a culture of appreciation and respect.

3. Turn Toward Versus Away

When people are just kind of hanging out, they actually are often letting their needs be known to one another either nonverbally or verbally. They are doing this a lot of the time. They're making what we call **bids** for emotional connection. We discovered this in our apartment lab, thanks to John's former student Janice Driver. This is a fundamental unit of connection, of emotional connection. They are asking for attention, interest, conversation, humor, affection, warmth, empathy, help and assistance, support, and so on. These tiny moments of emotional connection really form an emotional bank account that really gets built over time. Here are some examples: "There's a pretty boat." No response—that's turning away. Or a crabby response: "Will you be quiet? I am trying to read!" That's turning against. On the other hand, "Huh!" That's turning toward. Sometimes that's as good as it gets. Or, "Wow, that **IS** a beautiful boat. Hey baby, let's quit our jobs and get a boat like that and sail away together, what do you say?" That's enthusiastic turning toward. All this builds an emotional bank account. In our newlywed study, six years after their weddings, 17 couples had divorced. Their rate of turning toward in our apartment lab had been 33% six years earlier. The couples who were still married? Their rate of turning toward in our apartment lab had been 86% six years earlier: 33% versus 86%—that's a huge difference!

The *fundamental process of turning toward* is increasing awareness and mindfulness about how your partner makes bids. Also, turning toward involves seeing the longing behind a bid that may be a bit negative or unclear. One doesn't need to have high standards, because turning toward naturally leads to more turning toward. There's a positive feedback loop. So one can start small, and it will build over time.

Incidentally, the test of a good theory is that it ought to be disconfirmable and it ought to be supported by experiment. Also, every concept in the theory ought to be reliably measurable—with convergent measurement methods—and validated. That is the case for turning toward in our theory, the 33% versus the 86%. What is also important is that a good theory ought to make unexpected new predictions that turn out to be true.

What were our unexpected results? We discovered, much to our surprise, that love maps, fondness and admiration, and turning toward were the basis for—get this—humor and affection during conflict. That might not seem very important to you. But we had discovered that in good relationships people make their partner laugh and that reduces physiological arousal. Humor is incredibly important in relationships. A cool result, but how do you use that in therapy? Can you just ask people to smile and laugh more the next time they have conflict? No. It's been tried and it doesn't work. The answer that Janice Driver found was that humor and affection during conflict are highly correlated with turning-toward bids in nonconflict interactions (Driver and Gottman, 2004).

Second, these first three processes of friendship were also the basis for romance, passion, and good sex. To convince yourself of this result, begin by asking yourself how you would make your relationship more romantic in the next two weeks. What would you do? What we discovered was surprising. We really didn't expect this—these first three levels of the Sound Relationship House are the key. There's a book called *1001 Ways to Be Romantic* by Gregory Godek (2012). Number 24 is addressed to guys. It goes, "What could be more romantic than getting your wife a golden locket with your picture in it?" Now imagine: (1) John hasn't asked Julie a question in 10 years, so he fails love maps, strike 1. (2) Last night they were out to a dinner party and as she was telling a story John said, "Don't tell that story. You don't know how to tell a story. Let me tell it." So John fails Fondness and Admiration, strike 2. (3) John doesn't notice her bids, so he fails turning toward, strike 3, he's out. And then he gets her a golden locket with his picture in it. So now we ask you, is that going to be a romantic event? We don't think so. She'll probably drive the SUV over it a few times, really flatten out that locket. Or use it on her dart board.

So these three components of friendship affect the way people are when they disagree. If they are friends, they actually have a lot more access to their humor, to their affection—all the positive things that really make it possible to have disagreements or to live with them in a much more constructive and creative way. This is about earning and building up points that are like assets in the emotional bank account.

4. Sentiment Overrides

What happens when friendship isn't working? People go into "negative sentiment override." What the heck is that? Robert Weiss in 1980 suggested that couples are in one of two states: Negative or positive sentiment override.

In negative sentiment override, the *negative* sentiments we have about the relationship and our partner *override* anything positive our partner might do. We are hypervigilant for put-downs. We tend not to notice positive events. Robinson and Price (1980) discovered that unhappy couples don't see 50% of the positive things that objective observers see. We tend to distort and see neutral, sometimes even positive things as negative. We are overly sensitive.

In positive sentiment override, the *positive* sentiments we have about the relationship and our partner override negative things our partner might do. We give our partner the benefit of the doubt, assuming positive intentions. We don't take negativity personally but merely as evidence that our partner is stressed. We tend to notice negative events but not take them very seriously. We tend to distort toward the positive, and see even negative as neutral. We are not overly sensitive.

We initially thought that ONLY friendship would determine if people were in the negative or positive perspective. But here we were wrong. Our research showed that if conflict was a negative absorbing Markov state, they would also be in negative sentiment override, or the negative perspective. It's fine to be wrong; that's why we wanted our theory to be disconfirmable.

People are in negative sentiment override for good reason—the friendship *or the conflict* isn't working. Then we tend to see our partner as our adversary, not as our temporarily annoying friend. So our theory suggests not to try to apply cognitive modification to get people from negative to positive sentiment override. The theory suggests that it won't work unless fundamental friendship processes are working. If friendship is working, you automatically get positive sentiment override. If friendship isn't working, you automatically get negative sentiment override, because you are running on empty in the friendship. That's our prediction.

5. Manage Conflict

We use the term "manage" conflict rather than "resolve" conflict because relationship conflict is natural and it has functional, positive aspects. We need conflict. For example, it helps us learn how to better love and understand our partners, deal with change, and renew courtship over time. We try to manage but not eliminate conflict. Also, as Robert and John studied couples over many, many years, most couple conflicts (69%) were perpetual; they never got resolved.

Robert and John's first finding: the MASTERS of relationships are gentle toward one another. They reassure, soften start-up (including pre-emptive repair); they accept influence, self-soothe, repair and de-escalate, compromise. This is the opposite of George Bach and Peter Wyden's (1983) *The Intimate Enemy*. Bach had couples take turns airing resentments. They even hit each other with foam rubber bats called "batakas." That resulted in greater resentment. As Carol Tavris's (2010) excellent book, *Anger, the Misunderstood Emotion*, explains, there is no catharsis in anger. That doesn't mean we need to expurgate anger from our emotional repertoire, as some writers have claimed, but it means we need to make it constructive, from the outset with gentle startup.

Second finding: not all conflict in relationships is the same. Our research revealed that 69% of the time when couples were asked to talk about an area of continuing disagreement, what they discussed was a "perpetual" issue. This is a problem that has to do with fundamental differences between a couple, differences in personality or needs that are fundamental to their core definitions of self. They are issues without resolution that the couple has often been dealing with for many years. Couples continue to talk about the same issues, occasionally making some progress, or at least the situation might get somewhat better for a short time, but then, after a while, the problem reemerges. In each case, the discussion is an attempt to establish a dialogue with the problem, which, admittedly, will never go away nor be fully resolved. What is needed is exactly what Andy Christensen talked about when he developed acceptance-based couples therapy (Christensen & Jacobson, 1988; Christensen, Doss, & Jacobson, 2014).

Most relational conflict is not resolvable. Our research also agrees with Dan Wile, who presciently wrote in a book called *After the Honeymoon* that "choosing a partner is choosing a set of problems" (2008, p. 12). He noted that problems would be a part of any relationship, and that a particular person would have some set of problems no matter who that person married. Wile wrote:

> Paul married Alice and Alice gets loud at parties and Paul, who is shy, hates that. But if Paul had married Susan, he and Susan would have gotten into a fight before they even got to the party. That's because Paul is always late and Susan hates to be kept waiting. She would feel taken for granted, which she is very sensitive about. Paul would see her complaining about this as her attempt to dominate him, which he is very sensitive about. If Paul had married Gail, they wouldn't have even gone to the party because they would still be upset about an argument they had the day before about Paul's not helping with the housework. To Gail, when Paul does not help she feels abandoned, which she is sensitive about, and to Paul, Gail's complaining is an attempt at domi-

nation, which he is sensitive about. The same is true about Alice. If she had married Steve, she would have the opposite problem, because Steve gets drunk at parties and she would get so angry at his drinking that they would get into a fight about it. If she had married Lou, she and Lou would have enjoyed the party but then when they got home the trouble would begin when Lou wanted sex because he always wants sex when he wants to feel closer, but sex is something Alice only wants when she already feels close.

Wile also wrote, "there is value, when choosing a long-term partner, in realizing that you will inevitably be choosing a particular set of unsolvable problems that you'll be grappling with for the next ten, twenty, or fifty years" (2008, p. 13).

Along with Wile, we also claim that:

> *Relationships work to the extent that one has wound up with*
> *a set of perpetual problems one can learn to live with.*

When a problem is a perpetual problem, instead of **solving it**, a couple needs to learn how to dialogue well about their different subjective realities, rather than becoming gridlocked on this perpetual issue. The masters of relationship seem to be able to come to some acceptance of their problem. They are able to simultaneously communicate acceptance of the partner and the desire to improve this problem, often with amusement, respect, and affection. However, if they cannot establish such a dialogue, the conflict may become **gridlocked**, and gridlocked conflict eventually leads to emotional disengagement.

Doing a Dan Wile—A Powerful Method

A therapeutic technique we owe to Dan Wile's ingenuity is to speak for a partner when that person is unable to get his leading-edge feelings across because he is stuck in the attack-defend mode. Wile's technique is designed to "solve the moment," rather than trying to solve the entire conflict issue. In moving to self-disclosure mode Wile adds positive affects and mixed feelings, as well as negative affects. The method is very powerful. It models moving out of attack-defend and into self-disclosure, which can help end gridlock and build trust. We can see in the process of interaction how people move against one another, or toward, or withdraw from one another by the very comments they make and the emotions behind their comments. Julie added one modification of doing a Dan Wile, which Dan has adopted. After we get the message right in speaking for a client, we then ask them to say that to their partner in their own words. We do that to make our therapy more dyadic, less therapist centered. That, we hope, can minimize relapse after therapy.

The masters of relationships know how to move from gridlock to dialogue on their perpetual problems. The masters of relationships are able to express a fundamental acceptance of their partner's personality even though they are asking for change. As we mentioned, this is consistent with Christensen's model for acceptance-based couples therapy. They also soften the importance of the change request. Here are the differences between gridlock and dialogue about a perpetual issue.

Gridlocked conflict.

The topic of the conflict is of no help in knowing if the conflict is in gridlock or dialogue. The perpetual conflict can be about anything. To an outsider it may seem like a very small issue. But within the relationship it really seems like a big issue. One visual image for gridlock is two fists in opposition. In gridlock conflicts, people feel basically rejected by their partner. They are probably feeling like their partner doesn't even like them when talking about that gridlocked issue. They will have the same conversation over and over and over again. It seems like they are spinning their wheels and not making any headway on it. There is no possibility of compromise. Over time people become more and more entrenched in their positions and even more polarized, more extreme. Conversations on this issue lead to frustration and hurt. Here's the major index of gridlock: There's very little shared humor or amusement or affection or giving appreciation when they talk about this problem.

There's no positive affect going on in a gridlocked conflict. That's the key to measuring gridlock.

Over time, with gridlock people start vilifying one another. They start thinking negative thoughts about their partner, especially when they talk about this gridlocked issue. Most common in vilification that researchers have found is people start thinking of their partner as selfish. That finding is essential in our analysis of gridlock as a loss of trust.

Dialogue with a perpetual issue.

Dialogue with a perpetual issue is different from gridlock in one major way. In dialogue there is a lot of positive affect (amusement, laughter, affection, empathy), whereas in gridlock there is almost no positive affect. Couples who dialogue about a perpetual issue seem to be trying to arrive at a better understanding of the issue or to reach some temporary compromise. They have an amused "oh, here we go again" attitude that involves a lot of acceptance, taking responsibility, and amusement, as well as a serious attempt to make things better and accommodate to their personality and need differences.

Why are people in gridlock? Previous clinical writing has suggested that these gridlocked couples have some kind of psychopathology that keeps them from taking the partner's perspective, such as an inability to empathize, or a deficit in theory of mind. Perhaps, various clinical writers have suggested, these gridlocked folks are narcissistic or have a personality or character disorder.

However, our basic research revealed that there is a very good reason most people cannot yield on their gridlocked problems. John analyzed 960 gridlocked conflicts and called the reason for the gridlock the "hidden agendas." But now we understand that the hidden agendas have an existential meaning. We now realize that behind each person's gridlocked position lies something deep and meaningful—something core to that person's belief system, needs, history, or personality. It might be a strongly held value or perhaps a dream not yet lived. They can no more yield and compromise on this issue than they can give up the bones of who they are and what they value about themselves. Compromise seems like selling themselves out just for the sake of peace with this person, which is unthinkable to most people.

When a relationship becomes safe enough and one partner clearly communicates that he or she wants to know what's the underlying meaning of the partner's position, the partner can finally open up and talk about his or her feelings, dreams, and needs. Persuasion and problem solving are postponed in favor of the goal of understanding one another's dreams about each person's position on the issue.

We have an intervention called the Dreams Within Conflict intervention. It is based on the realization that not all relationship conflicts are the same or require the same skill set. Existential conflicts like these are fundamentally different. In this intervention we simply add some questions for the listener to our Gottman-Rapoport Conflict Blueprint. Here are these questions:

- What ethics, beliefs, or values do you have that relate to your position on this issue?
- Is there some story behind this that relates to your history or childhood in some way?
- What are all your feelings on this issue?
- Tell me why this is so important to you.
- What would be your ideal dream here?
- Is there a deeper purpose or goal in this for you?
- What are your core needs on this issue?
- Is there a disaster scenario connected with not having this dream realized?

6. Make Life Dreams Come True

A crucial aspect of any relationship is to create an atmosphere that encourages each person to talk honestly about his or her dreams, values, convictions, and aspirations, and to feel that the relationship supports those life dreams. We are back to love maps, but in a much deeper way here. One of our favorite films is *Don Juan DeMarco*. In that film Johnny

Depp plays a mental patient who thinks he is Don Juan and Marlon Brando plays his doctor. Depp transforms Marlon Brando's life. Brando is about to retire. One day, after Depp talks to him about women, Brando goes home and converses with his wife, Faye Dunaway, in their garden. He asks her what her life dreams are. After a silence she says, "I thought you'd never ask." Making life dreams come true first takes asking the question and remembering the answer.

This is especially true for anyone today who wants to be close to a woman. We are living through a very important historical period when women are becoming empowered (at least in enlightened countries)—empowered psychologically, politically, economically, and socially. It's been a hard-fought battle; for example, women only got the right to vote in Switzerland in 1970.

7. Create Shared Meaning

Finally we come to the attic of the SRH, where we build a sense of shared purpose and meaning. A relationship is also about building a life together that has a sense of shared purpose and meaning. Victor Frankl (2006) said that the pursuit of happiness is empty. He suggested that we find happiness along the way as we pursue deeper meanings in life. Everyone is a philosopher trying to make some sense out of this brief journey we have through life.

This level of the SRH is about creating shared meaning in the relationship. People do that in many ways, as Bill Doherty (1997) wrote in his fine book, *The Intentional Family*, including creating formal and informal rituals of connection, creating shared goals and life missions, supporting one another's basic roles in life, and agreeing on the meaning of central values and symbols (like what a home REALLY is). This search for meaning is important as well in dealing with prior trauma and its effects on relationships, as pointed out by the research of Richard Tedeschi in his work on posttraumatic growth (Tedeschi, Park, & Calhoun, 2008).

Here we return once again to building love maps, but at a deeper level. Understanding what matters the most to partners is essential to creating a meaningful life together. And that takes partners asking each other lots of questions. So the seventh level of the SRH loops back to the first level, love maps. (The SRH should probably be called the "Sound Relationship Bagel" since it's now circular.)

Trust and commitment.

As we reviewed earlier, trust and commitment were added to the SRH theory only recently, once we learned how important these two dimensions are and how to measure them using game theory, and incorporated Caryl Rusbult's research into our research.

THE FULL ASSESSMENT OF A RELATIONSHIP

Now that we've described our theory, how do we use it to assess a couple and determine the goals of their therapy? As we described earlier, the therapist can use our standard interviews, questionnaires, and a sampling of conflict to ask and answer the following questions before proceeding with defining the treatment goals of the therapy. Here are some of the general questions the assessment covers.

The Weight-Bearing Walls of the Sound Relationship House

Trust. Is trust an issue? Do the partners attune, accept, or dismiss negative emotions? Is there a history of betrayals, and, if so, what type of betrayals? Is there a history of affairs? Is there a meta-emotion mismatch? Do they attune on an everyday basis?

Commitment. Is there an issue with commitment to this relationship? Is there an issue with commitment to the therapy? Does the therapist think that they are doing negative comparisons?

Some Elements Inside the Sound Relationship House

Friendship and intimacy. What is the current status of love maps, fondness and admiration, turning toward versus away, passion/romance, sexual frequency, sexual satisfaction, relationship satisfaction, loneliness, thoughts about divorce/separation?

The positive or negative perspective. Are they in negative sentiment override?

Conflict management. What is the current status of spillover, start-up, Four Horsemen, flooding, accepting influence, compromise, and repair attempts? What are their specific conflict issues?

Past unprocessed regrettable incidents. What is their list of potential past attachment injuries or regrettable incidents that they have not processed yet? (Sometimes these emerge in later sessions of the therapy.)

Shared meaning. Have they created rituals of connection, shared roles in life, goals?

Individual issues and comorbidities. The therapist asks about each partner's primary family history and potential issues from childhood, attachment insecurities, alcohol and drug addiction, behavioral addictions (like gambling), suicide potential, domestic violence that is characterological, domestic violence that is situational, emotional abuse (isolation, degradation, sexual coercion, threats/property damage), and mental illness comorbidities: depression, anxiety disorder, trauma and PTSD, borderline personality disorder, psychosis, schizophrenia, bipolar disorder.

THE GOTTMANS' RELATIONSHIP CHECKUP

Beginning in 1980, our lab developed and validated a set of questionnaires that can (miraculously, now that Julie has painstakingly written all the text) provide a clinician with a profile of a client couple's relationship strengths and challenges. The real challenge in our lab developing these questionnaires was to avoid what Gerry Patterson (1982) called "the glop problem," which happens when all the data covary so strongly that we can't get any description other than the trivial one, "your relationship is unhappy." That feedback wouldn't make a therapist sound very smart or insightful. The other trick was to *validate* the questionnaires against the more expensive measures in our lab, the observational coding of the Oral History Interview, the SPAFF coding of emotional behavior, and so on. We have now accomplished these goals.

It takes a person about 1.5 to 2 hours to fill out these extensive questionnaires. For the couple, this is NOT an aversive experience. On the contrary, they find it interesting and illuminating. We, and our therapists, almost never have any problem with people refusing to take these questionnaires.

These questionnaires are now available online, automatically scored, with suggestions to the couple's clinician for a treatment plan. With scores calculated and well-established cutoffs, we use a red circle to mean that this is *an area that needs improvement* and a green circle to indicate that this is *a strength in the relationship*. We also note asymmetries between partners.

At the time of this writing, 30,000 couples have taken these questionnaires. The website to access them is Gottman Relationship Checkup (https://checkup.gottman.com). Clinicians can apply to sign up to be able to use this website. The website is NOT for couples to use without the guidance of a therapist.

Areas Assessed and Scored

Friendship and intimacy.
1. Relationship satisfaction and happiness
2. Divorce potential
3. Love maps
4. Fondness and admiration (affection and respect)
5. Turning toward or away
6. Satisfaction with romance and passion
7. Satisfaction with the quality of sex
8. Satisfaction with the frequency of sex
9. Emotional disengagement and loneliness

Conflict.

1. Harsh start-up
2. The Four Horsemen of the Apocalypse
3. Flooding
4. Accepting influence
5. Compromise
6. Negative sentiment override
7. Repair attempts
8. My family history
9. Specific conflict areas (with client-supplied comments)
   a. Emotional connection
   b. Stress management
   c. Relatives and extended family
   d. Jealousy
   e. Emotional or sexual affairs
   f. Basic values and goals
   g. Housework and child care
   h. Financial issues
   i. Having fun together
   j. Spirituality, religion, ethics
   k. Children
   l. Distressing events
   m. Gridlock on perpetual issues

Shared meaning.

a. Rituals of connection
b. Roles in life
c. Goals
d. Important life symbols

Individual areas of concern.

a. Drug and alcohol abuse
b. Drug and alcohol frequency screening
c. Suicide potential

   d. Domestic violence situational

   e. Domestic violence characterological

   f. Emotional abuse

      i. Social isolation

      ii. Degradation and humiliation

      iii. Sexual coercion

      iv. Property damage, threats

   g. SCL-90 scales (assesses potential psychopathology)

The detour scales (additional areas that need work).

   a. Chaos and control

   b. Trust

   c. Commitment

   d. Meta-emotions (a mismatch about their feelings about the emotions)

Contracting.

Once the therapist has conducted the assessment, the therapist can suggest the goals of treatment and check these out with the couple. To do this, the therapist works jointly *with* the couple, summarizing the assessment with the SRH diagram (Figure 10.1), noting which SRH levels are strengths and which need work, and checking to make sure that the therapist and couple agree about the goals of treatment.

Implications for Therapy

HERE'S A MINIMAL FLOWCHART OF HOW TO PROCEED IN COUPLES THERAPY

Our goal in this section is to present a brief flowchart of how couples therapy can proceed. We're going to keep it minimal here. We are not trying to be thorough, but instead, we're trying to give the reader a rough idea of the essential components of what we do. We hope the reader will see that we can use our theory to actually make a difference, a 4SD difference. In subsequent chapters we'll fill this all out a bit more.

1. Start with dysfunctional conflict, if it exists.

   a. If the couple has a problem just with conflict, and no spillover into their events-of-the-day conversation, begin with the Gottman-Rapoport Conflict Blueprint.

   b. If the conflict is pervasive (there is spillover), or there is gridlock with either a power or a love hidden agenda, add the Dreams Within Conflict questions to the Gottman-Rapoport Conflict Blueprint.

2. Process past regrettable incidents. Most couples have unprocessed past regrettable incidents. Process these with the Aftermath of a Fight or Regrettable Incident exercise, combined with using Dan Wile interventions to speak for the person who is worst at getting his or her leading-edge feelings across. A booklet for couples is available at Gottman Institute (www.gottman.com) called "The Aftermath of a Fight or Regrettable Incident." Consider whether there is a meta-emotion mismatch and, if so, help them develop a common emotion culture with each other. Your clients may need the help of the Eugene Gendlin (2007) book, *Focusing*, if one of them (the emotion-dismissing person) has trouble identifying his or her feelings or has trouble putting feelings into words that are consistent with what's going on in his or her body.

3. **Ritualize the weekly state-of-the-union meeting.** A one-hour meeting where they talk about the current status of their relationship this week: (a) say what went right this week; (b) give one another five appreciations; (c) if there was a regrettable incident, use the "Aftermath" booklet to process it; (d) if there is a current issue, use the Gottman-Rapoport Blueprint to process it; and (e) end the meeting by asking one another, "What can I do this week to make you feel loved?"

4. **Work on friendship/intimacy.** Begin by talking about everyday emotional connection. Show them the diagram in Figure 10.2. Use the Gottman "Guide to Great Listening."

5. Continue by introducing the Expressing Needs Card Deck (available free as a phone app). Continue building Friendship/Intimacy, by using the Love Map Card Deck, and the Open-Ended Questions Card Deck (all 11 decks are available free for iPhones and smart phones; type "Gottman" into a search).

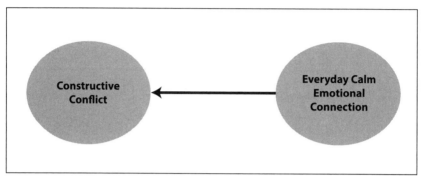

Figure 10.2. Constructive Conflict chart

6. **Work on the shared meaning system.** If they need to create rituals of connection, consider as a minimum the following three rituals:
   - A ritual for reunions at the end of a day. The 6-second kiss.
   - Weekly emotional connection meeting using the Expressing Needs Card Deck.
   - Daily: The stress-reducing conversation.
7. **Create important rituals of connection.**
   a. Set up a ritual for a weekly romantic date.
   b. Build rituals for initiating lovemaking, saying no gently, and being able to talk about sex.
   c. Work on sex, romance, and passion. If sex, romance, and passion are issues, use the seven exercises in the Gottman Institute: Gott Sex? (https://gottsex.com/).

A CLINICAL CASE

We have many tools that facilitate couples working on issues. However, we want to show you that in our general system theory for couples, the therapy we actually are doing is an EXPERIENTIAL THERAPY that is centered on the concerns and emotions that the couple brings into the therapy session. Our therapy is not didactic and instructional, although our Art and Science of Love workshop is more didactic. Yet, even these workshops are experiential and are focused on the couple's emotions. We have many clinicians that help couples during these workshops, a ratio of about 14 couples per therapist. The theory and the materials that facilitate emotional connection and effective conflict management are just a framework for helping the couple talk about the concerns and emotions they bring into each session of treatment.

The couple described here entered therapy after they participated in our Bringing Baby Home program (see Chapter 14). They were still having problems with their relationship. The wife, whom we will call Marlena, had been an actress, and was ending her 2-year leave and returning to a very successful career in a local theater company. Her husband, Jim, was a very successful criminal trial lawyer.

Assessment

Questionnaires

Based on cutoffs, we will summarize each questionnaire result for Marlena and Jim using these categories: (1) STRENGTH for a strength for both partners in this relationship; (2) CHALLENGE for a challenge for both partners in this relationship; (3) M → J for it being a bigger challenge for Marlena than for Jim; and (4) J → M for it being a bigger challenge for Jim than for Marlena.

Friendship and intimacy
1. Relationship satisfaction and happiness **M → J**
2. Divorce potential (Weiss Cerretto) **STRENGTH**
3. Love maps **STRENGTH**
4. Fondness and admiration (affection and respect) **CHALLENGE**
5. Turning toward or away **CHALLENGE**
6. Satisfaction with romance and passion **M → J**
7. Satisfaction with the quality of sex **M → J**

8. Satisfaction with the frequency of sex **J → M**
9. Emotional disengagement and loneliness **CHALLENGE**

Conflict

10. Harsh start-up **CHALLENGE**
11. The Four Horsemen of the Apocalypse **CHALLENGE**
12. Flooding **CHALLENGE**
13. Accepting influence **CHALLENGE**
14. Compromise **CHALLENGE**
15. Negative sentiment override **CHALLENGE**
16. Repair attempts **CHALLENGE**
17. My family history **M → J**
18. 19 areas
    a. Emotional connection **CHALLENGE**
    b. Stress management **CHALLENGE**
    c. Relatives and extended family **STRENGTH**
    d. Jealousy **STRENGTH**
    e. Emotional or sexual affairs **STRENGTH**
    f. Basic values and goals **STRENGTH**
    g. Housework and child care **CHALLENGE**
    h. Financial issues **CHALLENGE**
    i. Having fun together **CHALLENGE**
    j. Spirituality, religion, ethics **STRENGTH**
    k. Children **CHALLENGE**
    l. Distressing events **STRENGTH**
    m. Gridlock on perpetual issues **CHALLENGE**

Shared meaning

e. Rituals of connection **CHALLENGE**
f. Roles in life **STRENGTH**
g. Goals **STRENGTH**
h. Symbols **STRENGTH**

166

Individual areas of concern (STRENGTH indicates this area is not a concern)

    h. Drug and alcohol abuse **STRENGTH**

    i. Drug and alcohol frequency screening **STRENGTH**

    j. Suicide potential **STRENGTH**

    k. Domestic violence situational **STRENGTH**

    l. Domestic violence characterological **STRENGTH**

    m. Emotional abuse

        i. Social isolation **STRENGTH**

        ii. Degradation and humiliation **STRENGTH**

        iii. Sexual coercion **STRENGTH**

        iv. Property damage **STRENGTH**

    n. SCL-90 scales (assess potential psychopathology) **STRENGTH, except for disturbed sleep for both partners**

The Detour Scales (suggest additional areas that need work)

    e. Chaos and control **STRENGTH**

    f. Trust **STRENGTH**

    g. Commitment **M → J**

    h. Meta-emotions (a mismatch about their feelings about the emotions) **STRENGTH**

OUR SUMMARY

Marlena is more unhappy in this relationship than Jim.

FRIENDSHIP/INTIMACY. In the area of friendship/intimacy, Marlena is displeased with the amount of *romance* and the quality of sex, while Jim is displeased but mostly about the *frequency* of sex (he wants it more often than Marlena). They know each other very well, but they don't feel very loved or respected, nor do they feel that their partner is turning toward their bids for connection. Emotional connection is a big challenge. No wonder both of them feel lonely.

CONFLICT. Conflict is a huge challenge for this couple. They are both in negative sentiment override. They are flooded, and conflict is harsh and includes the Four Horsemen. They don't accept influence, don't repair very well, nor are they able to reach compromise.

SHARED MEANING. Their shared meaning system is a real strength in this relationship for shared goals, symbols (like what is a home), and supporting the roles they play in life. However, there aren't adequate rituals of connection.

FAMILY HISTORY. Marlena but not Jim described a painful and somewhat traumatic childhood history. That needs to be explored.

DETOUR SCALES. While there is trust and not much chaos in this relationship, Marlena is currently less committed to the relationship than Jim.

Their Narrative

Both Jim and Marlena say that since little Suzie arrived three years ago, their relationship hasn't been very close. Part of the problem is that, according to Marlena, Jim doesn't listen to her feelings very well. Things may change now that she is returning to acting, because she's been both bored and exhausted being a full-time mom. Jim is tired of all the fighting and too little sex.

Oral History Interview.

For Jim it was love at first sight. He saw Marlena acting in a play, thought she was beautiful, very sexy, and a great actress, and he went backstage and became an instant groupie. Marlena was slower to fall in love, but she fell in love when he planned a surprise weekend trip for the two of them on their third date.

He sprang this on her, and she was initially wary, but then fascinated, and agreed to go at the last minute. Jim had booked them to go on a two-week extravaganza safari in Kenya, where he had spent two years in the Peace Corps. On that trip she saw a new side of Jim. She met the villagers he worked with and experienced his great love of nature, conservation, and animals. She said he then swept her off her feet. Their sex life was wonderful in the beginning. They both said that they just felt so at ease with one another in bed.

After that experience, travel and adventure became a mainstay of their courtship. Jim even took acting classes and learned a lot about being an amateur community theater actor from Marlena. Marlena said that Jim was very open. They seemed able to have enormous fun together.

All that changed once they became parents. Little Suzie was a "spirited" child. The pregnancy was hard, and they weren't very close during that period, but they loved being parents. However, they took turns sleeping with Suzie, and they both were always sleep deprived. They hardly talked to one another, didn't get to finish sentences, and hadn't been on a date in three years. Sex was at a minimum, always hurried, the "last chore of the day," said Marlena. They fought all the time.

Family History

Jim was an only child. His father was a career soldier, and his family moved around a great deal. He described himself as an army brat. Mom was a stay-at-home mother, and he was always very close to her. When asked who comforted him when he needed it, he said it was only his mother, never his father. He was also close to his dad, but said that he needed to overcome his father's tendencies to be dogmatic and authoritarian. His dad taught him how to fight in elementary school when he needed to stand up to a bully. He respected his dad. His father liked debating and respected a strong argument. That's how Jim became a master debater in high school and college. He was always good at math and strong in sports. He described his as a good childhood. In college he developed a strong interest in Africa and decided to join the Peace Corps after college and go to Africa. He needed to debate this choice with his politically conservative father, but his dad eventually supported his choice.

Marlena came from a large Irish family. She had three sisters and two brothers. She was the oldest child, and she was always saddled with taking care of the younger children. She described her mother as very preoccupied with her work as a pediatrician. Her mom was the primary breadwinner in the family. She remembers her mother as always tired and irritable. Her mother called her "overly needy" and encouraged her to develop hobbies. When asked who comforted her when she needed it, she says it was her father. Her parents argued a lot, and these arguments always ended with her father giving in. She hated seeing that. Although her father also worked very hard as a teacher, and he had somewhat of a problem with alcohol, but he did most of the child care, taking the kids to school, and he always managed to be there when they came home from school. She described her dad as very warm and loving, but overly compliant. Her relationships with her siblings were still very close, except for one of her sisters.

Conflict Discussion

Their conflict session began by Jim laying out their issues and presenting an analysis of who is most at fault for each issue. He spoke like a lawyer in a courtroom presenting his opening argument and explaining what he will prove to a jury. He responded to Marlena by debating with her. The following is an excerpt.

Jim: I think we have two major issues here. The first is that we have let the fun parts of our relationship go. We aren't having as much fun, and I think that's my fault. I was always the one who took responsibility for planning the things we did that were exciting, and you always enjoyed that. I've slacked up on my responsibility because I want to make partner. Work has taken over my initiative in our relationship. The second issue is how we fight, and I think you get the blame for that. You store things up until you're a total nut case when you present your argument, you escalate, you yell and get hysterical. That serves to make me want to avoid you, so I work harder. That work, on top of all the duties we each have in child care makes me exhausted, and I just have no patience for the way you argue. Then neither of us want sex. That's it in a nutshell.

Marlena: You've got it all figured out, just as you always do. You rest your case.

Jim: I do. I rest my case (laughs). What's your position?

Marlena: Our problems come from me being very needy since I've stopped acting and become a full-time mom. I admit I am overly needy now. I'm probably real irritating. I won't be once Suzie is in preschool and I'm acting again. But our real problem is that you never listen to me. I'm this big pain in the ass to you. You have no patience for me. So instead I talk to my sisters and my dad, and they are really worried about how lonely I am.

Jim: You're going outside our relationship to complain about me. That's another one of our problems.

Marlena: I've got to talk to SOMEONE. All day long I'm relating to a toddler. Then you come home and I want to connect with you, but you immediately get on your computer.

Jim: So? You're not so perfect either.

Marlena: Okay, finding fault isn't going to help us.

Jim: You think all our problems are MY fault, right?

Marlena: Yes, I do.

Jim: So, I'm just trying to spread the fault around a little.

Marlena: No, you're being defensive.

Jim: No, I'm not.

Marlena: That's defensive right there. I rest my case.

Jim: (laughs) I've got to admit, you won that point.

Both: (laugh).

Contracting Session

The couple agrees with the therapist that the place to start is with conflict. They are very tired of fighting all the time. They want new tools for dealing with conflict. They also want to be closer to one another. They find the feedback process and the Sound Relationship House theory interesting and useful. They took the Bringing Baby Home workshop and it helped a lot, but their gains were only temporary.

First Treatment Session

In this session the therapist says that they are going to have that conversation again, but this time the therapist introduces the Gottman-Rapoport Conflict Blueprint. The blueprint is explained. They are to take turns as speaker and listener. The listener's job is to summarize and validate. The speaker's job is to stay out of attack-defend mode (no "you statements," no blaming, no criticism, "you always" or "you never" statements), but to describe how he or she feels about a specific situation and express a positive need (what you do need, not what you don't need). The need has to be as close to a recipe as possible, so the listener knows what actions the speaker wants done.

Jim has trouble understanding the role of the listener. The therapist explains two points. First, this kind of listening is not for framing a rebuttal (an occupational hazard of being a lawyer). This kind of listening is designed to UNDERSTAND the speaker, get into the speaker's perspective, in a compassionate manner, like a Vulcan mind meld in *Star Trek*. The listener should get in touch with the speaker's pain and empathize when validating. Second, the therapist explains that validating is not agreeing; it's not giving up your own perspective. It's being able to genuinely complete a sentence like, "I get it. From your perspective I can see why you feel this way and have these needs, because . . . "

The therapist also explains that it's most important to listen to NEGATIVE emotions and to try to understand what the longing is behind each emotion. The therapist hands out the booklet on great listening as something for them to read before the next session.

Marlena: So that's my whole point about listening to me, Jim. That's just exactly what I need from you. To listen to me. And to *want to* listen to me.

Jim: I do listen to you, up to a point.

Therapist: Stay with the blueprint. Take notes, listen. You get to be a speaker once she feels that you got it. Okay? Does that make sense?

Jim: Okay. Say all that again.

Marlena: Let me give an example. And this is about sex too. Last week I was walking in the Bellevue shopping mall, and I walked by these three guys, and they are sitting around this fountain and I walk by and they look up briefly and they look away. See, I'm not used to that. I'm vain. I'm an actress. I used to be a model. I'm used to guys totally staring longingly at me as I go by. And I run home. Suzie is at school and no one is home. So I get naked and look in the mirror, and I think, hey, I'm buff, why aren't these guys checking me out? I look even better than before I got pregnant. It's all back. What's happened? And then I think, what was on my mind when I walked by those guys? I know what was on my mind. I have this HUGE TO-DO LIST on my mind, and I think, yeah, and I always have that list or one like it on my mind, and then I'm mad at Jim, but I'm always mad at Jim. So I get that mind-set in my body and I look in the mirror again, and what message am I sending out? What did these guys see? What does Jim see? And I see it's, "Don't mess with me. I'm a mom! I got business to attend to. Don't mess with me! Back away!" So, I am not available to anyone. I am not sexy. I am like dry bones. And that's what I come to you with every day. That attitude. And what I get back from you is also, "Get the hell away from me! You annoy me!" That's what I get back. And that sucks!

Therapist: So what do you need from Jim?

Marlena: What I need is for you to tell me I am sexy, I am soft, you do want me, you do want to listen to me. I am important to you. That you do care. That I am not IRRITATING you! Even if I have nothing to say because I have been with a toddler for eight mind-numbing hours, you want me.

Therapist: Great job. Are you done?

Marlena: Yes, for now.

Therapist: Are you ready for Jim to summarize and validate?

Marlena: Yes, I am.

Jim: Okay. So your point is still that you're pissed at me. And you come at me when I get home from work, you're angry, and I respond like those guys. I look away. Is that it?

Marlena: Yes.

Jim: So I listened that time?

Marlena: I suppose so.

Therapist: Did he get it or didn't he?

Marlena: No, he missed a lot.

Therapist: Exactly. Don't be compliant like your dad is. Tell him what he missed.

Marlena: You missed that I don't feel beautiful anymore. I hate myself. I've become such a bitch. I feel like I'm being this OVERLY NEEDY BURDEN to you. And then I am angry, not at you, but because I feel so alone and so bored not acting. So I need you to be glad to see me at the end of a day, to feel like, "Ah, I have come home to Marlena, my love," and then to want to listen like this to whatever dumb thing I have to say about what the baby did today, or what I am upset about, and not be impatient, or dying to get alone with your case notes or your cell phone. But you're not like that. You can't wait to get away from me.

Jim: You done?

Marlena: Yes, I am now.

Jim: So your point is still you are pissed at me. And you come at me when I get home from work, you're angry, and I respond like those guys. I look away. I get on my computer or cell phone. Is that it? That's pretty much what I said before. What am I missing? This is so frustrating.

Marlena: No, you totally missed the point.

Jim: I tried to get the gist of what you were saying, without the extraneous details. It's what I do every day. I am a good listener.

Therapist: Jim. I think that the problem is that you're not writing things down as she speaks. So you're missing the *nuances* of what she's saying. You're hearing only a small fraction of what she is saying. And you're missing the important emotions. That may work in court, but in a love relationship, the listening has to be different. More like the way you listen when you're a tourist in a small town in Italy, and you are full of questions. Who built that church? Who designed these stained glass windows? Where's the market? And on vacation, you're not in a hurry, you're not impatient, you're relaxed and curious. So try to get it all. Not too short a summary; more of it.

Jim: Okay. That is different than the way I listen.

Therapist (doing a Dan Wile): Is it okay if I try to speak for you?

Marlena: Can't hurt.

Therapist: Okay, Jim. I want you to take detailed notes of what I say. And Marlena, correct me if I get this wrong.

Marlena: Okay.

Therapist: I'm trying to say that the listening thing I have been complaining about isn't all your fault. Write this down, Jim. It's NOT your fault.

Jim: (starts writing).

Therapist: What I'm trying to say with my story of the guys at the mall fountain is that in becoming a mom I have lost myself. I'm always too busy to just be myself. I have this air of total busyness, and I COME AT the world like a mother bear. Look out, don't mess with me. And I have lost who I am, your lover, the soft woman, the lady who loves who you are, who is fun to be with. I can just hear my mother saying, "See, I told you so. You are TOO NEEDY. You are completely an IRRITATING person. No one wants to be near you." And so I'm dying for you to come home and say, "NO, THAT'S NOT TRUE. I love her, she is an interesting person, she is desirable, I am very glad to see her, she is MY HOME. And I want to hear everything she says. She's not irritating. She is wonderful. And she's even more wonderful now that she is the mother of my child. I am so GRATEFUL to her. She made me a DAD, and I love little Suzie. I want to listen to her."

Marlena: (weeping) Yes, that's it! That's what I have been saying, trying to say. But you said it much better.

Therapist: Can you say that in your own words to him?

Marlena: Yes, okay, like he said, I want you to tell me that I am interesting, I am not annoying. I do hear my mother's voice telling me, "Jim isn't going to want to be with you. Why should Jim listen to you? No one wants to be with such a needy person." So it doubles, it triples how important it is to me that when you come home you want to listen to me. Even if what I have to say is boring because I have been with a toddler all day, and I'm in sweatpants, and my hair is a mess.

Jim: No one is more beautiful to me than you.

Marlena: That's what I want to hear. So if I tell you that Suzie duplicated the Lego structure I built in three minutes and how amazing that is, and how she concentrated, I want you to say, "Tell me all about it! Show me the Lego structure! Three minutes, that is incredibly AMAZING." Even if it isn't, that's what I want. And yes, compliments too like the one you just said.

Jim: Okay, so here's what I'm hearing. The details. One is that you've lost yourself since becoming a mom. You're on the warpath most of the time. You are filled with this list of tasks, and you hate it. You are a mother bear, and partly that's good because you're protective, and that's great. But partly that takes you away from who you are. You are not soft, you're in no mood to be my lover. Two, you're in sweats all day listening to this toddler, and it's mind numbing, but also it's not, it's also wonderful because she does amazing things that you want to tell me about, and have me be interested in, not impatient and anxious to get on my computer. So when I get impatient, it makes you feel so ALONE. And instead you need me to be glad to see you, and tell you what an amazingly beautiful woman you are, and that I'm horny for you, and want to romance you too, and above all hear all the things that are in your mind. And that makes total sense to me, because it just does. Did I get it?

Marlena: (crying) Yeah, yeah, yeah, you got it.

Jim: Finally.

Therapist: Knocked it out of the park! It's okay to hug.

Both: (hugging).

CHAPTER 11

What's Behind Demand-Withdraw:

Meta-emotion Mismatch

Emotion Coaching Versus Emotion Dismissing

This chapter will explore what is behind the mismatch between many men and many women we see in therapy in the carrying capacity for partner's negative affect. Our answer is meta-emotion. Here's that META term again. We've already had meta-communication in the old general systems theory. Now we will meet a new META. We will discuss how this idea applies to both to couples and to families.

META-EMOTIONS: FEELINGS ABOUT FEELINGS

DISMISSING THE NEGATIVE

If you examine photographs from the late 19th century, when photography first became widely available, you will notice that no one is smiling. As Mark Twain once commented, "A photograph is a serious document." Today, however, no one on our planet would think to pose for a photo without the requisite posed smile. Arlie Hochschild in her 1983 book, *The Managed Heart*, pointed out that the early airline industry REQUIRED stewardesses to smile; it was part of the required "equipment." As Paul Ekman observed, most of the smiles people produce under these posed circumstances are the "unfelt smiles," rather than the full-faced Duchenne smiles, in which the eyes as well as the mouth are fully engaged in the smile (and you get the crow's feet at the eye corners).

Managed emotions have become a part of modern culture. There are hidden assumptions here that one's emotions are like a jacket that one decides to wear in the morning. If one assumes that emotions are that kind of choice, then why would one ever CHOOSE to feel sad, or choose to feel afraid, or choose to feel angry, or choose to feel contemptuous, or choose to feel disgusted? Why not always choose to wear a happy jacket? In accordance with the very American Norman Vincent Peale's 1952 book, *The Power of Positive Thinking*, one would obviously choose to be always cheerful, curious, optimistic, hopeful, happy, and even ecstatically joyful. One would always choose hope over despair, joy over sadness, tranquility over stress, and so on. Put a smile on your face.

Not all cultures on the planet feel that way about the so-called negative emotions. For example, Italians don't, and Israelis don't. These cultures tend to view emotions as something that we do not choose, and that the so-called negative emotions are especially informative about who we are at any moment. They believe in exploring these negative emotions, and trying to understand them—in ourselves and others—because they are important. They don't believe in suppressing negative emotions either. However, many other cultures on the planet have the view that negative emotions are potentially dangerous and need to be severely managed, or disasters will ensue.

This belief that emotions are purely a matter of choice actually has some dreadful consequences. One then becomes impatient with the negative emotions, in oneself and especially in others. One tends to dismiss these emotions and minimize their importance. In his 2010 book *The Gift of Fear*, Gavin de Becker reviews the work he has done with the victims and survivors of violent crimes. These are people who could have easily been raped or murdered. Some have escaped a predator whom the police later arrested as a serial killer. He notes that there was always a moment in the sequence of tragic events when the victim dismissed his or her fear. One story is about a woman who was carrying her groceries from her car to her apartment. A pleasant and good-looking young man she had never seen before in her apartment complex offered to help her carry her groceries. She felt uneasy but discounted her trepidations as silly. He nearly killed her. De Becker concluded that our best method for staying safe is to honor our fears and trust our intuitions when some situation feels unsafe. This is especially true for women. The world is a far more dangerous place for women than it is for men. A national probability study in the United States found that 40% of women in their lifetime will be seriously physically or sexually assaulted. In the military that estimate is 50%.

Our research showed that in close relationships THE major incompatibility in marriage is a mismatch in how people view the negative emotions. Among heterosexuals, mostly what leads to divorce is husbands being emotionally dismissive of negative emotions in their women, and women feeling abandoned by this meta-emotional attitude. That is the major cause of past emotional injuries in these couples, injuries that usually go unprocessed in most relationships, unless they get good therapy—which they mostly don't get. In America there are 900,000 divorces each year, and we estimate that fewer than 10% ever talk to any therapist, clergyperson, or mental health counselor about their problems.

One husband John saw in therapy said, "When my wife walks into a room, I scan her face. If I see anything negative there, I get up and leave as quickly as I can, because I know this is not gonna be good. We're either on for some major explosion, or she's gonna whine and complain about something or someone. Nothing is ever right for that woman, or good enough. I want you to fix her. That's our only problem, really."

In the first study we planned for our family psychophysiology laboratory, we decided to study families as well as couples. Each parent was to be separately interviewed about their own experience of sadness and anger, their philosophy of emotional expression and control, and their attitudes and behavior about their children's anger and sadness. Their behavior during this interview was taped and later coded with a meta-emotion coding system designed by a central member of our laboratory staff, Carole Hooven.

In our first study of the effects of the parents' marriage on children, we discovered a great variety in the experiences, philosophies, and attitudes that parents had about their emotions and the emotions of their children. One pair of parents said that they viewed anger as "from the devil," and that they would not permit themselves or their children to express anger. Their child was quite docile in her interactions with her parents but appeared quite angry and bossy in her interactions with her best friend. A similar negative view toward anger was echoed by other parents. Some parents in our study said that they put their children in time out just for being angry, even if there was no child misbehavior. Other parents felt that anger was natural but ignored the experience of anger in their children. Other parents encouraged the expression and exploration of anger. There was similar variety with respect to sadness, and the information we gathered about sadness was not redundant with the information we gathered about anger. Some parents minimized sadness in themselves and in their children, saying such things as, "I can't afford to be sad," and "What does a kid have to be sad about?" Other parents thought that emotions like sadness in themselves and in their children were important and viewed themselves as emotion coaches of their children about the world of emotion. In our pilot work there also appeared to be gender differences: Fathers seemed less likely to be aware of their own sadness or to assist when their children were sad; fathers who were oriented toward emotion seemed more interested in their children's anger than in their sadness. Mothers seemed to be more concerned with their children's sadness than fathers. These were our initial impressions.

So we decided to focus on studying parents' feelings about feelings, which we called their meta-emotions. Meta-cognitions are our thoughts about thinking. In social interaction research, the term "meta-communication" refers to communication about communication. We began to also use the term "meta-emotion structure" to refer broadly to similar executive functions of emotion, ones that included concepts, philosophies, and metaphors about emotions, as well as emotions about emotions. Concepts similar to meta-emotion have been discussed by Mayer (2004) in ideas about emotional intelligence.

What we mean by the meta-emotion structure construct, specifically, is the parents' awareness of specific emotions, their awareness of these emotions in their child, and their coaching of the emotion in their child. "Emotion coaching" refers to talking to the child about the child's emotions, helping the child to verbally label the emotions being felt, accepting the child's emotions, discussing the situations that elicited the emotions, and having goals and strategies for coping with these situations.

The effects of inducing anger may vary across subjects, not only because anger is not induced uniformly across people, but because people's emotions about their own anger vary so much. Take the startle experiment. In a startle experiment the experimenter will fire off a high-intensity stimulus, like a gunshot, behind the subject's head. That results in a startle reflex. However, after displaying the startle reflex, people will have various emotions because of having been startled. Some people laugh with pleasure, some laugh with embarrassment, some become afraid, some are disgusted, and some become angry. This second emotional response is a meta-emotion. It is an emotion about an emotion. Whenever we elicit an emotion in therapy, we are also dealing with emotions people have about having experienced that emotion. We always engage the person's meta-emotion structure, whether we study it or not.

META-EMOTION STRUCTURE

A meta-emotion structure is an organized set of feelings and concepts about emotion, and this idea includes the idea of an emotion philosophy. For example, a mom may be disgusted by his or her 5-year-old's anger and believe that children of that age should not express anger, that it is disrespectful, destructive, and bad. Then she would think it is fine to punish her daughter for showing anger. It's the same to this mom as misbehavior.

Another mom may view his or her 5-year-old's anger as acceptable and as an important moment for talking about the child's emotions and understanding what the child is feeling.

We also study people's metaphors about emotion. For example, one father in our research referred to sadness as if it were a limited resource, like how much money one might have to spend. He talked about his belief that his children should not "waste" their sadness on trivial things but instead "invest" their sadness only in important things. For this father it was almost a sin for his child to be sad about missing Mom one morning, because that was wasting the limited resource of sadness on a trivial, unimportant everyday event. He said that if his daughter's pet had died, that would be a wise investment of sadness. But merely missing Mom was showing poor judgment on the child's part on what to spend this valuable and limited resource on. This "limited resource" metaphor for sadness led this father to act disapproving most of the time, when his daughter was sad—yet at other times to be compassionate and understanding of her sadness.

Would his daughter understand his concept, or would she only see his disapproval? His metaphor for sadness had a profound effect on his parenting and on his relationship with his daughter. This metaphor is an example of a pattern of meta-emotions and an organized set of thoughts about these patterns of meta-emotions, and we refer to each of these various patterns as a meta-emotion structure.

This meta-emotion concept was generalized to couples by Dan Yoshimoto. We eventually interviewed people about their feelings, history, and philosophy with emotion, in general, and with the specific emotions, with anger, sadness, disgust, fear, affection, love, pride, and joy, with expressing, noticing, and experiencing negative and positive emotions. And we asked about the possibility of having an emotion-centered life, or a life without it. We also asked about the couple's relationship and emotions. Could they talk to their partner calmly about their sadness, their anger, their joy? Was their partner proud of them? What was the expression of love and affection like in the relationship?

Yoshimoto found two general patterns, the attuned pattern, which was accepting of negative emotions, and the dismissing pattern, which was disapproving or minimizing about negative emotions. We're focusing on the NEGATIVE emotions here, but in general we found that people who were dismissing with negative emotions also tended to feel uncomfortable with some of the very positive emotions (affection, praise), if their expression was unconstrained. For example, one emotion-dismissing husband said that he was uncomfortable with "displays" of affection in public, or uncomfortable if laughter was "too loud." The attuned, emotion-accepting pattern had these features:

- They try to notice small amounts of negative emotions.
- They value talking about all emotions.
- They ask questions about emotions.
- They talk about their partner's emotional needs.
- They accept all feelings and wishes as okay.
- They try to validate others' emotions by putting themselves in their partner's shoes and saying that their partner's feeling makes sense.
- They try to understand first and then problem solve.
- They believe that one's emotions are a personal guide for finding meaning.

The emotion-dismissing pattern was far more ACTION ORIENTED and had these features:

- They try to avoid having or dwelling on negative emotions.
- They minimize their importance, preferring to substitute a more positive emotion for the negative one.
- They distract themselves if they have a negative emotion, so it won't take over.
- They think "Suck it up and get on with life," or you could get stuck in the negative emotion and never be able to get out of it.
- They have an ACTION ORIENTATION ("do something, just do anything").

- They try to not have any personal needs, or be needy.
- They believe you can have any emotion you want.
- So therefore be positive, don't dwell on negativity, it's dangerous.
- They are impatient with negative emotions in self and others.
- They think staying in a negative affect state is poisonous.

The demand-withdraw occurs with meta-emotion mismatches

Our findings were very simple. One partner is attuning (coaching) and the other is dismissing (even about their children's emotions). The mismatch alone predicted divorce or stability in the next four years with 80% accuracy.

CASE EXAMPLE FROM OUR LOVE LAB: THE IMPORTANCE OF ATTUNEMENT

Here is an example of a couple in our first study (with 100 couples) using this couple's meta-emotion. This couple was very unhappily married. They were both in the bottom 1% in marital satisfaction in this study. This couple was also very low in both husband and wife being able to attune when they were each sad (the husband in the bottom 30th percentile, and the wife in the bottom 19th percentile) and for husband and wife being able to attune when they were angry (the husband in the bottom 28th percentile, and the wife in the bottom 21st percentile). In this excerpt from the husband's interview, he says that he cannot talk to his wife when he is sad. He feels that she will confront him (call him out) when he is sad, so he chooses not to share it. He also mentions not being appreciated, encouraged, or respected by his wife.

Husband Meta-emotion Interview

In this excerpt the interviewer (I) is trying to find out what sorts of things make the husband (H) feel sad, and whether he can talk to his wife (W) about his sadness. It's very difficult for him to separate being able to talk about his sadness without also becoming angry about feeling disrespected by his wife.

I: What sorts of things make you sad?

H: Hearing all this crap about my job. All the time. I don't feel that I get the respect I need or deserve from my wife. I didn't get the time I needed even though I had this trip coming. The thing that makes me the saddest is when I feel I'm getting shortchanged out of being married. I'm not able, you know, to continue to grow. Go back to school. My wife, she's quittin' her job. She's going back to school and the burden falls on me. To cover all the bills. All the money, you know, I do side contracting, so I'm trying to do all these things to keep the money flowing. And she doesn't want to even see that as viable. You know, by that I mean that she doesn't encourage me, "Hey, you know, you're doing a great job." My side jobs, I make great money, but she's, "Oh no, you're going to be out late tonight. When you going to be home?" Those types of things, they make me sad or angry. I suppose a little bit of both. Where I just want to run away.

So, we can see that this man is very angry with his wife and feels highly unappreciated. For him the marriage feels unfair.

I: In general, what are your thoughts and feelings about being sad? How do you feel about your sadness?

H: How do I feel about my sadness? I feel all right about it. It's kind of a slowdown time for me. And I get pretty nostalgic. Like an AM radio station, think back to better times and better days, a flight back to the past, and then I feel sad.

Personally he feels okay about his own sadness. He doesn't dismiss or suppress it.

I: How does your wife respond to you when you're sad? Respond to your sadness?

H: Oh, yeah, well, she calls me out. "Oh, there you go being moody again. Blah blah blah, yak, yak, yak." (laughs) She doesn't really acknowledge it. Therefore I choose not to share it.

The husband laments his inability to get his wife to be supportive of him, especially when he is sad. Instead, he complains that she confronts him in an attempt to get him to buck up and be strong. Later in the interview, he says that he is also worn down by her anger.

Wife Meta-emotion Interview

In the following excerpt from his wife's meta-emotion interview, she talks about his being unable to not take her sadness personally. When he hears about her sadness, she says, he feels he's done something wrong. When she is sad, she says he feels blamed by that, and he just does not know what to do about her being sad.

I: What sorts of things make you sad?

W: Lots of things every day. With me, crying is a way for me to express my sadness. It makes me feel a lot better. And it's something I usually like to do on my own. I don't like to share it with someone and start bawling (laughs). But I'm the kind of person where if I feel sad, or I can get in the shower and I'll just bawl my head off. (laughs) I feel much better.

Personally, she is very comfortable with her own sadness. She will continue to express this personal comfort she feels about being sad.

I: How do you feel about your sadness?

W: I think of sadness as a very healthy and normal emotion personally. My husband . . . he's helpless when I get sad. Or a number of things like that, so a lot of times I'm hard on myself and I just think, "Why am I being so emotional or what have you?" That doesn't happen to me very often. I allow myself to be sad and feel sad.

The interviewer is now getting the idea that she believes that her sadness is difficult for her husband to handle.

I: So, how does he respond to you with actions? What would I see and hear? Would your husband know if you were sad? Would he pick up on it?

W: Yeah, he would pick up on it. Not necessarily know what to do about it.

The interviewer now wants to get some detail and examples of what she perceives happens when her husband notices her sadness.

W: I would say really, probably, he would be really busy. He would make himself busy and he would retreat more. Because again I think for him, if I'm sad he internalizes that and thinks of it as, "Oh gosh." And a lot of times *he doesn't know what to do.* And so he deals with it in a way that he feels he can deal with it. Rarely would he be loving and affectionate. I don't think he would do that. Even though he is, I consider him, I mean if I said to him, "Oh, I need a hug," or "I need affection," no problem, he's no problem. But he doesn't figure that out on his own. Like he would think to do that.

He dismisses her sadness.

I: How do you feel about this response?

W: (angry facial expression) I would certainly like for him to be more affectionate. And loving and understanding. And not internalize it.

I would certainly like for that to be different. I think I've communicated that to him. But for him that takes a lot of effort.

She feels that he blames her for feeling sad, and that he asks her to justify being sad.

W: There's times when I'm depressed and he says, "Why are you depressed?" And I don't know *why* I'm depressed. I mean sometimes I really don't. I'm just in a downer, I'm in a bad mood. I'm just down, I'm just blue. He looks at it as, "I'm not making her happy," basically. And he's not sure what to do, so he's thinking, "I'll just let her get through this time and she'll be back to herself."

Flooding

This husband was also in the top 90th percentile of all people in the study in being flooded. On the other hand, his wife was not very flooded (bottom 30th percentile). Their physiological data during their conflict discussion fit this pattern as well—he was flooded and she was not.

Oral History Interview

On the Oral History Interview, for the positive friendship codes they were both in the bottom half of all people in the sample, and for enemyship codes (viewing one's partner as a hostile adversary) he was in the top 1%, and she was in the top 7%. This excerpt from the interview is characterized by them not being very positive or expansive about their relationship or their first meeting. There were long pauses as the interviewer tried to get them to talk expansively about their early relationship history and their impressions of one another. The interviewer is working hard to elicit much of anything from them.

I: Just want to start at the beginning with you guys and ask how you met, how you got together.

(She pokes him.)

H: Well, we met through one of my best friends. Probably my best friend. On the platonic level, though. She was going out with somebody. How old were you then?

W: 18.

H: I was a senior in college. She was a young lily little freshman. And I was in the lunchroom. I didn't have any coins. She was loaded down with coins. She loaned me some coins. That was the first time we'd met but not the first time I'd seen her.

I: When was the first time you'd seen her?

H: I saw her walking through the hall.

There are no spontaneous compliments emerging, so the interviewer sees if there are any.

I: So she kind of stood out to you?

H: No. Well, yeah, she stood out but . . .

W: You don't want to admit that.

She picks up on his reluctance to compliment her.

H: She walked around all stuck up and stuff (imitates a swagger).

W: He's lying.

The husband is not earning very many points with his wife.

H: She was kind of stuck on herself. I always tell her about that. I played football and I got my fair share of attention. She really didn't go for all that. She went about her business.

This may be a compliment. It's hard to tell.

W: I'd seen him before. But I don't recall where or when. I didn't pay a lot of attention, especially to the football players.

She was unimpressed by him.

H: Yeah. She had this little hat on, looked like the good girls, a little tight jeans and a little vest, I remember thinking, "Man, she looked good." Matter of fact I even told my friend, Steve, I said, "I'm gonna marry that girl." I didn't know what I was getting myself into. Saying something crazy like that.

There is finally a compliment, and some nostalgia, but she isn't going to join in with him in reminiscing about their early relationship.

W: After dating for a while we were off then, we just stopped.
H: Broke up the engagement.
W: Exactly, broke up the engagement. Broke up and decided no, we need to see other people and we never stopped seeing each other.
H: But also saw other people.
W: But also saw other people.
I: Why did you break up?
W: A lot of it was that we were really too young. Totally young and immature. I thought I was ready for marriage and totally was not. Felt like it was the same way with him. It was a blessing that we didn't get married when we were originally engaged. Yeah. We were just too young and not ready. For the—
H: Rigors of—
W: (laughs) the rigors of . . . marriage.

They begin to talk about how hard it has been being married to one another. This is not a very positive Oral History Interview.

Conflict Discussion

The observational coding of their conflict discussion showed that it was highly negative (he was in the top 4% and she was in the top 14% on negativity) and not very positive (he was in the bottom 2% and she in the bottom 9% on positivity). In the following excerpt, they keep interrupting one another, and they escalate the conflict by getting increasingly angry.

H: Okay, household responsibilities. I mean what else is there to say that we didn't already say?

W: (laughs) I thought it was very interesting that you said about the bills. How you had relinquished that over to me and you appreciated that. It had taken a load off of you, because you never told me that. Even though I have known that, you have never told me.

H: A lot of things you haven't told me.

W: I'm just saying that goes to appreciation.

H: We're not talking about appreciation.

Even getting started is difficult for them. She is fishing for a restatement of a compliment from him for her now doing the bills. She is looking for more appreciation, but he becomes defensive very quickly.

W: No. It has very much to do with appreciation. To do with household responsibilities. And my whole feeling that comes out of us not doing our fair share is resentment and feeling that I'm not appreciated. And since I have taken that household responsibility over, it has been a huge difference. And although you've never said that, you've never acknowledged it, that's my example of, you know, the daily things I do, just that daily thing of getting them out of the mailbox. (laughs) And organizing them.

H: (yawns).

W: You know, that's a daily thing. (laughs) Did one today and not even organizing it and not writing checks down, just keeping that whole system organized. And you've never once said . . .

She is going to press this point that she has not received enough appreciation from him for taking over the bills. He rejects this request, claiming that he also received no appreciations from her for all the time HE did the bills.

H: No, I did that before also, though. And you never said anything to me about it.

W: I know, but I'm talking efficiently though. I'm talking about half the time you didn't know what you paid. . . .

She needs to make the point that when he did the bills, he did a bad job, whereas she did the job efficiently. She has just moved into attack mode, and she is now unlikely to get any appreciation from him.

H: (laughing, shaking his head).

W: When you paid, when it was due, when we got it.

H: That's not true.

W: (eye roll) Oh, that's so true!

H: I did it, and . . .

W: No.

He disagrees with her, and he brings up his point that when he was doing the bills, they had far less money, and he also feels unappreciated for working nights now to bring in more money, and, because he is working both the day job and the extra night job, he has had to ask her to take over doing the bills.

H: And the other thing is the money just wasn't there.

W: Well, we didn't win a lottery since I took them over. We have the same amount of money.

H: No, but things changed. When you first started taking it over, that's when I started working the part-time job. We had the extra money. You were working *little* part-time jobs. And that's . . .

W: Okay, so you do deny that. No change has happened since I took it over, is that what you're saying? (derisive laugh).

H: What I'm saying is well, yeah, sure.

She is not getting the appreciation she wants, so she pushes her point. He begrudgingly says things have indeed gotten better now that she is doing the bills, but then the conflict has escalated.

W: I don't know what that means. Does that mean, yes some changes have taken place, or no, some changes have not taken place? One or the other.

H: Some change has taken place, yeah.

W: For the positive, not.

H: Right.

W: Positive changes have taken place.

H: Yeah.

W: Okay. (nods) Well I'm just saying it's nice to hear this. I hadn't heard that. So that just goes along with my feeling not appreciated, but the thing that would make me feel better about it is, one big thing about it that is my pet peeve.

She now feels encouraged by receiving this begrudging appreciation, and now she will bring up another issue: housework. She tries to soften this with humor. He responds defensively.

W: Last night after I had gotten home from work and had gotten the girls and done my whole thing that I do every day and dinner and you came home, house was straightened and you came home and you (laughs) put your bag in the middle of the floor (laughs harder).

H: (smiling).

W: Your gym bag in the middle of the floor. And your coat on the dining room chair. And that is such a pet peeve of mine. I mean, why can't you just, and then I proceeded to hang the jacket up in the coat closet and put your bag in the bedroom. I'm just saying that would be one thing that would be really helpful for me.

H: Yeah, well I don't do that all the time.

She acknowledges that he does usually clean things up. But then she escalates again, and he stonewalls.

W: No, you don't ever do that. Actually I could say, if you do that, that is just very rare. And I don't think it would really be a major deal, it would just be like thinking, "Like okay, I'm taking this jacket off and I'm right by the coat closet. I'll just go ahead and hang it up." I mean, you know what I'm saying? I mean, it's not like it would be a major task. But it would really, like, because that's just a pet peeve. You know just something daily that you could do. When you come in, just put your things away. And I don't mean, your bag can be in the middle of the bedroom, that's fine, but not the pit stop in the living room, right in the middle of the floor.

H: (looking away, stonewalling).

She tries a repair before turning back to her major pet peeve.

W: That's helpful for me. Of course, I want you to cook on Friday, um, and I would like you to tidy up on Fridays.

H: I do.

W: I'm not saying that you don't. I'm just saying that I do appreciate those things when you tidy up on Fridays and you make dinner because I do that every day, every day I do something to tidy.

H: I know.

W: And every day I make dinner. So I don't think that's too much to ask that you do it on Fridays.

H: (nodding).

W: So, what is your . . .

Now he is going to launch a defensive counterattack, labeling her point as just "tit for tat," meaning she is keeping score on who does what, and he finds that unfair.

H: On Saturdays, Fridays, I cook. I clean up Saturdays. I try to get up and make breakfast. I try to let you sleep in.

W: I appreciate that.

H: Sundays I get up and make breakfast . . .

W: When I said what is your, I meant what do you want me to do differently, that's what I meant, not like what your things are that you think irritate me, or . . .

H: I want you to stop just trying to, I just get tired of everything being tit-for-tat, "Well I do this, I do that, I do this," and I just constantly feel like I'm always having to defend my position. I understand. I know what you do. I understand that. And I try to do what I can do, but by the time I come home it's 6:30, on weekdays . . .

He begins to feel that he is getting through to her, so he presses his point.

W: Right.

H: You know what I'm saying?

W: I can understand that. But can you understand?

She feels encouraged because she has given him some appreciation, but she doesn't feel that she has gotten the appreciation she deserves. So she says, "I can understand that," but then she adds, "But can you understand?" However, he wasn't finished with his point, so he needs to tell her that her adding "But can you understand?" is an interruption of his point. As he pushes his point, she also pushes her point, and now the conflict escalates further.

H: Hold on, hold on. I'm not finished.

W: Okay. All right.

H: See and this is what I'm talking about, the communication piece.

W: Right, I know, because I do not . . .

H: Because when you cut in . . .

W: I have to say something now . . .

H: No. Because when you cut in . . .

W: I have something to say here . . .

H: Hold on! Shut up!

W: (smiling) See, that's what I'm saying.

H: Because I'm on a thought process.

W: I know.

H: I'm on a thought process and you cut in.

W: Okay.

H: Okay?

W: Go ahead.

That last line was a good repair on her part.

H: So let me finish my thoughts. I think we need the interviewer back in here because things get done.

W: No, no.

H: And you're telling me.

W: Shhh. You're going off on a tangent.

H: Shhh.

They are both now trying to repair the escalation and calm down. However, they haven't calmed down long enough. She is encouraged by their repair to push her point that she cleans up far more than he does. He is having none of that.

W: When you get home at 6:30 in the evening . . .

H: The girls have to be fed by then. I try to, I try to—just like last night—pick up the room. I try to pick up around the place, you know, when people come over, you know, I'm the one who is cleaning the bathroom, picking up the places that people are gonna see. You know, and you make me out to be like this dirty slob, when you know that's not the case.

W: (laughs).

H: You know that's not the case. I can be just as sloppy as you can be sloppy. And you try to act like you're Miss Immaculate Clean. And you know that's not the case.

W: I didn't say that.

H: Okay?

W: I just clean up and you don't.

H: Yes I do. I pick up just as you do. You pick up—

W: You pick up when it's totally out of control and I try to pick up every day so that on Friday I don't have to spend the whole weekend cleaning, 'cause that's not what I'm gonna do with my weekend.

H: Just like the other night when you were gone. Did you come back to a clean kitchen?

W: Certainly I did.

H: Okay.

W: Just as who made dinner for you before I left?

H: See, you're tit-ing for tat-ing again.

W: No, see.

H: I'm just stating the fact.

W: Okay.

H: Was it clean?

W: Yes, it was.

H: So I did pick up, so I didn't just pile things up until they got to a big pigpen, like you say I always do.

W: Um hmm.

H: Okay, so acknowledge that.

W: Okay.

They seem to have accepted that they both contribute mightily to keeping things straightened up. However, it's not over.

H: On the weekends—

W: (rolls her eyes).

H: I try to pick up, I try to let you sleep in, I try to do my fair share of cooking—you don't see that.

W: Are you done? Can I speak again?

H: No. Those are the things that make me resentful.

W: Okay. Tell me when I can talk.

H: Go ahead.

She needs to push the point that she does more than he does.

W: Okay. You were saying that you do, but your problem is that I don't appreciate what you do do. But can we agree that I do more than you do?

H: I've already said that.

W: Okay.

She has won her point, but they are both now angry and escalated physiologically.

H: How many times do I have to say that?

W: Okay. I'm trying to make my point here, so can you listen now? Shhh! (holds hand up) So we both have agreed that I do more than you do, a considerable amount more than you do. And you say that you do appreciate what I do, you do show appreciation. Is that what you're saying?

She is going to summarize and consolidate her win. The husband is resisting.

H: (pouring himself a glass of water, taking his time, then looking at her and laughing) I would say . . .

W: It's real clear, you do show it or you don't.

H: I just feel that that's something we both need to do.

W: No. No.

H: We both need to practice.

W: No, no, no, no, no. See, finally answer my question. Do you appreciate what I do?

H: Do I *show* appreciation?

W: Exactly.

H: Okay.

W: 'Cause it's easy to say "I appreciate" but—

H: I don't show appreciation.

W: Okay. Now the same would be true of yours. You're saying of me that I don't appreciate what you do, although you do far less than I do.

H: (silent).

W: You have your things you do, you clean the bathroom. Occasionally. You do the yard work. You take out the garbage (pause).

H: (stonewalling).

She has won the battle, but lost the war. Why did this discussion go so badly? Because they have not connected emotionally during the conversation. They do not have a high trust metric.

However, in this conflict discussion we see a full-blown win-lose pattern. Not only are they avoiding giving sincere appreciations, which would have de-escalated the conflict, but, as we will see in Chapter 12, they are operating with a pattern which is not only low trust but creates and nurtures a betrayal metric. We didn't intervene with this couple because they were part of our basic research. In Chapter 12 we will examine more about the dynamics of betrayal.

HOW DO YOU TREAT A META-EMOTION MISMATCH?

How do we move beyond this basic research into the therapeutic context? This is one place where the problem seemed insurmountable because, without treatment, it was such a good predictor of relationship breakup. However, in therapy it turned out not to be very difficult to solve this meta-emotion mismatch using three steps. That was a big surprise. Step one follows.

Step One: Communicate the idea that Understanding Must Precede Action. It turned out to be easy because both an UNDERSTANDING and an ACTION approach to emotions are right. The question is merely one of timing. The motto the therapist proposes is that UNDERSTANDING MUST PRECEDE ACTION. Understanding one's emotions help one know what the goals are, they provide direction, and then action is the next step. Improving listening is an important first step toward understanding.

Step Two: Build A Common Emotion Culture. Because these mismatches in meta-emotion are so common among unhappily married couples, we also needed a way to help the couple system develop a common emotion culture. When the couple has children, emotion coaching is usually the window we can use to change the emotion-dismissing person. Emotion coaching is easy to learn, and it has fairly immediate payoffs for the dismissing parent. The coaching moment builds trust with a child who may be quite distant from that parent.

Step Three: Teach Emotion Coaching. The other window to bridging this meta-emotion mismatch is through talking about each person's experience growing up, and how they were comforted as a child, and how their parents responded to their emotions, how their parents showed them they were proud of them and loved them. Through this meta-emotion interview, each partner can talk about their own experience with emotions, both as children and as grown-ups. The interview can also turn toward their own relationship and what they would prefer from one another. Therefore, step one is to do a meta-emotion interview with each partner, in the other's presence. Step two is to teach the four basic skills of emotional connection, and then to ritualize this emotional check-in with one another in a once-a-week meeting. The four skills of emotional connection are: (1) putting one's feelings into words and self-disclosing to one's partner, (2) asking open-ended questions of one's partner, (3) exploring one's partner's feelings and thoughts, and (4) empathizing with those emotions.

For conflict, by using the Gottman-Rapoport blueprint, it is possible to have the emotion-dismissing person learn to talk about emotions without any escalation. When both people get listened to, the conflict can be calm as well as emotional; there is no flooding. The emotion-dismissing person is usually action oriented, and that is a good thing. The emotion-dismissing person only needs to learn that understanding must precede advice. When listening occurs for both partners, then the conflict does not escalate, and there is no need to fear or dismiss negative emotions.

CHAPTER 12

The Power of Turning Toward

As we observed couples in our apartment lab in Seattle, we needed to train the camera operators in a new way. That training revealed something very fundamental about relationships. For the first time in our lab, couples were freely moving around. They were wearing Holter monitors that assessed two channels of electrocardiogram, so they could move around freely. Three cameras could follow each person's movements through this lab and zoom in or out. There was a kitchen, a dining area, and a sink area. There was a couch and living room chairs, and a big beautiful picture window that overlooked a park and the Montlake Cut. The Montlake Cut has boats of all shapes and sizes moving from the salt water of Lake Union to the clear water of Lake Washington. It's a beautiful window for people watching, and for boat watching.

Rapidly, the camera operators, who were also trained emotion coders, discovered that there was a virtual carnival of events as one person attempted to get the partner's attention, start a conversation, or get the partner to respond in some way. As soon as this event occurred, which we called a "bid for connection," the camera operator would shift one of the cameras so we could see the other person's reaction to the bid. As we described earlier, John and Janice Driver started calling the responses to bids "turning toward," which meant ANY response at all, or "turning away," which meant NO response at all, or "turning against," which meant an irritable or crabby response.

As we mentioned, in that newlywed study with 130 couples we found that the 17 couples who divorced six years after the wedding had turned toward 33% of their partner's bids. Those who stayed married had turned toward 86% of their partner's bids. Our conclusion was that turning toward bids is like building an emotional bank account. And the more assets in the emotional bank, the better.

Driver also discovered that if one gets a couple to turn toward more bids when they are not arguing, there will be more spontaneous humor during conflict. This is just a correlational result. Yet what we think at this time, although we haven't yet tested it, is that the secret to laughing together during conflict is to get people to turn toward bids more.

Couples differed widely in how many bids per minute they produced. During dinner, some couples produced 200 bids in 10 minutes, while other couples produced 2 bids in 10 minutes. We believe that if people are in a relationship where there is a lot of turning away, they will start bidding less. We created a videotape with two clips on it. One clip we called "Spain without interest," and the other clip we called "bread with interest." In the "Spain without interest" clip a wife says she would like to go to Spain sometime. The husband answers that he had been to Spain, but arrived in the middle of a military coup attempt, and had to walk to his hotel through soldiers with fixed bayonets. The wife expresses no interest and the husband becomes quiet. In the "bread with interest" clip a couple are talking and responding in a very excited manner to a conversation about what bread they ate as children (Wonder Bread and sloppy joes) compared to the great bread they can now get in Seattle with hard crusts and soft interiors. They are making bids rapidly, and also they are very responsive to one another's bids. These were two entirely different marriages.

TURNING TOWARD BIDS IS REQUIRED IN ALL THE SEVEN EMOTIONAL COMMAND SYSTEMS

There is a great film called *Sliding Doors*, starring Gwyneth Paltrow. It's a relationship film, but it has a science fiction premise. That premise is that every choice in effect creates a new parallel universe; it's an idea popular in some theories of a "multiverse" in modern physics. In that film we start by seeing Paltrow in bed with her boyfriend. They are getting ready to start their day. It turns out to be a terrible day for Gwyneth for two reasons. One reason is that she gets fired from her job in an all-male company in London. The second reason is that her boyfriend is getting ready to cheat on her. We see him getting two wine glasses ready and the other woman getting ready for the tryst. Meanwhile Gwyneth is rushing to catch a train on the London Tube, but she misses the train. The sliding doors close her out. She goes up top to hail a taxi, but before she can enter the cab a mugger tries to nab her purse. What an awful day for her. She holds on to the purse, but the mugger hits her on the head and she is bleeding, so the cabbie takes her to a clinic for a few stiches.

Now the film shows Gwyneth coming home. The other woman is gone. Her boyfriend is surprised she's home so early, and she tells him she had an awful day—she got fired. We learn that Gwyneth is the sole breadwinner, while he is writing his novel. In great British fashion, he offers to comfort her by making a pot of tea. He suddenly notices he has made a mistake and left both empty wine glasses out on the coffee table, so he tosses one of the wine glasses in the laundry hamper. Gwyneth later notices one wine glass out and asks him about it. Yes, he to lies her. He had a glass of wine to relax due to his writer's block tension. In a later scene Gwyneth will discover the wine glass in the laundry hamper and put two and two together, but for now his cheating is safely undiscovered.

Then suddenly the film shifts to the scene of Gwyneth again running for a train in the London Tube, and this time she makes it through the sliding doors. What's going on? This is a parallel universe in which she makes it onto the subway train. She walks in on her boyfriend and the other woman in this universe, and there is a huge row, after which Gwyneth throws him out. Eventually the two worlds come together in a very strange way that suggests that fate is real.

After seeing this film, John was thinking that in a relationship there are many SLIDING DOOR MOMENTS. Such a moment is when a choice presents itself to turn toward, away from, or against a bid for connection. Here are a few examples. One evening, while getting ready for bed, John was about to finish a murder mystery by one of his favorite authors, Michael Connelly. John is a Connelly groupie. He put the novel on his bedside table and started toward the bathroom. Before entering the bathroom John saw Julie in the mirror brushing her hair, and he noticed that Julie looked sad. This was a sliding door moment. Did he want to deal with her sadness right now? No, not particularly. He wanted to finish the novel. But then he imagined the parallel universes represented by the choice. He could avoid walking through the sliding doors, get into bed, and finish the novel. That would be delicious, he thought. But then, he thought, what if he felt amorous? Then he'd turn to Julie, but she would be sad, and not in the mood for making love, so John would feel rejected. No, he thought, "I don't like that universe," so he walked through the sliding door, took the hairbrush from her hand, and started brushing her hair. He knew she loves that, and she leaned back against him. He asked her what she was sad about, and she told him. They talked and connected, and then they went to bed. John finished his novel, and it was delicious as a Connelly novel always is. Sure enough, he did feel amorous, and, because he had turned toward her, they both felt close to one another and their night had a happy ending.

These sliding door moments are ubiquitous in relationships. Another example that illustrates the positive feedback feature of turning toward is that one day John walked by Julie, who was taking clothes out of a dryer, and she was audibly grumbling. There's a bid. Not a very direct bid, but it's a bid. John asked her what was wrong and she declared that she hated folding laundry. John does not mind doing housework as long as he can do it in a self-indulgent manner. He agreed to fold the laundry. She smiled. John put on some Bill Evans playing piano, and sat down on the bed to fold the laundry. He had a moment of peace. Julie drifted in eventually and also sat on the bed. John thought he could read her mind. He thought, "I bet she's thinking I'm going to ask her to help fold, even though she told me she hates doing that," so he faked her out and didn't ask her to help.

Eventually he and she both just enjoyed the music. Julie reminisced about the great concerts they'd heard at Dmitrio's Jazz Alley in Seattle. Remember hearing McCoy Tyner there, she asked? Sure, John replied, he has the biggest hands I've ever seen. Eventually we started doing this more often, John folding and both of us listening to jazz, a lovely peaceful moment in time together. Here's our law of turning toward: Turning toward leads to more turning toward. So you do not have to have very high standards for turning toward. Enter the loop at any level, and it just gets better and better. Not too many things in life are like that.

Furthermore, often there is not very much difference between turning toward and turning away. Here's another example from our marriage. We were grocery shopping together and Julie asked John, "Are we out of Cascade?" John had no idea, so he said, "I have no idea," but he took a box and put it in the cart. That additional act said, "I don't know if we're out of this stuff, but, if you're worried about it, what the heck, let's get a box." That's turning toward, a little, but it counts. If John had simply said, "I don't know," that wouldn't have been a negative act, but it would have been a missed opportunity to walk through a sliding door.

What are the implications of turning away from a bid? Well, usually, probably not much. Even the masters of relationships are not perfect at turning toward. However, we did notice that a lot of turning away, and especially a lot of turning against, resulted in some nonverbal behavior we described as "crumpling," that is, a bodily kind of disappointed caving in. These moments could be called "microattachment injuries," just small moments when our partner is not there for us. Many of these moments are innocent, mindless moments that are not mean-spirited. However, a mindful awareness of how and when our partner expresses a small need can, over time, make a huge difference.

TURNING TOWARD IN ALL THE EMOTIONAL COMMAND SYSTEMS

So, is all turning toward equal? The answer is no. It turns out that turning toward needs to happen in all of seven emotional command systems in a relationship. You might be asking yourself at this point, What *seven* emotional command systems? We'll tell you.

The late Jaak Panksepp wrote a landmark book called *Affective Neuroscience* (1998). In that book he reviewed a massive amount of evidence that showed that all us mammals have seven fundamental emotional command systems for turning toward. The command systems can function independently or together. Joan DeClaire and John Gottman (2002) gave them names in their book *The Relationship Cure*. The seven emotional command systems are described below in the form of a bipolar range:

1. **THE SENTRY.** TASK: Build a safe haven versus fear. Attachment theory is concerned with this system. Its primary hormone is adrenaline.
2. **THE NEST BUILDER.** TASK: Create secure bonding versus separation panic/grief (oxytocin, vasopressin, cortisol are the hormones of this system). Attachment theory is also concerned with this system. Its primary hormones are oxytocin and vasopressin.

These first two systems are the emotional command systems of attachment theory. The SENTRY comes first because all us mammals need to keep watching for danger, simply because it's a matter of life and death. Panksepp had a $100 bet with his grad students to see if anyone could condition a rat to back up toward its food. No one could do that, because mammals have to use their nose and eyes to constantly watch out for danger. A small error could mean suddenly facing a dangerous predator or a rival who wants your food.

The second system, NEST BUILDER, is what makes a mammal a mammal. We are nurturant, we love, we take exquisite care of our young pups. We lick them, kiss them, cuddle them, and would do anything it takes to defend them and keep them close. We think babies are adorably cute, and they make these juices flow. In a nursing mammal, oxytocin makes her milk flow. We melt when we're close, and we're sad and sometimes even panicked when we're separated. We grieve if we lose an attachment figure, as is common in bereavement.

These two are powerful systems. And they're related to one another. Oxytocin totally shuts down the brain's fear system. That's part of limerence, falling in love. We feel safe, we feel taken care of, protected, cherished. As we mentioned previously, oxytocin promotes trust, sometimes even too much so. Oxytocin is also the hormone of bad judgment. Spray oxytocin up someone's nose instead of saline and they will give their money away to an untrustworthy person. We secrete oxytocin after an orgasm, which is part of the reason we may not see the red flags (if we're having sex) during courtship that this person is not to be trusted.

These are two very powerful emotional command systems and they are central to attachment theory. As Panksepp points out, they have a common physiology and neuroanatomy in the brains and nervous systems of all us mammals. They are a part of our evolutionary heritage. However, these two systems are not everything. We think that to be a competent couples therapist, it is very important for the therapist to become an expert on the remaining five emotional command systems as well. Each of these systems is like the colors of an artist's pallet. They are separate, but they can work together.

Moving Beyond Attachment Theory

Here are summaries of the other five neuroaffective systems Panksepp described.

1. **THE EXPLORER.** TASK: Supports seeking, search, curiosity, new learning, and adventure versus boredom (dopamine is the major neurotransmitter of this system). We *Homo sapiens* are the great storytellers and meaning makers. We do both as part of our intense curiosity. We are big explorers, even going into outer space despite the obvious dangers.
2. **THE JESTER.** TASK: Foster play, silliness, and humor versus rigidity (dopamine again). All mammals play, and need to play; we need to laugh, to have fun, to be silly, to see the absurdity in everything.

3. **THE SENSUALIST.** TASK: Create and foster sexual connection, lust, romance, passion versus loneliness (the hormones are testosterone and estrogen).

4. **THE COMMANDER IN CHIEF.** TASK: Build a climate of peaceful respect, fairness, and justice versus tyrannical dominance. Compete, and establish one's status and competence (the hormones are adrenaline and serotonin).

5. **THE ENERGY CZAR.** TASK: Create energy balance and health versus depletion and illness.

Clearly these systems can work together, when, for example, we seek a mate. Then the explorer and the sensualist are unified. When a mother bear defends her cubs from a powerful predator, she uses the nest builder together with the sentry and the commander in chief. They can also work separately. For example, we do not believe that behind anger there is always insecurity and that we need to soften anger in therapy to get a partner to hear that anger. There are many cases when anger is just anger, for example, when we react to crime, injustice, or racism, or unfairness in the relationship. Then we believe that partners need to be able to listen to anger nondefensively. As therapists we do not have to "unearth" the insecurity behind anger for it to be understood by a partner.

We labeled emotional command systems 3 to 7 "beyond attachment theory" because we disagree with those who believe that for couples therapy one needs only the sentry and the nest builder. For example, some believe attachment security will guarantee that couples will develop a great sex life naturally, will know how to play and have fun automatically, will have adventures and learn together, and be able to manage stress just fine without any further therapeutic intervention. We just have no evidence that this is the case. We think that the therapist must plan to get all of these systems to work well in order to increase our effect sizes beyond the pitiful current half a standard deviation effect size. To us that means that as a couples therapist you have to become a master of all seven emotional command systems.

Panksepp's amazing integration of affective neuroscience and evolution has shown that these are our primary affective command systems. They also have a very clear neurological basis in mammals.

In *The Relationship Cure*, John and DeClaire suggested that people differ in how much they have strong needs in each of these emotional command systems, so relationships have to negotiate the rocky terrain of varying emotional command needs. For example, in our relationship Julie is the true physical adventurer, while John is an adventurer from the neck up (that is, intellectually). On a road trip to Yellowstone, we once talked about out fondest dreams. Julie announced that her fondest dream was that for her 50th birthday, she wanted to take 10 women on a trek through Nepal to Mount Everest base camp and beyond. John's dream was to create nonlinear differential equation models of couples' interactions. Julie has a very highly developed Explorer Emotional Command System, while John's Sentry Emotional Command System is highly developed. John can easily tell you 10 ways you can die at a picnic. He sees the world as a dangerous place, and while reading the morning *New York Times* at breakfast John is likely to say, "Julie, here's another place we're never going to on vacation."

John's first reaction to Julie's dream was, "Are you out of your mind? They are killing people in Nepal. Some guy just slaughtered the whole royal family!" However, gradually John came to understand what these majestic mountains meant to Julie, what Buddhism meant to her, and when she returned he saw a picture of her at the top of Mount Kalapitar at 18,600 feet. He'd never seen her look happier. Being a single parent for a month was worth it, just to see that huge smile. However, John waited until she returned safely to read Jon Krakauer's book *Into Thin Air*, which is about a horrible climbing disaster on Mount Everest. This turning toward life dreams in our emotional command systems is a mutual thing in our relationship. When John wanted to start keeping a kosher home, Julie joined him in doing so.

We all have varying needs in all emotional command systems, and they change over the life course. Like all mammals, we all need to play and laugh. The Jester Emotional Command System must be honored. We all need adventure. The Explorer Emotional Command System must be honored. We all need romance, passion, and great sex. The Sensualist Emotional Command System must be nourished. Every relationship needs to become a safe haven; the Sentry must be respected. Every relationship needs to feel close, connected, and securely attached. The Nest Builder must be revered. Every relationship has to feel fair, just, and equitable. The Commander In Chief must be valued. And in every relationship we need to manage our energy. We have to be able to replenish that energy when we are weary, or we'll burn out. We need one another's help to manage the stresses of everyday life, the "slings and arrows of outrageous fortune." The Energy Czar must be treasured.

Our emotional needs span all seven emotional command systems, and turning toward is a powerful tool for learning to love one another better and better as we grow old together.

BUILDING A GREAT SEX LIFE: IT'S NOT ROCKET SCIENCE

In an amazing book, *The Normal Bar*, Northrup, Schwartz, and Witte (2014) conducted an online study with 70,000 people in 24 countries. They were curious about what might be different about couples who said that they had a great sex life, compared to couples who said that they had a bad sex life. If we ignore the great limitations of self-report data, their results have some fascinating implications. This massive study as well as our work opposes the advice that Esther Perel gives in her book *Mating in Captivity* and in her clinical work in general, when she assists couples in improving their sex life. Perel tells couples not to cuddle. She also believes that emotional connection will stand in the way of good erotic connection. However, here is a finding from the *Normal Bar* study:

> **Fact: Couples who have a great sex life everywhere on the planet are doing the same set of things. Couples who do not have a great sex life everywhere on the planet don't do these things.**

The critical experiment has yet to be done, so these are just correlational results. Nonetheless, we've blended these findings with our own research to suggest that therapists recommend the following to strengthen their couples' sex life:

1. Say "I love you" every day and mean it.
2. Kiss one another passionately for no reason.
3. Give surprise romantic gifts.
4. Know what turns partners on and off erotically.
5. Be physically affectionate, even in public.
6. Keep playing and having fun together.
7. Cuddle often
8. Make sex a priority, not the last item of a long to-do list.
9. Stay good friends by building love maps and fondness and admiration.
10. Talk comfortably about their sex life.
11. Have weekly romantic dates.
12. Take romantic vacations.
13. Be mindful about turning toward.

In short, for a good sex life, couples need to turn toward one another to connect emotionally and physically, with love and affection. Remember, only 6% of noncuddlers have a good sex life. So Perel's intuition, that for a strong erotic life couples shouldn't cuddle, runs counter to international data. What is very clear from the *Normal Bar* study is that having a great sex life is not rocket science. It is not difficult. However . . .

**Fact: Couples who have a bad sex life everywhere
on the planet neglect intimacy.**

The Sloan Center at UCLA studied 30 dual-career heterosexual couples in Los Angeles. These couples had young children. The researchers were like anthropologists, observing, tape recording, and interviewing these couples. They discovered that most of these young couples:

1. Spend very little time together during a typical week.
2. Become job centered (him) and child centered (her).
3. Talk mostly about their huge to-do lists.
4. Seem to make everything else a priority other than their relationship.
5. Drift apart and lead parallel lives.
6. Are unintentional about turning toward one another.

One researcher on this project told John that it was his impression that these couples spent only about 35 minutes together every week in joint conversation, and that most of their talk was about errands and tasks that they had to get done.

So, if we put these two studies together, what does it tell us? We think it says that as clinicians we need to tell our couples NOT to avoid one another, but instead to follow these very simple actions that everyone on the planet apparently does to make their sex lives great. Emily Nagoski's wonderful book, *Come as You Are*, talks about the dual process model of sex. In that model each person has a sexual brake and a sexual accelerator. In some people the brake is more developed, and in some people the accelerator is more developed. It's important to learn what for you and for your partner steps on that sex brake, that says, "No, I'm not in the mood for lovemaking." It's also important to learn what for you and for your partner steps on the accelerator, that says, "Oh yes, I'm in the mood for lovemaking." We have a free iPhone and smart phone app designed for that purpose. It consists of over 100 questions to ask a woman about her brake and accelerator, and over 100 questions to ask a man about his brake and accelerator.

Those questions are one of seven exercises in our *Art and Science of Lovemaking*, available on the website, Gottman Institute: Gott Sex? (https://gottsex.com/).

COUPLES THERAPY WITH GAY
AND LESBIAN COUPLES

Many gay men and lesbian women are involved with and/or living with a partner in committed relationship, a trend that has only increased since the onset of the horrific AIDS epidemic. Robert Levenson and John conducted a 12-year longitudinal study of gay and lesbian committed relationships. Theirs was the first longitudinal, observational study of gay and lesbian couples. While studies that use only self-report measures find that there are essentially no differences between heterosexual and same-sex couples, with observational methods surprising distinct differences did emerge when the couples were compared with married heterosexual couples, matched in relationship satisfaction and length of time together. Here is a summary of these unexpected differences Robert and John found (Gottman et al., 2003a; 2003b) using their mathematical model (discussed in this book, Chapter 8, on change).

START-UP. In our conflict discussion, they found that both gay and lesbian couples started with much less negative and more positive affect; that is, the gay/lesbian *uninfluenced* steady states were positive, while the heterosexual couples' uninfluenced steady states were negative; we didn't expect that. Also, there were no significant differences between gay and lesbian couples on this uninfluenced steady state variable. Specifically, the gay and lesbian couples were significantly less belligerent and less domineering, and showed less fear/tension, less sadness, and less whining compared to heterosexual couples. That described the same-sex couples *before* influence processes began. What about how they influenced one another?

INFLUENCE. The gay and lesbian couples also influenced one another in far more positive directions following the start-up than was the case for heterosexual couples. This was especially true of the lesbian couples, who did even better than either the gay or heterosexual couples in creating positive social influence.

REPAIR. The gay men's effectiveness when repairing was much greater than either heterosexual or lesbian couples.

REPAIR THRESHOLD. Men tended to repair at a lower threshold of the partner's negativity, whether they were gay men or heterosexual men, compared to lesbian or heterosexual women.

DAMPING EFFECTIVENESS. Gay and lesbian couples were more effective at damping positive affect than heterosexual couples. This effect means that it was homosexual couples, more than heterosexual couples, that turned toward one another more and got down to the business of problem solving, rather than avoiding the issue.

OVERALL INFLUENCE. Examining the slope parameters for influence either with positive or negative affect, a fascinating influence pattern emerged just for same-sex couples. This pattern was a greater use of POSITIVE affect to influence, whereas heterosexual couples used NEGATIVE affect, rather than positive affect, to influence the partner. Here's the amazing conclusion here: This means that heterosexual couples are more likely than same-sex couples to be at risk for a pattern of negative escalation (see Chapter 13 in which we identify that escalation pattern as a Richardson's arms race, characteristic of actual war). We also found that lesbian couples were both angrier AND used more humor and showed more excitement/joy than gay male couples, so we concluded—not surprisingly—that lesbian couples were more emotionally expressive than gay male couples.

How do Robert and John's findings fit with other research on gay and lesbian couples? As you probably know, over the past decade there has been a major cultural shift in the way same-sex couples' relationships are viewed in the United States of America, culminating in the historic 2015 Supreme Court decision legalizing marriage for gay and lesbian couples. As Filmore, Baretto, and Yassi (2016) noted, as this shift has taken place, professionals within the clinical community need to meet the growing needs of same-sex couples for counseling, guidance, and therapy. Many others articles have been written calling for new methods to meet the special needs of gay and lesbian couples (for example, Gotta, et al., 2001; Riggle, et al., 2016). Despite these calls, no such therapy has emerged.

For a special therapy for gay and lesbian couples to emerge, we need basic research on these couples. What else do we know about gay and lesbian couples? The classic questionnaire-based study of American couples by Blumstein and Schwartz (1983) actually concluded that same-sex couples are not very different from married couples on most issues. In fact, the group that actually stood out as most different was heterosexual cohabiting couples, where commitment to one another was generally weak, compared to the other groups of couples in the study (married heterosexual, gay male, and lesbian).

This general conclusion that heterosexual couples and same-sex couples are not very different from one another has been replicated in a series of self-report studies by the late Lawrence Kurdek. In 2004 Kurdek wrote an article titled, "Are Gay and Lesbian Cohabiting Couples Really Different From Heterosexual Married Couples?" He compared gay and lesbian cohabiting couples without children with heterosexual married couples with children on variables from five domains indicative of relationship health at three separate longitudinal time points. He reported that for 50% of the comparisons, gay and lesbian partners did not differ at all from heterosexual partners. Furthermore, as in Robert and John's study, for 78% of the comparisons on which differences were found, gay or lesbian partners functioned *better* than heterosexual partners did. What about relationship stability and happiness? Kurdek did suggest that same-sex couples are less stable than married heterosexual couples, but he concluded that, in general, the processes that regulate relationship functioning are identical across gay, lesbian, and heterosexual couples.

Levenson and Gottman's conclusions were the same as Kurdek's when they used questionnaire data. There were very few differences between gay, lesbian, and heterosexual married couples. However, the observational data suggested that same-sex couples were less defensive, less hostile, and less domineering, and demonstrated a better sense of humor during conflict than heterosexual married couples. That conclusion echoed the results of an article Kurdek wrote in 2005. He concluded that, compared to heterosexual married couples, same-sex partners divided up household labor more fairly, and they reported resolving conflict more constructively. Same-sex couples reported similar levels of relationship satisfaction, got less support from family members, but more support from friends compared to heterosexual married couples.

One theme of this book is that we NEED to do this basic research BEFORE we design a therapy. So, indeed, these basic findings were then used in creating a therapy for same-sex couples. How effective was that therapy?

Intervention Effects With Gay and Lesbian Couples

We want to briefly review preliminary research we have done in collaboration with Sam Garanzini and his partner Alapaki Yee, directors of the Gay Couples Institute of San Francisco. The Gay Couples Institute of San Francisco has followed the Gottman therapy model of the Sound Relationship House. Even though these are preliminary data, they are important because, amazingly, there are currently no outcome data for couples therapy with gay and lesbian couples. At the beginning of selected therapy sessions, the couples filled out our standard relationship satisfaction scale, the Locke-Wallace (Locke & Wallace, 1959).

As we have noted, in the couples and family therapy research field the effect sizes of interventions have been small, usually of the order of 0.5 standard deviation units (Pinsof & Wynne, 1995a, b; 2000). There was a randomized clinical trial of a psychoeducational intervention with gay male couples by Whitton et al., (2016), who reported an even smaller effect size of 0.19 from pre- to post- and 0.18 from pre- to three-month follow-up. These are very small effects.

We will summarize the results of an uncontrolled study of this therapy over a five-year period with 108 gay and lesbian couples that was conducted at the Gay Couples Institute of San Francisco by certified Gottman therapists. Figure 12.1 displays the results in just eleven sessions of therapy with gay and lesbian couples. These effects on the Locke-Wallace were statistically significant.

Just how significant were these results? One measure—as we have noted—is the effect size of the intervention (see the Preface of this book). As usual, the effect size of this intervention was computed using the change in relationship satisfaction from Time 1 to Time 5 (Session #11) divided by the standard error of the residual from the analysis of

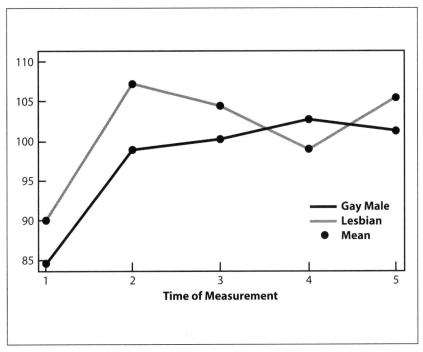

Figure 12.1. Average Locke-Wallace relationship satisfaction over time for gay and lesbian couples in Gottman Couple therapy.

variance. This statistic is called Cohen's *d*. In Sam and Alapaki's study we computed *d* as follows:

$$d = (M1 - M2)/\sqrt{MSE},$$

where the numerator was a difference in mean scores of relationship satisfaction and the denominator, MSE, was the mean square error term from the analysis of variance.

We compared the first therapy session mean (following our assessment sessions) with the final eleventh session mean. For the gay male group, we computed Cohen's $d = (101.42 - 84.52)/13.70 = 1.23$, and for the lesbian group, we computed Cohen's $d = (105.50 - 90.08)/13.70 = 1.13$. According to Cohen (1992) and Sawilowsky (2009), this effect size is in between a large effect size (0.80) and a very large effect size (1.20). Our effect size is over six times larger than Whitton's for gay male and lesbian couples. Garanzini explains these large effect sizes by saying that "90% of the couples need only 10% of the skills of the Sound Relationship House." He adds, "However, the 10% varies from couple to couple." The length of treatment (eleven sessions for most couples) is comparable to what has been noted for couples therapy with heterosexual couples (Doherty & Simmons, 1996; Simmons & Doherty, 1990). Of course these results are just a beginning. Sam and Alapaki are planning a randomized clinical trial in the future.

Another result obtained in our study was that the effect sizes were either unrelated to prior co-morbidities, or positively related. That means that couples with prior co-morbidities did *better* than those couples without prior co-morbidities. For example, there were greater gains for couples facing prior substance abuse than for couples without prior substance abuse. That is very good news. However, this result is not that unusual; Fals-Stewart, O'Farrell, & Lam (2009) found similar effects with heterosexual couples.

CHAPTER 13

Examining Relationship Stability

In this chapter we will reveal two previously hidden instabilities in couple relationships. Our analysis will require talking about a typology of couples and examining the risks of each type of couple.

THE FIRST OBSERVATION-BASED TYPOLOGY OF COUPLES

In 1974 Harold Raush reported the results of the first observational study of a couple's transition to becoming parents. He also was the first to utilize information theory to examine sequences of interaction. Raush created a typology of couples. It was kind of a Goldilocks theory because there were just three types, and—just like Goldilocks's three bowls of porridge—Raush thought that only one couple type was good and healthy.

1. *Volatile*—they were overly emotional, too hot, probably unhappy.
2. *Avoiders*—they were overly distant, too cold, and probably also unhappy.
3. *Validators*—close, but rational, just right, probably happy.

Raush believed that the validators were the only healthy type of couple, but he really had no empirical basis for that judgment. In fact, Raush graciously let John reanalyze his audiotapes with John's more emotionally based coding system. John then compared these data with data he was collecting from other couples at the time. While Raush used simulated conflicts, John used actual conflicts of the couples, and videotape instead of audiotape. Over many years of such comparisons, it turned out that Raush was only partly right (Gottman, 1994). Here were the facts.

Stable Couples and Their Risks

John's research (Gottman, 1994) showed that there were indeed couple types, and some of them were similar to the types Raush had described. Initially John also found evidence for three types of couples, and he used Raush's terminology: volatile, validating, and avoiding. However, John found that *all types* were stable, but only if the ratio of positive to negative affect during conflict discussions was greater than or equal to 5.0. Their kids were also fine, by the way, as long as that ratio was 5:1 (or greater). Remember, that was our definition of homeostasis.

Later research in our lab showed that there were actually four types of HAPPILY MARRIED STABLE heterosexual couples in John's data, because there were actually *two types* of couples John had initially called conflict avoiders. These couples actually did not avoid *conflict*; instead, THEY AVOIDED PERSUASION AND COMPROMISE. Both previously labeled "conflict avoider" types agree to disagree and do not try to persuade their partner. Both types avoid problem solving, and they do not move on to compromise. One type is *accepting* of the partner's negative emotions, while the other type is *dismissing* of the partner's negative emotions. The accepting type has an emotionally much closer relationship than the dismissing type. Both types are equally likely to be stable and happily married.

The two types of persuasion avoiders:

- **PERSUASION AVOIDERS & NEGATIVE EMOTION ACCEPTERS.** These couples avoid persuasion, and they do not downregulate positive affect's influence during conflict.

In their events-of-the-day conversation they are accepting toward negative emotions expressed by the partner. They don't avoid conflict. They will talk about an issue thoroughly, but then they don't try to convince their partner. They do not compromise; they agree to disagree once they understand their partner's point of view. They are very separate individuals, although they feel emotionally close to one another, and they are not very interdependent.

- **PERSUASION AVOIDERS & NEGATIVE EMOTION DISMISSERS.** These couples are also persuasion avoiders, but they **do** downregulate positive affect's influence during conflict. In their events-of-the -day conversation they are dismissing toward negative emotions expressed by the partner. They also avoid both persuasion and compromise during conflict, AND they avoid talking about their negative emotions at all. They also do not compromise, they also agree to disagree, but they don't try to understand their partner's point of view. They are also very separate individuals, whose lives are more in parallel, but not unhappily so.

There were also two other types of stable couples who did not avoid persuasion. They were:

- **VOLATILE COUPLES.** These are quite a lot like the couples Raush described as volatile. They are persuasion-seeking couples who love to debate, tooth and nail. In fact, if they are paired with someone who wants to give in, they find that very unsatisfying, and see that person as not really caring enough to take them on. They are very **interdependent**, and they tend to stay very romantically in love for life. They can also be quite jealous.
- **VALIDATING COUPLES.** They listen first, and then debate and compromise. They do not avoid persuasion, but

they time it to follow some good listening. They are also good listeners to their partner's emotions, but not quite as accepting as the emotion acceptors.

ALL four types of couples were STABLE and HAPPY if their positive/negative ratio during conflict was greater than or equal to 5.0, and that was usually the case. This ratio goes along with and can be indexed by whether they have HARSH or GENTLE START-UP in the conflict discussion. Then these couples avoid a negative absorbing Markov state. Furthermore, most of the time all four types were in fact stable and happy. John also found that their kids were also okay on measures of child adjustment. Raush worried about the kids of volatile couples.

The Revealed Instability of the Volatile and Validating Couples

Here is a surprising source of instability in the interaction of all couples who use negative affect to influence one another. To understand this source of instability, we need to review the mathematics of war.

The Richardson's Arms Race Model

In 1960 a very important book was republished about war and other deadly quarrels. Lewis Richardson's book was titled *Statistics of Deadly Quarrels*. What is amazing about Richardson's work is that he was able to create a very simple mathematical model that fit all the actual data of war and deadly quarrels. "Deadly quarrels" was a term he used to include major incidents of deadly feuds, banditry, gangsterism, and homicide. He was concerned with predicting both the onsets and the terminations of deadly quarrels as well as wars.

He modeled escalation to war and mass killing as a simple math model of actions and reactions, with no regulation. His analysis of all wars prior to World War II showed that he could fit the actual data very well with this very simple model. In case you're interested, his equations are in our Appendix 2. He found that when a feud, or a quarrel, or a war, or an arms race begins, its outcome is inevitable and deadly. Despite the fact that the math of this unregulated escalation is simple, the outcomes of these types of human conflicts are devastating, and the physical consequences and human suffering are by no means simple. Richardson's research actually gave us some ways of avoiding war.

Here is the reason this work on war is so important for our typology of couples' conflict interactions. John's friend the mathematician K. K. Tung published a math book in 2007. Tung's Chapter 10 is all about our mathematical model. Tung showed that the equivalent of an arms race escalation of negativity is a possibility for all couples that have a nonzero negative influence function in the negative affect ranges. That means that the only nonescalating and naturally stable kind of couple are the two types that John previously labeled conflict avoiders.

Imagine our shock at this discovery. Most writing about couples, starting with Harold Raush, had suggested that conflict avoiders were *dysfunctional* at some level. Instead, Professor K. K. Tung revealed their hidden strength. Conflict avoiders have very resilient relationships.

What's going on here? Turns out that all couples who exert their persuasive power using negative affect have a potential instability, due to the Richardson arms race pattern. For these couples a runaway spiral of negativity is possible. They can avoid this destructive spiral of escalating negativity only if they have very positive start-ups and repair effectively. Hence, both validating and volatile couples are inherently unstable because they have this potential for a Richardson-type arms race dynamic. This 5:1 ratio counters the arms race by the feedbacks of positive start-up and repair. However, *there is still that inherent instability that could lead to escalated quarrels, or a cycling pattern of quarreling and making up.*

THINK OF WHAT THIS MEANS! This means that any couple that uses negative affect to influence one another is at risk for a Richardson arms race, in which negative affect is runaway and not regulated. They can *offset* the negative arms race, but only by creating a very delicate balance, using repair very early, before negativity has a chance to escalate. They can also make start-up more positive, they can accept more influence from positive affect, and they can repair and damp effectively (turning toward). However, they are creating a very delicate balance. Once again, intuition, in this case Raush's, was totally wrong.

Tung showed us that persuasion avoiders (previously valled conflict avoiders), namely both partners influencing one another through only positive affect, is the only relationship that is NOT inherently destabilizing. All other relationship types have this arms race possibility that must be offset in therapy.

The Two Unstable or Unhappy Types: Mismatched Influence Functions

So far, we have revealed a hidden instability in couples who use negative affect to influence one another, the Richardson arms race pattern with negative affect. Here is another surprising result. Our math showed that all the three stable Raush types (volatile, validating, avoiding) had MATCHED INFLUENCE FUNCTIONS. This was a revealed symmetry in the bilinear part of their influence functions. The initial three types had matched influence functions, so they were matched in power sharing. Figure 13.1 shows the diagram of only the bilinear part of the influence functions. They match across partners. That was a surprising discovery.

Here's a refresher on how to read these graphs. The right-hand side of the graph is the amount of influence that positive affect has on one's partner. If it slopes up, the effect of the positive affect is positive on the partner. If it slopes down, the effect of the positive affect is negative on the partner. If it is flat, there is no effect of positive affect on the partner. The left-hand side of the graph is the amount of influence that negative affect has on one's partner. If it slopes up, the effect of the negative affect is positive on the partner. If it slopes down, the effect of the negative affect is negative on the partner. If it is flat there is no effect of negative affect on the partner.

This matching across partners meant that there would be no demand-withdraw pattern for these three types of couples! They are totally matched in the way they try to influence one another.

We also discovered that there were two other types of couples, and both types had MISMATCHED influence functions. These *two* types

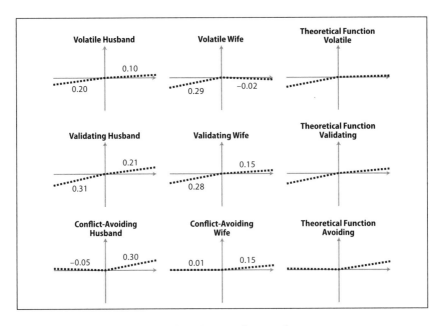

Figure 13.1. Volatile/Validating/Conflict-Avoiding graphs

of couples had influence function asymmetries across partners and their ratio of positive/negative was less than or equal to 0.8. Both types of couples would be characterized by the demand-withdraw pattern. One type of couple turned out to be stable, but unhappy, while the other type of couple divorced. How were these two types different?

The Two Mismatched Couple Types

What were the fates of these two types of mismatched couples? Without treatment, we discovered that "hostile" couples stayed married but stayed unhappy, whereas "hostile-detached" couples eventually divorced. We have suggested that there are different types of couples and that these differences exist because of the preferred social influence patterns of each partner. You are likely to see couples in therapy who are either hostile, whose mismatched influence patterns have led to either escalated conflict

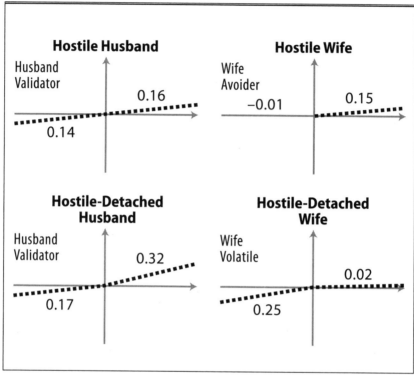

Figure 13.2. Hostile and Hostile-Detached graphs

(the negative absorbing Markov state), or hostile-detached couples who are also very withdrawn from one another and are leading parallel lives. Both types of MISMATCHED INFLUENCE couples are characterized by the DEMAND-WITHDRAW PATTERN. One partner will engage, while the other will withdraw. These mismatched influence functions are picking up demand-withdraw as well as meta-emotion mismatch.

Yet only the hostile-detached couple will also display the Richardson arms race with negative affect. In each case it will be necessary to work on both everyday emotional connection, that is, build friendship and intimacy, *and* use the conflict blueprints (Gottman-Rapoport, Dreams Within Conflict, and Aftermath of a Fight or Regrettable Incident). However, it will also be necessary to help the hostile-detached couple deal with many past regrettable incidents.

CHAPTER 14

Enter the Baby

Now here is a major challenge to our new general systems theory. Can we move smoothly, theoretically, from couples to families? Can we just consider the new baby to be another person—just a tiny one—in the same system? Does that even make sense? If not, then what modifications do we have to make to move from couples to families? As you will see, the answer is we can move forward.

None of the great figures in the development of general systems therapy for families was a developmental psychologist, so they didn't have much to say about kids. Many questions simply went unaddressed. When was it okay to bring a child into family therapy? Would it hurt a child who was, say, 5 years old to witness her parents arguing, even with a therapist to help? At what age was cognitive development adequate for a child to benefit from the process? Did the very processes of therapy have to be modified so a child could understand what was going on, much like children's books had to be written specially for kids? Could one actually do therapy with a dysfunctional mother, father, and baby? What would be dysfunctional in interactions with a BABY? How could one even conceptualize this system?

In the last 50 years all of these questions have been answered. The answer to all these questions is very surprising, and also very encouraging. Yes, we can extend general systems theory to include the baby. The emerging new theory has exquisite precision and beauty. We now understand the emotional needs of infants and young children. We understand how to move this knowledge through adolescence and young adulthood as well. We do have an empirically based general systems theory of the family. We now understand how some child pathologies develop and what factors put children at risk for psychopathology. Furthermore, we can use that theory to inform psychotherapy with ailing families. In this chapter we begin this extension of general systems theory to the family.

CHILDREN VIEWING
THEIR PARENTS' ARGUMENTS

Let's revisit those questions we asked earlier. Would it hurt a young child to witness her parents arguing, even with a therapist there? A partial answer has been provided in a series of investigations of children viewing conflict between adults conducted by E. Mark Cummings of Notre Dame University (Cummings, 1987; Cummings and Davies, 1994; Cummings, Goeke-Mory, and Papp, 2003, 2004; Cummings, Lannotti, and Zahn-Waxler, 1985; Cummings, Papp, and Kourus, 2009; Cummings, Zahn-Waxler, and Radke-Yarrow, 1981). Cummings has discovered that, in general, this is a very distressing event for most children before adolescence. It is also unpleasantly physiologically arousing. He has recommended that parents generally try to have arguments out of children's earshot and, if the children do witness a marital argument, that the parents make up physically by kissing and hugging in front of the children, particularly if the children are preadolescent. On the other hand, adolescents may benefit from seeing a marital discussion that does get calmly resolved. That usually means the parents role play a discussion they have already had, not one they are uncertain of.

Cummings, Goeke-Morey, and Papp (2003; 2004) reported the results of mothers' and fathers' reports of marital conflicts in the home. There were reports about over 1,000 conflicts, including several hundred conflicts that took place in front of the children. The study included 116 families with children 8 to 16 years old. The kids' emotional responses were far more negative if the fights included threats, personal insults, verbal hostility, defensiveness, nonverbal hostility, withdrawal, or signs of physical distress, compared to fights that consisted of calm discussion, giving support, and showing affection.

What is the bottom line about bringing children into therapy in which they can witness their parents arguing? Here we are talking of sessions of family therapy in which the therapist may have the parents arguing about a major area of disagreement, and then consider inviting the children into these kinds of conflict interactions. We are not ruling out all kinds of child involvements. Our general advice about including children into family therapy sessions, based on the research is:

DON'T DO IT! UNLESS THE PARENTS' NEGATIVE INTERACTIONS ARE ALREADY AFFECTIVELY DOWNREGULATED

If what we recommend is true, then how are we family therapists to work with children? Here come our answers to this question.

ENTER THE BABY: THE HIDDEN DISASTER SCENARIO

So far, yes, in this book we have focused on couples. We have contended that the Sound Relationship House theory is adequate for describing the couple system and for doing therapy with couples. In all of that theorizing we had at most a two-dimensional game theory table, and two differential equations as well as a two-dimensional phase space force field portrait. But what happens to the system when we add a third person, for example, a baby, or even more children?

Are we just adding a new dimension with each child? Can we extend our work to families? The answer is yes, we can, and the secret of that extension concerns the *family's* meta-emotion structure and a parenting style called "emotion coaching," a term we coined that has become quite popular these days. In this chapter we will review our work with families, beginning with the work we have done with father-mother-infant interaction and the Bringing Baby Home intervention. In creating this exten-sion of general systems theory to the family, we will be adding another important concept, which developmental psychologists call EMOTION REGULATION. Once again, the baby's and the child's physiology will be critically important for the clinician to understand.

PSYCHOLOGISTS DISCOVER BABIES

A remarkable thing happened in the early 1970s. With the advent of inexpensive video cameras and videotape recorders, researchers began doing basic observations of babies and the parent-infant relationship. They were astonished to discover how there was an elegant mutual regu-lation of attention and emotion in the face-to-face interactions of parents and young babies. The organization of the family system that emerged was simply spectacular!

In 1974 Michael Lewis and Leonard Rosenblum published their landmark edited book, *The Effect of the Infant on Its Caregiver*, and a few years later in 1977 the late Daniel Stern published his book *The First Relationship*. All of these initial findings about the fabric of face-to-face interaction have held up over the following decades, and they have been considerably expanded. Part of this field, an important part but not the whole story, has concerned the development of attachment theory. How-ever, the wonderful nature of microorganization of interactions between parents and babies has gone far beyond any theory designed to simplify it. In many ways, just as with couples, this waterfall of new information and theory building began with the task of description and the discovery of essential patterns. Again, the mathematics of information theory proved essential to uncovering this new approach. Dan Stern wrote:

> The new approach taught me that the actions occurred in sec-onds and split seconds. If mothers and babies interacted on this micro-local level, then micro-techniques of analysis were needed. As a psychiatrist, I had been taught to identify behavioral (clin-

ical) "units" such as "intrusiveness," "sensitivity," and "rejection." These were too large, too global, too vague for what my colleagues and I were doing now. The new behavioral units became gaze aversions, head turns, speed of physical approach, duration of facial expression, small shifts in arousal, and so on. Now we could unpack "intrusiveness" and see what tiny behaviors made it up. (1977, p. 3)

Hence, as we move from couples to include babies and then the developing child, we will discover the principle that

THE COUPLE IS THE CRADLE THAT EITHER HOLDS AND NOURISHES THE DEVELOPING CHILD, OR FAILS TO DO SO.

It is stunning that the microdescriptions of family interactions could provide a powerful template for understanding both normal development and the emergence of some psychopathologies, particularly as we understand the complex interactions between genetics, child physiology, and the particular social environment and culture into which the infant is born.

As a field, we learned—first and foremost—that the infant is not at all the passive tabula rasa (blank slate) we had assumed, but instead, through its temperament, the infant *actively* shapes its own social world. Emerging new research now even shows that the nature of the couple's interactions during pregnancy strongly affect the intrauterine environment through the actions of stress hormones. Even the music a mother hears—which the fetus cannot hear—affects the movements and heart rate of the fetus. We used to think that 50% of intelligence was due to genetics. When we take into account the nature of the pregnant mother's intrauterine environment, that percentage due to genetics drops to 26% (Paul, 2011).

In this chapter we will take you through the breathtaking advances in developmental psychology that have cultivated and helped us to complete the new general systems theory we have been describing for FAMI-LIES. There is a lot to learn about babies and about how they reciprocally affect and are affected by the parents.

MUTUAL REGULATION OR DYSREGULATION OF AFFECT

To give you a flavor for this early research, we discuss two figures from a landmark chapter by Brazelton, Koslowski, and Main (1974). We will not reproduce the figures. However, the quotes from the essay will give you a feel for these patterns. The entire time period in each figure is just 5 seconds. In the first figure we see a mom and baby who are very sensitive to one another. The authors wrote:

> In Figure 5 the mother and baby are looking at each other, smiling and vocalizing together. The baby begins to cycle and reach out to her. At "a" he begins to turn away from her. She responds by looking down at her hands and she stops her activity (briefly). This brings him back to her at "c." . . . The kind of sensitivity to each other's needs for attention and non-attention that a couple might exhibit is represented by these cycles. (p. 63)

In their Figure 5 there is a synchronicity to the mom and baby's interactions that can result in prolonged bouts of attention and exciting play. She allows the baby to look away when he needs to. When he's back, then she is very engaged. On the other hand, in the next figure from the same chapter, the authors commented, "The kind of insensitivity of the mother to the baby's turning away represented by Figure 3 seems to prolong the period of looking away" (p. 63). Indeed, in their Figure 3, while the baby looks away the mother maintains her high-energy engagement, even spiking it at "d." The baby, in turn, looks away for approximately 40% of their (5-second) interaction. The baby tries to calm down, in part, by looking away.

How widespread is this kind of mismatch between a mom and a baby? In a section of Dan Stern's book titled *Missteps in the Dance*, he described the interaction of an *intrusive* mother as follows:

> The dance they had worked out by the time I met them went something like this. Whenever a moment of mutual gaze occurred, the mother went immediately into high-gear stimulating behaviors, producing a profusion of fully displayed, high-intensity, facial and vocal infant-elicited social behavior. Jenny invariably broke gaze rapidly. Her mother never interpreted this temporary face and gaze aversion as a cue to lower her level of behavior, nor would she let Jenny self-control the level by gaining distance. Instead, she would swing her head around following Jenny's to reestablish the full face position. (1977, p. 135)

In these examples we can see both the potential delicate precision of a long bout of exciting and innovative play, and also how easy it is for a well-meaning mother to ignore her infant's cues and proceed in her own way, which—as we will see—dysregulates the entire interactive family system.

AND BABY MAKES THREE

What actually happens when a baby arrives? Our book titled *And Baby Makes Three* was the first study we conducted together and the first book we wrote together. In the course of our research we got to know 222 babies. It was great fun. It can renew your faith in our species. We began our collaboration with one very basic study and two intervention studies. In our basic study we followed 130 newlywed couples—a representative sample of Seattle's population—for six years as many eventually became pregnant and underwent the transition from just being partners to becoming partners plus parents. We first observed them a few months after their wedding in a small apartment lab at the medical school campus of the University of Washington.

The lab had a large picture window overlooking the beautiful Mont-lake Cut, where couples could watch boats make the journey from the salt of Lake Union to the clear water of Lake Washington. Couples spent 24 hours in this lab, which was designed to resemble a bed-and-breakfast getaway—except it had three cameras bolted to the wall that followed every movement, every bid for connection. They wore Holter monitors collecting two channels of electrocardiogram as they moved around. We took urine samples to measure stress endocrines, and we took blood samples to study their immune system.

What a huge transition it is to become parents! Enormous! To fully understand this transition we had to learn about pregnancy, about what it's like for a couple to go through pregnancy together (or not so together). We also had to learn how to study babies. Fortunately, one of John's oldest friends, Edward Z Tronick, was one of the world's intellectual leaders in understanding babies and how they were parented. Tronick agreed to help John and his student, Alyson Shapiro, study babies and parent-infant interaction.

We kept the same Levenson-Gottman standard lab for examining couple interactions. We added a paradigm for studying how moms and dads interacted with a 3-month-old baby, dyadically and triadically. The paradigm was called Lausanne Triadic Play (LTP), developed in Lausanne, Switzerland, by two psychologists we collaborated with, Elisabeth Fivaz-Depeursinge and Antoinette Corboz-Warnery. They wrote a great book called *The Primary Triangle* (Fivaz-Depeursinge & Corboz-Warnery, 1999; Fivaz-Depeursinge, Corboz-Warnery, & Keren, 2004).

In their LTP play paradigm the baby is seated in an infant seat and two cameras are merged in a split screen. One camera is focused on the baby and another on the mother-father dyad. We added the collection of heart rate physiological data only from the baby during the LTP. The LTP has four phases, one where the father and baby play alone and the mother sits back, one where the mother and baby play alone and the father sits back, one where both parents play with the baby, and a fourth in which the parents talk to one another, ignoring the baby. It was a lot of fun

Figure 14.1. Angry baby face   **Figure 14.2.** Happy baby face

learning how to code baby affect from John's friends Edward Tronick and Steve Porges, both masters in studying babies and their physiology. There was a lot to learn.

As you can see from the photos in Figures 14.1 and 14.2, the emotions of babies are very easy to read. They are excellent broadcasters of their emotions. Furthermore, parents interacting with their babies are also an open book. All it takes to understand this is a camera and an open mind.

In our first study of the transition of these newlyweds to parenthood, we followed couples as they went through pregnancy, and then video-taped them in our standard couple lab during pregnancy and again when their baby was 3 months old. At 3 months we also studied the parents dealing with a conflict interaction in our standard couple lab setting. We kept following the babies as they developed. In this chapter we are just going to give the reader a flavor for what we discovered in basic research extending our systems theory to the family triad.

In that first study we did NO INTERVENTION. However, then we analyzed our data, comparing the masters who sailed easily through this huge transition with the disasters who had a great deal of trouble adjusting to becoming parents. What was completely shocking was that two-thirds of our couples had a precipitous drop in relationship satisfaction in the first three years of their baby's life. In our videotapes, coded blind and compared to the tapes of childless couples, there was also a precipitous rise in hostility during conflict.

Yet a third of couples sailed through this transition. Furthermore, even a few months after the wedding we could predict which group a couple would be in once they became pregnant. Using these analyses, again comparing the masters to the disasters of the transition, we designed our 10-hour-long workshop for couples going through the transition to parenthood. The workshop was called Bringing Baby Home. That workshop has now been taught to nearly 1,500 workshop leaders in 25 countries. Our workshop was all about mothers and babies, but we also had a very strong focus on moms and on fathers too. In studying fathers, we were guided by John's friend Ross Parke, whose 1996 book, *Fatherhood*, is still one of the best books summarizing research on how important dads are. It turned out that no one is more surprised by these research findings than men about to become fathers. Fathers are very important. It turns out that men really shine in play.

Maybe the reader was surprised when we said that we did no intervention in our first study. Why would one need to do intervention when a baby arrives? Isn't this just a moment of total bliss, and doesn't it ensure that the family will be happy as long as the baby arrives healthy? As we mentioned, the very surprising answer is no. Think of how amazing it is that a whopping 67% of couples going through this transition to parenthood experience a huge drop in relationship satisfaction in the first three years of the baby's life.

Think of this! If that characterizes most American couples, then this is a virtual epidemic! Only 33% were what we would call masters of the transition and even the masters' lives were not without difficulties. We aren't the only scientists who have discovered this phenomenon. Our colleagues Jay Belsky (Belsky & Kelly, 1995) in Philadelphia and Carolyn Cowan and Philip Cowan (1999) at Berkeley also discovered it.

THE GOOD NEWS: BRINGING BABY HOME

Our friends Carolyn and Philip Cowan pioneered the first effective couples group intervention for couples going through this transition; their work inspired ours. As we noted, we began our first basic (nonintervention) study when the couples were newlyweds, starting just a few months after their wedding, following them for six years, and then studying them during pregnancy. We compared these couples to couples that did not become pregnant during the time (controls). Figure 14.3 shows the drop in marital satisfaction for those who became parents. The red line drops from 130 to 70. That's a 60-point drop, or four standard deviation units (4SD, $4 \times 15 = 60$). If we could reverse that, we'd have a 4SD effect size. And that's exactly what we wound up getting! Remember our call for a 4SD therapy in our preface? Well, here it is.

To study our couples during pregnancy, we designed a new Pregnancy Oral History Interview, asking couples how becoming pregnant was going. It turned out that our coding of husbands in this interview was a great predictor of the couple's changes in marital satisfaction. Declin-

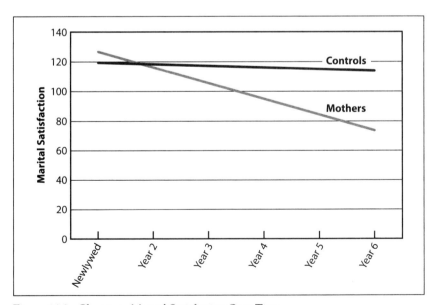

Figure 14.3. Change in Marital Satisfaction Over Time

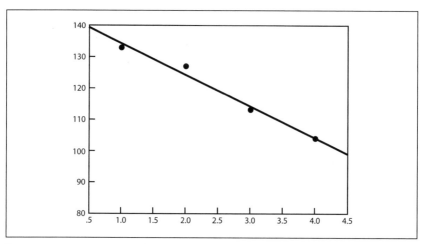

Figure 14.4. Average marital satisfaction for couples where husbands had negative pregnancy oral history interviews.

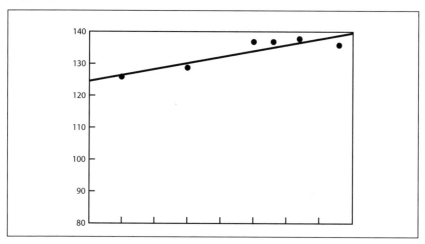

Figure 14.5. Average marital satisfaction for couples where husbands had positive pregnancy oral history interviews.

ing wife satisfaction was predicted by the husband's negativity during the Pregnancy Oral History Interview, the husband's disappointment with the marriage, and his description of their life as chaotic.

On the other hand, his fondness and admiration of her during this interview predicted her increasing marital satisfaction. His love maps of her, that is, his knowing her well through her pregnancy, predicted her increasing marital satisfaction, and her love maps of him, that is, knowing him well through the pregnancy, all predicted her increasing marital satisfaction.

Husbands were so important in this transition that Alyson Shapiro (for her master's thesis) looked back at our newlywed tapes to see whether we could predict which husbands would be positive and which would be negative during the pregnancy. Alyson could absolutely make that prediction. Those husbands who were more positive than negative to their new brides, and more complimentary toward them in the first Oral History Interview we conducted a few months after their wedding, were exactly the same guys who sailed through this transition to parenthood. Recently, we compiled everything we had learned about how important these guys were in a book Julie and John wrote together with Doug Abrams, Rachel Carlton Abrams, and Lara Love (Gottman, Gottman, Abrams, Carlton Abrams, & Love, 2016) titled *The Man's Guide to Women*.

Looking at the data qualitatively, the husbands with more negative Pregnancy Oral History Interviews described the changes in their wives' bodies in unflattering terms ("She looks like a whale") and said that they were not sexually attracted to her when she was pregnant. The more positive Pregnancy Oral History husbands described the changes in their wives' bodies in flattering terms ("She's beautiful when she's pregnant" and "She just glows now") and said that they were even more sexually attracted to her when she was pregnant. The differences were quite dramatic.

From the pregnancy conflict discussion we found that our specific emotions (SPAFF) coding could predict with high accuracy—accounting for approximately half the variance—how much their baby would laugh or cry during the 3-month LTP, and also, since we recorded the baby's heart rates during the LTP, the baby's vagal tone. Clearly, there are individual differences in temperament that we have no control over, some of which are genetic.

Yet, later, after we designed the Bringing Baby Home intervention, we found that for parents who attended it, compared to control group couples, their baby's vagal tone was significantly higher, as was the baby's eventual complex linguistic development. The Bringing Baby Home workshop was designed in collaboration with two amazing family life educators at the Swedish Medical Center, Carolyn Pirak and Joan Parthemer. They knew much more about what pregnant women needed than we did, and they were very active in designing the Bringing Baby Home workshop. We gratefully accepted their leadership.

In two randomized clinical trials, our lab showed that this workshop was highly effective for 77% of the couples who attended it. The remaining 23% (in the second study) benefited from an added parents' support group, supervised by one of our therapists, John Slattery. Furthermore, this workshop and support group kept dads involved with their babies (daughters as well as sons). To our knowledge it's the only intervention to do so. As we mentioned, this workshop has now been tested in many countries and in all cases found to be highly effective in reversing the drop in marital satisfaction, greatly reducing both postpartum depression and divorce. THE NEWS: WE WERE GETTING A 4SD EFFECT SIZE. We had developed our first 4SD therapy!

THERAPY WITH THE FAMILY TRIAD

Babies don't come with a handbook. There's no user's manual. When we brought our baby daughter home from the hospital, Swedish Medical Center gave us a videotape. We looked at one another and said, "What do we do now?" Julie said, "Put in the videotape." And so we did, but we were disappointed that the tape only told us about all the services that Swedish Medical Center offered. There was no information about the baby or on how to parent this infant. We set out to develop the videotape we needed, and we did just that.

Parents have to learn how to interact with their baby mostly by trial and error. As we noted, in 1999 Elisabeth Fivaz-Depeursinge and Antoinette Corboz-Warnery published their first amazing book called *The Primary Triangle*. In their book they described their microanaly-

240

ses of mother-father-baby interaction using the LTP. They wrote about how families coordinate their play with the baby or fail to do so. They described how parents read babies and how babies read their parents, and the challenges of coordinations, miscoordinations, and repair in a dance of coregulation:

> How do the partners coordinate their actions from moment to moment? How do they mis-coordinate their actions? How do they repair these false steps? . . . Indeed, when we begin to search for the moment-to-moment interaction for co-regulation, we again discover a universe of minute micro-processes. This world is most clearly revealed by "false steps," "errors," or "mis-coordinations." Mis-coordinations between partners are much more likely than smooth coordinations; after all, we are separate individuals. Consequently, as E. Tronick and his colleagues have emphasized, mis-coordinations would not only be inherent in interaction *but profitable for development*; what counts is whether cooperative repair is initiated efficiently (Tronick and Cohn, 1989). Repair might reestablish the function or possibly amplify it. (Fivaz-Depeursinge & Corboz-Warnery, 1999, pp. 16–17, italics added)

Let's take a small example from their work. When 3-month-old babies see two parental heads of roughly the same size approaching them in play, the baby seems to know "play with both." The baby shifts gaze from one parent to the other, focusing mostly on the mouth areas of parents' faces (where most of the emotional information resides). However, if one parent withdraws (visually creating one small head and one bigger one) the baby gets confused and is likely to fuss and cry. The same result occurs if one parent intrudes and takes over the other parent's game with the baby. The baby is a sensitive barometer of harmony. As the baby gets older, even at 9 months, Fivaz-Depeursinge and Corboz-Warnery found that some babies even actively will include the withdrawn parent by socially referencing and inviting the withdrawn parent into the play. For example, the baby may have a nice interaction with mom, and then maintain that joyful facial expression, but shift gaze to the withdrawn dad, who then sees this as an invitation to join in the play. Fivaz-Depeursinge and Corboz-Warnery called these babies "young family therapists."

As we observed moms, dads, and babies interacting in the LTP, guided in our scoring of videotapes by Tronick's work and Fivaz-Depeursinge and Corboz-Warnery's, we had the added advantage of being able to measure the baby's heart rate during the play and we were guided by Porges's work on infant vagal tone.

THE THIRD AXIS IN FAMILY PHASE SPACE: THE BABY'S AXIS

We also used our phase space portraits math model to analyze the LTP data, and we reported these results in our book *The Mathematics of Marriage* (Gottman et al., 2002). That book also extended the math model to a longitudinal study of gay and lesbian committed couples. In that book we showed – with the same equations – that:

1. When the moms were unhappily married, their start-up just with their baby (mother-baby phase) was far more negative emotionally than when the moms were happily married. So the babies were starting out with a compromised mom. It seems that she couldn't be at her best with her baby when she was unhappily married.

2. Happily married moms in the *triadic play* (the phase with dad included) were in synchrony with their husbands; in contrast, the moms with low marital satisfaction were out of sync with their husbands. As Fivaz-Depeursinge and Corboz-Warnery showed, this "out of sync" between parents' behavior involves either one person withdrawing from, or one person intrusively interrupting, a game that the other parent has begun, all of which lead to the baby's crying and physiological arousal. Babies like their parents to be in sync, not competing with

one another and not having one parent withdrawing from the play.

3. There was also a significant interaction with the baby's *unin-fluenced attractor with dad*. This means that babies themselves with happily married dads actually also *started* the play with dad more positively than if their dad were unhappily married.

4. When moms were unhappily married, dad's negative affect during the triadic play contributed to mom also becoming more negative toward the baby. That is, she *amplified dad's negativity* when she was unhappily married, whereas she *compensated for his negativity* when she was happily married. Again, just like with couples, in happy families we also see a balance of positive and negative affect when the parents are happily married, a regulation that compensates for negativity.

5. In playing with dad, babies were also far less negative in response to their dads' negativity when their dad was happily married, compared to when he was unhappily married. So babies seem somehow already buffered from their dad's negative affect in a family where the parents are happily married. This is very cool.

6. In unhappily married couples, mothers were more responsive to increasing negativity in the baby by becoming more negative toward the baby themselves, a reciprocation of negativity, rather than a buffering, which happened with happily married moms. This situation was amplified when the father had also been negative in his dyadic interactions with the baby. This is an extension of the negative absorbing Markov state to the baby.

7. In the triadic play, among happily married couples, the baby's direct influence on the mother was *positive*, regardless of the father's affect. Moms get buffered *by babies* from dads' negativity if the couples are happily married. Isn't that totally cool? Among unhappily married couples, the baby's influence on the mother was negative when the dad was negative, and posi-

tive when the dad was negative. So, only if unhappily married are moms highly coupled in how their baby influences them, and that influence is coupled directly to the dad's affect. This effect on the unhappily married mom was most pronounced when the baby's affect was most negative. So we can see how this can become a highly negative cycle in an unhappily married couple: Dad's negative affect will transfer to the baby and become amplified when the mom interacts with her baby, if she also starts negatively. It could be a TRIADIC Richardson arms war runaway cycle of negative affect. This is again an extension of the negative absorbing Markov state to the baby.

The equations we used in these analyses were *exactly* the same equations we used for analyzing the couple interactions in previous chapters, with the SAME INFLUENCE FUNCTIONS! The only difference is that we used the Shapiro coding of the LTP for our data. Therefore, the extension from couples to families works beautifully! We had extended our general systems theory from couples to the family.

GENERAL SYSTEMS THEORY OF FAMILIES: IT'S THE SAME FABRIC

We learned that the fabric of the couple system is the same stuff that starts the family system once a baby arrives. The couple duplicates the same type of interactive pattern they established as a couple once they begin interacting with their baby in the LTP.

However, their interactive pattern as a couple, if she is carrying the baby in her womb for 9 months, suggests another kind of linkage that affects the developing fetus. The emotional climate between the couple during pregnancy may be affecting fetal development itself. The link happens, in part, because the stress hormone *cortisol*— which is a steroid glucocorticoid hormone—easily crosses the intrauterine barrier. Cortisol is produced in response to stress by the zona fasciculata of the adrenal gland and functions to increase blood sugar, to aid in metabolism, to suppress the immune system, and to reduce bone growth. A pregnant woman stressed by negative marital conflict passes these stresses on to the fetus by changing the quality of the intrauterine environment.

Our powerful ability to predict from the conflict lab interactions in the third trimester to the 3-month-old infant's affect (how much the baby laughs, smiles, or cries) and the ability of the infant to self-soothe via high vagal tone (respiratory sinus arrhythmia) suggests that the quality of the intrauterine environment could be the mediating variable in those predictions. This kind of linkage is not unique to our laboratory. As Keenan, Jacob, Grace, and Gunthorpe (2009) wrote:

> More than a dozen independent studies link prenatal maternal stress and anxiety to differences in later child development, even when controlling for confounders such as postnatal mood. . . . Negative child outcomes associated with prenatal stress include infant regulation problems (crying, sleeping, feeding), decreased attention, more impulsivity, negative affect or temperament, and lower cognitive test scores or language abilities. (2009, p. 39)

Our Bringing Baby Home workshop powerfully changes that destructive marital dynamic that can affect the quality of the fetal environment.

THE DEVELOPMENT OF
PSYCHOPATHOLOGY IN INFANTS

Our results are completely consistent with other data on parent-infant interaction. The parent-infant interaction system is a very sensitive indicator of the emotional state of the parents. What are the consequences of a miscoordinated parent-infant system? What has to go wrong for the development of psychopathology?

Edward Tronick is one of our nation's leading experts on parent-infant interaction. He has shown that maternal depression has a big effect on babies. In his brilliant "still face" research method, a mom will present a neutral and frozen face to her baby. Most babies, even 3-month-olds, go through a repertoire of tactics to engage the still-face mom. You can watch them on YouTube. Babies are quite charming at getting a response from a parent. They coo and smile, grin, and flirt. It's fascinating, and most grown-ups have a hard time doing a still face in response to a baby. When mom stays unresponsive, the babies eventually get very upset. When mom soothes the baby and becomes responsive again, the baby starts interacting again, and the relationship gets repaired quickly. On the other hand, Tronick found that the babies of depressed moms don't change much in response to the still face. They are probably used to a nonresponsive mother.

Richard Davidson discovered a lateralization of brain waves (EEGs) in most adults, with relatively greater LEFT frontal activation during the APPROACH emotions (curiosity, interest, and anger) and relatively greater RIGHT frontal activation for the withdrawal emotions (fear, sadness, and disgust). Davidson also discovered that when asked to just think about a typical day, depressed people had relatively greater RIGHT frontal activation than left, whereas nondepressed people had relatively greater LEFT frontal activation than right.

Both Tiffany Field and, independently, Geri Dawson studied the interactions of babies with clinically depressed moms, and they also collected EEG (scalp brain waves) from baby and mom. It turned out that just like their depressed moms, *babies* of depressed moms had greater RIGHT than LEFT frontal activation. Dawson even found this pattern when the baby was observing soap bubbles rising, something that would amuse and delight most babies, and would cause greater LEFT than RIGHT frontal activation (curiosity, amusement). With the babies of depressed moms, while watching soap bubbles rise Dawson found a *right* frontal EEG pattern. These babies were fearful or sad watching the bubbles. This is a very dramatic set of results. Olson, Sameroff, Lukenheimer, and Kerr (2009) wrote:

> Infants who experience frequent dys-regulated interactions with caregivers may be at risk for delays in the development of self-

regulatory competence. . . . Conversely, Feldman, Greenbaum, and Yirmiya (1999) measured individual differences in maternal responsiveness to micro-shifts in infant affect at 3 and 9 months and found that synchronous interaction predicted self-regulatory competence at age 2, even when the effects of infant temperament were controlled. In other prospective longitudinal studies, unresponsive mother-infant interaction has been linked to self-regulatory problems in middle childhood (Carlson et al., 1995; Jacobvitz & Sroufe, 1987; Olson, Bates, & Bayles, 1990) and adolescence (Olson, Bates, Sandy, & Lanthier, 2000; Wakschlag & Hans, 1999).

What we are saying is that the mother, father, and baby create an exquisitely tuned interactive system. When both parents' interaction is coordinated, sensitive, and responsive to the baby's developing ability to self-soothe, the baby builds vagal tone. The system is finely tuned. The baby rewards the parents with long bouts of delightful play. Nothing engages parents more than this kind of play. It includes cycles of great fun and love. Then from out of nowhere the baby may become over-stimulated, fuss, and get increasingly upset. The nurturant mom and dad soothe the baby together, allow the baby to look away, and then return to them. Gradually, as the baby's vagal tone builds, the baby can self-soothe and turn back again.

THE SYSTEM SOMETIMES REPAIRS ITSELF

When the system is miscoordinated, the triad family system repairs. As we noted, Fivaz-Depeursinge and Corboz-Warnery showed that even at 6 or 9 months some babies participate in actively making these repairs.

Tronick discovered that REPAIR is the sine qua non, the as-good-as-it-gets process for creating securely attached babies. Attachment security was identified by John Bowlby, and later measured by Mary Ainsworth, to describe the safe haven in a relationship that makes it possible for infants to explore and learn (Ainsworth, Bell, & Stayton, 1971). Attachment security describes a RELATIONSHIP, not an infant. It is quite possible for a baby to be securely attached to one adult and not to another. Tronick discovered that moms who repaired miscoordinated play at 3 months had securely attached babies at 12 months. Moms who did not repair miscoordinated play at 3 months had insecurely attached babies at 12 months. The system is quite malleable.

INTERVENING IN THE PRIMARY TRIAD

Unfortunately, the family system doesn't always repair itself. In 1989, two scientists, Sameroff and Emde, edited a book titled *Relationship Disturbances in Early Childhood*. They began to explore how to conceptualize the primary triad and HOW TO INTERVENE to create the kind of finely tuned parenting that would nurture health in the developing mother-father-baby SYSTEM. That book was later followed by another edited book by Sameroff, McDonough, and Rosenblum (2004) detailing many effective clinical strategies for changing this young family system. Intervening early is smart, and it's effective.

SUMMARY

What have we concluded in this chapter? We can definitely extend our general systems theory to the family once a baby arrives. In fact, for most couples the arrival of the first baby is a disaster. Yet it is a disaster we can totally avoid with our Bringing Baby Home program, described in the first book we wrote together, *And Baby Makes Three*. We can change the couple and avoid problematic interactions with their baby.

Furthermore, it is possible to actually intervene into the developing family and avoid the development of some psychopathology in the baby. The system of interaction between mom, dad, and baby is so finely tuned that it is possible to change it so that the parents are warm and respon-sive to the baby. These hopeful and positive changes are possible with our new general systems theory for the family.

What about continuing to extend our general systems theory to the family as the child develops? That's exactly where we are headed.

CHAPTER 15

The Family as the Baby Develops

We learned in Chapter 14 that we could actually extend our general systems theory from the couple to the family triad once a baby arrives. We needed to add several concepts to perform this extension seamlessly, including understanding the development of emotion regulation in children. Yet the extension was totally doable. It works, and it is on a solid empirical and theoretical footing. That's really exciting, and these ideas give us an understanding of the developing family system.

But what about the family system as it develops? Can we continue to understand families using this new general systems theory? If that were true, it would really be something. Does this understanding extend beyond the family, as the child emerges to interact with other adults and other children?

The answer is a resounding yes. The family processes we have described launch the child into the world. Formed in the cradle of the family's interactions, the young child may be propelled into the world as an emotionally intelligent animal, ready to master its own nervous system so it can engage creatively and prosocially. Alternatively, the family may have shaped the baby to respond poorly to the world: ready to overreact neurologically with reliance on far more primitive systems of fear and loathing. The secret lies in the emotional world of the developing family.

THE DISCOVERY OF EMOTION COACHING

With Lynn Katz in the 1980s we started looking at parent-child interaction and child development and its relation to the couple's dynamics. We started with 4–5-year-old kids, and studied them up to age 8, and then Lynn continued to study them up to age 15.

We were encouraged by the work we were doing with the first baby, so we continued to study mother-father-child interaction with older kids. That work began when John was still a professor at the University of Illinois. John combined the study of couples' interaction, but added parent-child interaction, and his observational research on peer interaction in children.

Our Space Capsule

At the University of Illinois John used a mock-up of the Apollo space capsule. In this space capsule lab, we had kids we were studying don astronaut suits with NASA labels, and sit in the space capsule mock-up, while their parents interacted with them, standing on small ladders. The fantasy game delighted young children, and the best part was that they were able to sit still and concentrate for long periods of time as we recorded their facial expressions and physiology. We showed the children emotion-eliciting films. The parents taught their kids how to play a very pro–dental health video game in which the kids got to shoot down junk foods, armed with tubes of toothpaste. First the parents learned how to play the game. Then we observed them teaching the game to their kids.

For this study John and Lynn developed an interview of the parents about how they felt about the emotions, the meta-emotion interview. We already discussed the meta-emotion interview when we talked about couples. That was Dan Yoshimoto's extension of the meta-emotion interview that Lynn Katz and John developed for studying parents. So, the parenting meta-emotion interview came first, back in the 1980s, when John was a professor at the University of Illinois. The research on families also continued at the University of Washington, in Seattle.

The original meta-emotion idea was that, although emotional expressions and emotional experiences appear to be fairly universal in our species throughout the planet, the way people feel about the emotions is probably not cross-culturally universal. We coded our meta-emotion interview with a system designed by Carole Hooven, who was a staff member in our Seattle lab (we continued this research once John moved to Seattle).

We also showed the kids movies when they were alone in the space capsule designed to elicit emotions in the children. For example, the "Flying Monkeys" scene from *The Wizard of Oz* was a good elicitor of fear, while the "Better Bring a Bucket" restaurant scene from *Monty Python's The Meaning of Life* was a good elicitor of disgust. We also taped the kids playing with either their best friend or a child stranger their own gender and age. We coded these tapes with an observational coding system that had been designed by John and his former graduate student, Jennifer Parkhurst (Gottman & Parkhurst, 1980; Gottman, 1983). John's 1983 monograph, *How Children Become Friends*, employed these coding systems to describe two studies on how young children become friends, or fail to do so. That monograph was the first observational research on children's friendship, which was further elaborated across development in the book *Conversations of Friends* (Gottman & Parker, 1986). The peer world of kids is crucial for their healthy emotional development. This peer world is so intricate that we review the research John did on how children become friends in one of our appendixes.

Once again, as with babies, we discovered that the way the parents interacted with one another during conflict was a great predictor of how they would interact with their child. However, separate and important understanding resulted from knowing the parental meta-emotions of the parents. What we eventually discovered was a validation of the important clinical work done in the 1960s of child psychologist Haim Ginott. Ginott wrote two important books titled *Between Parent and Child* (1965/1994) and *Teacher and Child* (1975). Ginott's ideas were later further beautifully popularized by Faber and Mazlish in their 1980 book, *How to*

Talk So Kids Will Listen and Listen So Kids Will Talk. That amazing book still ranks 140 on Amazon's best-seller list. Let's talk about the science.

In our meta-emotion study there were two broad types of parents:

1. *Emotion dismissers.* These people tended to not have a very detailed vocabulary for describing their own emotional states during our interview. They also felt that paying attention to NEGATIVE emotions was potentially harmful. They used a lot of explosion metaphors to describe anger, and mental illness terms to describe sadness, disgust, and fear. They were trying to protect their kids from having the negative emotions. They said that they tended to use ACTION to avoid feeling these emotions or paying too much attention to them They said things like, "I just roll with the punches, and get on with life," and "I don't dwell on these negative emotions." They seemed to believe that the emotions were like a garment one chooses to wear. They said, "Why would anyone choose to be sad, or angry?" They said that they preferred and tried always to choose to be optimistic and cheerful. They also either did not notice their children's negative emotions (Mom: "Harry, has Jessica ever been sad? I don't think so." Dad: "Oh yeah, that one time she visited Grandma by herself, getting on the plane she looked a little sad.") or they were impatient with their children's negative emotions, tried to distract their children, give them food, or cheer them up if they noticed any negativity. Some parents' meta-emotion about anger was disgust, so they viewed their child's anger toward them as disrespectful and worthy of punishment, even if there was no other child misbehavior.

2. *Emotion coachers.* These people tended to have a detailed vocabulary for describing their own emotional states during our interview. They felt that paying attention to NEGATIVE emotions was potentially constructive. They believed that just experiencing all emotions fully was a good thing, and they

wanted their kids to also experience all the emotions. They weren't trying to protect their kids from having negative emotions. They said that they tended to INTROSPECT when they felt negative emotions. They said things like, "When I'm sad usually something's missing, and I need to figure out what that might be," and "When I'm angry usually I have a goal that's getting blocked." They seemed to believe that the emotions were like a GPS that guided them through life. They didn't try to avoid feeling these negative emotions. They also were tuned into their children's negative emotions and empathized with them, even when there was misbehavior. They helped their children put words to their feelings. They seemed to believe that all feelings were acceptable, but they set firm limits on misbehavior.

The data were actually more complicated than this broad-strokes picture, because some people could be considered dysregulated and therefore dismissing, but only with specific emotions. For example, some people hated anger, and viewed any anger directed toward them as disrespect (i.e., contempt); others hated sadness and would even leave the house if their child became sad. So the dichotomy is only an approximation to the richness of studying meta-emotion.

Despite these caveats, these two kinds of parents taught their children the video game in two entirely different ways. The dismissing parents gave their kid a lot of information at the start and then hung back, waiting for their kid to make a mistake. Then they became critical, sometimes relentlessly so. When anyone gets corrective feedback when they are just learning something new, they make more mistakes. Their kids' performance levels kept getting worse and worse. The coaching parents gave their kid very little information, just enough to get started. Then they hung back and ignored the kid's mistakes, and waited for the kid to do something right. At that point they came in and gave praise and encouragement, and just a little more information. Their kids' performance levels kept getting better and better.

Emotion-dismissing parents scanned for other people's mistakes and became critical of negative emotions in their partner. On the other hand, emotion-coaching parents scanned for what was going right and appreciated it in their partner. The conflict marital interactions of the emotion-dismissing parents were also more likely to contain the Four Horsemen than the conflict marital interactions of emotion-coaching parents. It was better for everyone, though, if parents were matched versus mismatched on meta-emotion styles. Mismatches in emotion coaching versus emotion dismissing of the parents were deadly to the marriage. These matches versus mismatches alone predicted marital stability or divorce with 80% accuracy. (However, in therapy it is not very hard to change this problem.)

Effects of Being Emotion Coached

It turned out that kids who had been emotion coached were on a totally different developmental trajectory than the kids who had been emotion dismissed. The emotion-coached kids turned out to become what can only be termed "emotionally intelligent." As we tape-recorded their play, we detected that they did much better with peers, either with a best friend or making friends with a stranger. And, as we followed them developmentally, they kept being emotionally intelligent with peers. This was no simple splinter skill that they learned. As John and Lynn pointed out, in preschool it's totally skillful to simply express negative emotions to a peer. "I don't like it when you do that" will get most preschool children to stop being obnoxious. But in middle childhood, once teasing and more complex peer social structures emerge, the proper response to being teased is to act cool, that is, as if you've had an "emotion-ectomy." These emotion-coached kids were fine in middle childhood. In adolescence, emotions become important for understanding who you are, who you are becoming, and how you feel in different relationships. Again, during adolescence, emotion-coached kids did very well with peers, even though the skill set had changed. Emotion-coached kids developed what could only be called "social moxie," a general emotional intelligence with peers.

Another one of our findings that John is particularly proud of is that when marriages ended in divorce, if even one parent was an emotion coach, their kids were almost totally buffered from the usual negative effects of divorce on kids. There were no ill effects on grades, or either internalizing (depression, suicidality) or externalizing (for example, aggression, bullying) symptoms. They were still sad about their parents breaking up, however.

THE DEVELOPMENT OF CHILDREN'S EMOTIONAL INTELLIGENCE

Why did we include a very detailed study of 4- and 5-year-old children's relationships with peers, with a best friend and with a stranger, and then, as we did, follow these preschool kids into middle childhood (age 8)?

We were trying to build a systems theory of FAMILIES, so why did we include children's peers? Here is our answer: We not only need to measure family variables when building a systems theory of families, but we also need to validate that theory. The developing child starts leaving the family, and gradually peers become more important than the family itself. How does the family launch, or fail to launch, the developing child? Could we extend our family systems theory to families with older children? The answer again is a decisive yes.

So, if we take a step back, we can ask, what domain of a child's life is the most important for potentially validating our family systems view? The answer is that developmental psychology research has consistently shown that probably the most important kinds of variables one can measure about a child to predict how the child will eventually turn out have to do with how that child gets along with other children. These findings were behind the emergence and recognition of the importance of EMOTIONAL INTELLIGENCE, a field pioneered by Dan Goleman (2005).

Figure 15.1. Children playing in leaves

Acceptance or rejection by peers is a very important risk variable for all children that can predict their future.

In a series of studies with his former grad student, Martha Putallaz, John studied how specifically young children would get accepted or rejected when they attempted to enter a group of other kids. They were able to identify specific social skills for effective entry and also the patterns of behavior that lead to peer rejection. Putallaz then discovered, for her doctoral dissertation, that the way parents, especially fathers, interacted with their very young children predicted how the children would be accepted or rejected when they entered school, as measured by the gold standard of these measures, the peer sociometric, an index of the social fabric of a classroom.

Acceptance and rejection by peers, and the ability to make a best friend, turn out to be very important variables in a child's well-being and happiness in school, and in predicting whether the child will do well, or wind up in a deviant peer group and doing badly in school and in life in general. A huge number of references establish this fact of the importance of children's peer relationships (for example, Asher, 1983; Asher & Coie, 1990; Asher & Gottman, 1981; Parker & Asher, 1987, 1993; Vanhalst et al., 2015).

Peer relationships were a major research area for John and some of his students. In a monograph for the Society for Research in Child Development titled *How Children Become Friends* (Gottman, 1983), John reported the results of decades of his observational research on the conversations of friends, done in collaboration with his former student Jennifer Parkhurst (see *The Conversations of Friends*, Gottman & Parker, 1986).

Therefore, to gauge the utility and validity of a SYSTEMS VIEW OF THE FAMILY, it is important to demonstrate that these marital and family variables we collect are actually VALID. We have to show that we can predict important variables in the development of the child. Peer relations are a very important class of such variables. We added behav-

Figure 15.2. Children painting together

ior problems, academic achievement, child attention abilities, and child health to our list of validity variables that our systems theory of families had to meet.

OUR RESULTS

One of our first major findings was that young children carry their parents' marital unhappiness in their bodies. This result truly amazed us. We could measure marital satisfaction in two equivalent ways, one with our standard relationship satisfaction questionnaire given to the parents, or we could measure parental marital satisfaction with our 24-hour urine sample taken from their 4-year-old. Kids with unhappily married parents were secreting more stress hormones than kids whose parents were happily married. Once more we see dramatically that the quality of the parents' marriage affects the entire fabric of the family and the subsequent development of the child.

We also discovered that parents' awareness versus dismissing of their own and their child's negative emotions was strongly related to both marital interaction and how they parented their child. Emotion-dismissing parents used low warmth, derogation, criticism, and intrusiveness when teaching their child something new. On the other hand, emotion-coaching parents used scaffolding and praising, lightly supporting and encouraging the child, attending to the child and responding to the child with what we called "positive directedness."

We discovered that meta-emotion and parenting variables taken at age 4 or 5 were predictive of child outcomes at age 8 (Gottman, Katz, and Hooven, 1997).

We also discovered strong links between the parents' awareness of their own emotions, their coaching versus dismissing their children's emotions, how the parents interacted during conflict in their marriage, their parenting behavior, and their children's physiology. Here's what we found.

We measured the children's autonomic and endocrine physiology carefully, to get a window into the physiological basis of emotion regulation abilities of the children. The children's autonomic nervous system and emotion regulation ability was linked to the children's behavior as judged by teachers to the children's academic achievement, and to their ability to focus attention. We also measured the children's autonomic physiology during parent-child interaction, when they were viewing emotion-eliciting films, and additionally their adrenaline and cortisol secretions during a 24-hour urine sample, all when the children were 4 years old.

These extensive physiological measures were predictive of standard behavior checklists measuring child internalizing (anxiety, depression) or externalizing (aggression) symptoms filled out by the parents and the child's teachers and a special questionnaire we designed for parents on how much the parents had to externally downregulate their child.

THE DEVELOPMENT OF THE CHILD'S EMOTIONAL INTELLIGENCE: EQ

As we mentioned, it is now well known that learning to interact successfully with peers and to form lasting peer relationships is a very important developmental task. Children who fail at this task, who are rejected by their peers, and especially those who are unable to make friends, are at risk for a number of later problems (Parker & Asher, 1987, 1993). Therefore looking at how a child relates to other children is very important. The peer context presents new opportunities and formidable challenges to children. Interacting with peers provides opportunities to learn about more egalitarian relationships than parent-child relationships; to form friendships with age mates, negotiate conflicts, engage in cooperative and competitive activities, and learn appropriate limits for aggressive impulses. It provides opportunities for learning that friends can be sources of great fun and adventure as well as comfort in times of need. Even very young children are able to obtain this kind of comfort in times of stress from their friends. For example, with his student Laurie Kramer, John found that the quality of friendships among 3-year-olds was the best predictor of adjustment to becoming a sibling (Kramer & Gottman, 1992). The child's best friend became a support system for the transition from a first-born only child to becoming a sibling. It's part of the key to having siblings without a disastrous sibling rivalry.

Thus, there is a major challenge in being able to make linkages from the family's emotional world to the child's peer world. The challenge is that, as the child develops, many of the child's peer social competencies become precisely the opposite of what children specifically learn in emotion coaching with parents. Even in the preschool period, entry into a peer group is successful to the extent that children do not call attention to themselves and their feelings, but instead watch the peer group, understand what they are doing, and quietly and nonintrusively imitate what they are doing, waiting to be invited in. These skills of observing, waiting, watching, and not expressing one's emotions or discussing them are even more important in middle childhood, when teasing becomes central. Any theory we develop has to contend with the problem that the specific skills children learn in emotion-coaching interactions with parents are precisely the wrong skills for succeeding with peers, and this is even more the case in middle childhood. Hence we propose that a social learning or modeling theory of the development of social competence will not do. It is doomed to failure. Our friend Steve Asher has systematically studied loneliness in children (for example, see Vanhalst et al., 2015). Chronically lonely children are stably sensitive to scenarios that involve inclusion or exclusion.

What do we offer as an alternative to a specific skills approach? We suggest that instead of a social skills theory for making developmental predictions and linkages from the family to the child peer system, a set of general abilities underlie the development of social and emotional competence with peers, and that these abilities form the basis of what Salovey and Mayer (1990) called *emotional intelligence*. While Salovey and Mayer's idea of emotional intelligence is a very long list of skills, we thought that the link in making these predictions would be much simpler: it would be the child's ability to regulate emotions and to self-soothe and focus attention during salient emotionally trying peer situations. We observed that the child's peer social competence in middle childhood in part was in the inhibition of negative affect (Guralnick, 1981), particularly aggression, whining, oppositional behavior, fighting requiring parental intervention, sadness, and anxiety with peers. Being teased in middle childhood is the ultimate proving ground for the child's ability to inhibit negative affect.

What John and Lynn Katz discovered was that emotion coaching by parents when the kids were in preschool actually created emotional intelligence in the children. The children did not just learn specific skills, they developed an emotional intelligence that they took with them through middle childhood, even though this period required new social skills. In adolescence, the emotional intelligence that they took with them required even more new social skills. That was an amazing set of findings about the power of emotion coaching.

What was different about children who could or could not do this making friends and getting accepted business? There was a fundamental set of abilities we discovered that had to do with understanding one's own emotions, being able to regulate them, being able to soothe oneself physiologically, focus attention, listen to what one's playmate is saying, being able to take another's role and empathize, being able to engage in social problem solving, or, as Asher has suggested, relating one's goals to one's strategies. These are the skills children learn with emotion-coaching parents, but they are not applied isomorphically to the peer world. They involve the child knowing something about the world of emotion, her own as well as others. This knowledge arises only out of emotional connection being important in the home. Yet the skills do not stay the same. They change with development, and they change quite dramatically.

In middle childhood, John and Lynn discovered that the child who has been emotion coached by parents has developed a general set of skills that appear to have nothing to do with expressing and understanding one's own feelings. However, they have to do with the ability to inhibit negative affect, to self-soothe, to focus attention (including social attention), and to regulate one's own emotions. In middle childhood these abilities are manifested by inhibiting displays of distress and inhibiting aggression when the child is teased, and instead acting emotionally unflappable, and in being able to enter an ongoing peer group with ease and awareness instead of with the lumbering bravado of the socially rejected child.

These emotion regulation abilities are, to some extent, temperamental and genetic. They are also shaped by parents beginning in infancy. This shaping begins in parents' ability to deal with an infant's distress with affection and comfort (Dunn, 1977) and continues into the face-to-face play with the infant in the first year of life (Gianino & Tronick, 1988; Stern, 1985). This thinking is consistent with many current theorists' writing about social and emotional development in infancy and the role of face-to-face interaction of infants and parents. Hence, we found that there are pathways from our meta-emotion variables to the child's physiological responses during emotion-arousing situations in the laboratory (parent-child interaction, emotion-eliciting films).

Therefore, we can extend our general systems theory and therapy to the family as the children develop. Furthermore, this extension passes a huge test of validity. We can use these data to understand the child's social world BEYOND the family and into the child's peer culture. The secret is emotion coaching.

IMPLICATIONS FOR THERAPY

Transition to Parenthood

The Bringing Baby Home workshop has now been taught to over 1,500 workshop leaders, who hail from 20 different countries. In studies that have been carried out, this workshop is actually effective at creating a 4SD intervention (Shapiro & Gottman, 2005).

Randomized Clinical Trials and Clinical Work With Emotion Coaching

It isn't enough to have all this work done on meta-emotion as the link that extends couples' work to families, unless we can actually demonstrate that there is a CAUSAL relationship between emotion coaching and child/family outcomes. Fortunately, that research has already been done by Sophie Havighurst in Melbourne, Australia. In a program of randomized clinical trials, Havighurst and her colleagues have actually demonstrated the efficacy of emotion coaching training provided to parents. Sophie's program is called Tuning in to Kids. Havighurst and colleagues created an emotion-coaching parent training program and demonstrated that this program was effective compared to control groups for internalizing problems in children such as depression (Kehoe, Havighurst, & Harley, 2014), and externalizing problems with children aged 4–9 years (Duncombe, Havighurst, Kehoe, Holland, & Frankling, 2016), somatic complaints in adolescents (Kehoe, Havighurst, & Harley, 2015), externalizing behavior in teens (Havighurst, Kehoe, & Harley, 2015), with toddlers (Lauw et al., 2014), and with fathers' relationship with their children (Wilson, Havighurst, & Harley, 2014). They also found that emotion coaching was as effective as behavioral intervention (Duncombe et al., 2016).

Emotion coaching was also evaluated in clinical practice throughout South Korea by Christia Choi. Choi effectively changed an orphanage in Busan and one in Seoul, both K–12 school in crisis, in which the children were acting out severely. With just six months of training the teachers and nuns in emotion coaching, the schools made a remarkable recovery. Furthermore, the high school orchestra the following year performed in Carnegie Hall. Subsequently, Choi trained 200,000 teachers throughout South Korea in emotion coaching. The work has also been applied programmatically throughout the United Kingdom by J. Rose.

UNDERSTANDING EMOTION COACHING CLINICALLY

We wrote about emotion coaching in a book John published called *Raising an Emotionally Intelligent Child* (Gottman & DeClaire, 2009). Emotion coaching is not complex; it consists of just five steps. First, emotion-coaching parents believe that a child's emotions are important moments for teaching and closeness. They welcome such moments. Second, they empathize with the child's feelings, even if there has been misbehavior by the child. Third, they help the child label all the emotions the child is feeling. Fourth, they set limits on misbehavior, communicating their own emotions about it, expressing their values, and setting up consequences for misbehavior. Fifth, if there is no misbehavior, they problem solve with the child.

As we mentioned earlier, emotion coaching was an empirical validation of the thinking of a great child therapist, Haim Ginott. We want to introduce you to Ginott's work. We want to give you some sense for how important it is to listen to and to understand a child. Children are very aware of the fact that they are small. They are very aware of the fact that they need their parents to survive. And so, because they know they are small, they have a mixed relationship with power and powerlessness. They also have a heightened sense of dignity.

Very few adults remember what it was like to be a child. Sometimes we ask adult audiences if they remember, and some hands go up. Of those adults who do remember what it was like to be a child, we ask them if they had anyone in their lives who treated them with respect, who listened to them, and fully loved them. Some of these hands stay up. We then ask these adults if they would be willing to share a story of the adult who treated them with respect and love. Usually they are willing, and the stories they tell are always powerful. There isn't a dry eye in the house as they recount the remarkable tales of these adults and of how much it meant to them to be listened to, to be treated with honor, to be told that they were important and special, and loved and accepted.

A great deal of the research we will talk about in this chapter is an empirical rediscovery in our laboratory of Haim Ginott's brilliant intuition. Ginott never did any research, but he remembered what it was like to be a child, and he understood how to connect with a child, and how to do so with honor, respect, acceptance, and love. He realized that the things he knew as a child therapist needed to become available to every parent and every teacher. We want to tell you the story of this remarkable man because insightful clinicians are at times our greatest source of hope and understanding. That is certainly true of Dan Wile, about whom we have talked about in previous chapters. And it is certainly true of Susan Johnson, whose emotionally focused couples therapy brought attachment theory to the couples therapy arena.

So what did Ginott say? Most parenting advice books are all about discipline. But, Haim Ginott said, although we want children who are obedient and cooperative, we want so much more for our children. We want them to be able to think for themselves, to be kind and compassionate, to have good values and ethics, to believe in themselves, to work hard and be successful, to have great relationships with others, and much more. Ginott's point is that we cannot accomplish these things with good discipline. Instead, the magic moments for accomplishing many of these goals are the moments when our child is emotional. These moments are our windows into the developing heart and mind of our child.

One day, 10-year-old Andy asked his father, "What is the number of abandoned children in Harlem?" His father began by giving his son a long lecture on social problems, only to realize later that Andy's question was personal, not intellectual. Andy's questions came from his own fear of being abandoned. Ginott suggested that the most important thing a parent can do is *listen*, listen for the emotion behind the words. What matters is emotion itself, that parents look for it, seek it out, listen to it, and respond genuinely and empathically with real understanding. All feelings and wishes are acceptable, but not all behavior is acceptable, and parents should set firm limits, conveying their values to the child.

Ginott also recommended that with children statements of understanding must *precede* statements of advice. We used this motto in therapy with meta-emotion mismatches. He also said that sometimes what cannot be granted in reality can be granted in fantasy. Suppose a parent is driving on a hot summer day with a child and gets caught in unrelenting bumper-to-bumper traffic. The child says, "Dad, I want some ice cream." Dad says very sweetly, "Honey, there's nothing I can do until we get home. Then I'll get you some ice cream." Not mollified, the child repeats the request more insistently: "I want some ice cream now!" Dad repeats himself, explaining why he cannot get the ice cream now. This exchange continues, with the child escalating, adding whining and crying as the exchange continues. Eventually the father is upset and threatening. An oppositional struggle has erupted. All this, Ginott said, might have been avoided if the father had originally said something like, "Yeah, ice cream sounds great. I wish I had some myself right now." The child, whose feelings are understood, would have said, "Yeah," and the father might have added, "Some chocolate ice cream would be nice," and the child might have continued, "Yeah, an ice cream sundae with sprinkles." Dad: "Yum."

Ginott said that when a child is in the midst of strong emotion she cannot listen to anyone, and she certainly cannot process good advice. The child wants us to understand the feelings and thoughts going on inside at this very moment. Ginott wrote:

> When a child tells us "The teacher spanked me," we do not have to ask him for more details. Nor do we need to say, "What did you do to deserve it? If your teacher spanked you, you must have done something. What did you do?" We don't even have to say, "Oh, I am so sorry." We need to show him that we understand his pain and embarrassment and feelings of revenge. How do we know what he feels? We look at him and listen to him, and we also draw on our own emotional experiences. We know what a child *must* feel when he is shamed in public in the presence of peers. So we phrase our words that the child knows we understand what he has gone through. Any of the following statements would serve well: "It must have been terribly embarrassing." "It must have made you furious." "You must have hated your teacher at that moment." (1965/1994, p. 27)

Ginott pointed out that a child's feelings do not disappear when he is told not to feel that way, or that it's not nice to feel that way, or that he has no proper justification for feeling that way. The common mistakes that parents make: to rush in and judge, to rush in with advice and solutions, and also just to rush.

Ginott's approach is so radically different from approaches that emphasize external configurations such as family rules or a list of consequences parents can apply to child misbehavior, or a way to structure family meetings so that the rules are democratic and not authoritarian, and so on. The difference is that Ginott's methods engage the parent with the *processes of the child's emotional world*. Once this process begins the parent is on a whole new course with the child. Ginott discourages parents from telling children what *they ought to feel*, because it makes them distrust what they do feel. Statements like, "You don't mean what you say. You love your little brother," or "This is not you. This is the devil in you acting up," or "If you mention that word 'hate' one more time you'll get the spanking of your life," or "You don't really hate your brother. Maybe you dislike him. You should rise above such feelings," convey to the child that she should not trust her emotions, but instead rely on what parents tell her she is feeling. Let's review Ginott's message to parents.

Process Is Everything

He said that we can only create KINDNESS in our child by treating the child in a kind manner. We can only create RESPECT in our child by treating the child respectfully. We can only create EMPATHY in our child by treating the child with compassion.

He said, DO NOT SAY:

1. What is wrong with you? You are so *stupid* to treat your guest rudely.
2. This will teach you to hit someone smaller than you [smack!]. Yes, Ginott said, it will do just that.
3. He told the story of a teacher who was trying to read a sensitive poem, and a child in the class named Stuart who was cutting up. She said, "Stuart, will you sit down, or are you just naturally slow?" However, Stuart was not listening to her—he was busy planning the details of her funeral.

Kids Have a Heightened Sense of Dignity, So Validate Their Emotions

Kids are very aware that they are little. They talk often of what they couldn't do when they were littler and what they can do now. They know they are growing and developing, and they have mixed feelings about that. They have a great concern with power and powerlessness. For example, Ginott told the story of a favorite uncle who visited and was sleeping in the family room. His 9-year-old nephew, Jonathan, came in bouncing a basketball. His uncle said, "Please stop, Jonathan. I am trying to take a nap." Jonathan bounced the basketball two more times before he stopped. Why did he do that? Ginott answered, Jonathan was trying to show that he was complying of his own free will. Why? Kids also need to save face.

Researcher Sam Vuchinich studied parents and kids at dinner-time and found that parents started over 75% of all the fights at dinner (Vuchinich, Hetherington, Vuchinich, & Clingempeel, 1991). These dinnertime battles were often over food. Why might that be damaging? Ginott said that kids will often conduct small experiments with their own self-concept, which often center around their preferences, some-times their food preferences. One child may say, "These peas and mashed potatoes are touching. That's disgusting! I'm not eating this." This child, Ginnot said, is saying, "I am the kind of kid who likes separate food. That's who I am." When a parent responds, "Eat all your food. That's the rule in this house," that parent is inadvertently saying, "I don't accept your experiment. I will tell you who you are!" Ginott says, what if the food right now looks like roadkill to a child? What is a parent teaching this child by making him eat roadkill? In short, Ginott said, parents do a lot of harm by invalidating children's feelings. They sometimes do that to "hold up a mirror of reality" to the child. Does the child need this mirror?

A child whines, "My finger hurts." The parent may reply, "Oh, no. That's just a small scratch. That can't hurt." Instead, Ginott says, the parent can say, "Yeah, sometimes a scratch can really hurt." Or a child is running around and says, "It's really hot in here." The parent may respond,

"Don't be silly," instead of, "It's hot in here for you." The parent may say, "Don't be afraid. There's nothing to be afraid of," instead of, "What's scary here for you?" To say that nothing is scary in here is to tell a child to ignore her own instincts. What if a grown-up says to a kid, "Come into my car—I have candy here for you"? Ginott says, we *want* our children to sometimes be afraid and not ignore their own instincts.

Fathers are often confused about their son's fears. They think if they are understanding about their son's fears the boy will turn into a wimp. In one of the parenting groups we ran, a father said his son kept being afraid of going to sleep because there was a T. Rex in his room. Our group asked the dad to have his son give him a tour of the scary shadows in the room, and to ask his son what he thought they should do. Next week the father reported that his son showed him the scary shadows when the lights went out and the dad said that they did actually look like a T. Rex. Also, the dad said that his kid came up with his own solution to this dilemma. His son said, "Let's read the dinosaur book real loud." Even if it was a dumb idea, it was the child's idea. The real test was the next two nights, when the dad reported that his son said he didn't need his dad to lie down with him anymore.

It's Very Hard for a Kid to Wait

Children operate on a slower time scale than adults. Yet a parent who waits for a child to help solve a problem, who waits for a child to come up with her own ideas is doing a great service. A parent who is not impatient with a child to come up with her own solution communicates: (1) you have good ideas; (2) you can solve problems; (3) I trust in your abilities; and (4) we are a team, and you are a part of the solution, not just a part of the problem. A parent who just sits patiently with a sad child communicates a great deal: (1) Being sad will not kill you. You won't be sad forever. Kids don't always know that. (2) It reassures the child—you are not alone; I understand what you feel. (3) Your feelings make sense. Trust your feelings. (4) Even with these feelings you are acceptable. A child is really crabby one evening and her dad says, "You are really crabby tonight. I know just how you feel. I have those days myself," and she replies, "I'm having a really horrible day, Daddy." Dad says, "It's okay."

We have written about emotion coaching in a number of publications, and have a videotaped workshop for parents and a manual available on our website, which is titled *Emotion Coaching*.

A SUMMARY OF THE FAMILY SYSTEM

The extension from a couples systems theory to a family systems theory requires us to understand the developing child's emotional and regulatory functioning, to understand regulatory physiology in children, and to understand parenting. The key dimension we bring to this understanding of parenting concerns the meta-emotion structure of the family. When we examine how parents interact with very young children, their responsiveness, warmth, acceptance, and scaffolding/praising parenting contrasts hugely with an emotion-dismissing, critical, and mocking parenting style.

We discovered that these styles are merely extensions of the couple system, not strange add-ons. It is all one fabric, one tapestry that a couple weaves either intentionally or unintentionally that extends the temporal forms they have created with one another to the children. These interactive patterns, as they extend to the children, create what attachment theorists have called attachment security, or they create insecurity. However, our findings go far beyond the usual recommendations of attachment theorists. Our findings suggest that it is not enough for parents to be warm and responsive. Parents need to be good emotion coaches. As Haim Ginott wrote, they need to communicate that all feelings and wishes are acceptable, but not all behavior is acceptable. Parents need to scaffold their child's development by sensitively supporting the child's growth and learning, and they also need to set limits on the child's behavior as they communicate the morals and values of their family. They also need to help the child develop the tone of the vagus nerve, and help develop the child's emotion regulation abilities and social communicative skills.

It all starts in the family, and it's all about being responsive to a child's emotions.

CHALLENGES FOR THE FUTURE: CUMULATIVE RISKS, RESILIENCE, AND CHILD OUTCOMES

So far we have been talking as if the only influences on the developing child are the couple and their parenting. We have been ignoring the broader environment and culture into which the couple and child are embedded. Yet, again during the past 50 years, we have learned an astonishing fact. This fact is so powerful that every family therapist needs to become aware of it and its consequences. It's a finding all about cumulative risks and their effect on our children.

Here is the finding:

The more cumulative risks a child experiences in daily living, the greater are the adverse effects on the child's development.

That is so simple, and it is so crucial, such an amazingly powerful conclusion! These life stressors include factors in six ecological subsystems: family process variables (such as support for autonomy, parental involvement in the child's life), parent characteristics (such as parents' mental health, parents' education), family structure (such as parents' marital status), family management of the community (such as informal friendship and kinship networks, adjustments to economic pressure), peers (such as antisocial versus prosocial peers for children), and community (such as average income and educational level of the neighborhood).

Arnold Sameroff produced a classic developmental work (Sameroff, Seifer, Zax, & Barocas, 1987). He discussed this work in a series of books that described his *transactional model of development* (Sameroff, 2009; Olson & Sameroff, 2009; Sameroff et al., 2005; Sameroff & Emde, 1989). In one of his most basic findings, he plotted on an x-axis the number of severe cumulative stresses a child might have experienced, and along the y-axis *any important positive child outcome measure*, such as school achievement, IQ, good behavior, child health, you name it. After three major life stresses there was always a precipitous drop in all positive child outcomes. Charlotte Patterson's now-classic article (Patterson, Vaden, & Kupersmidt, 1991) also documented the amazing accuracy these cumulative stresses on families can have in predicting a child's rejection by peers and general preparation for failure at school when the range of families in a sample was large enough to represent the whole population.

Evans, Dongping, and Wipple (2013) reviewed the research on the effects of cumulative stresses in a child's life and child outcomes of all sorts, work pioneered by Arnold Sameroff. Figure 15.3 demonstrates the adverse effects on child IQ of multiple risks. To repeat, what is startling is that the same results obtain for almost any positive outcome variable plotted on the y-axis. These child outcomes include psychological adjustment, self-competence, freedom from problem behavior, involvement in activities, and academic performance.

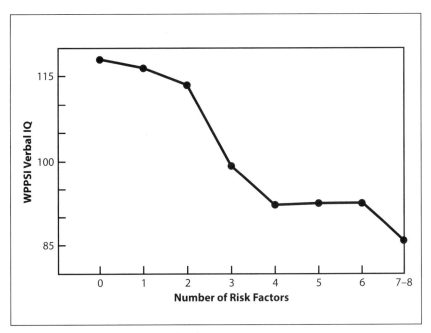

Figure 15.3. Cumulative Effects of Risk

What can we do to buffer children from these adverse effects? The answer is all about the development of the parents' and later the child's regulatory physiology. Emotion coaching is a powerful 4SD intervention.

BUT, THERE IS HOPE!
AND THE HOPE LIES IN EMOTION COACHING

MEANINGFUL DIFFERENCES IN YOUNG CHILDREN'S LIVES

We want to tell you about an important study that was published in two books, one titled *Meaningful Differences in the Everyday Experience of Young American Children* (Hart & Risley, 1994), and the other titled *The Social World of Children Learning to Talk* (Hart & Risley, 1999). The study was done by Betty Hart and Todd Risley. Todd Risley invented the whole idea of TIME OUT for kids when he was a grad student at the University of Washington. We bet you didn't know that anyone had to actually INVENT time out. But Todd Risley is the person who invented it. Pretty smart guy.

In their study, there were three groups of parents: (1) professional parents, who were highly educated; (2) lower-class blue-collar parents (called working class); and (3) welfare parents. In their study they started with babies 10 months old and charted (every month) the development of the babies' vocabulary. This is very hard to do, very labor intensive, because every baby develops his or her vocabulary in a very different way. Charting the development of the babies' vocabularies, they found that by age 3 years the babies of the professional parents had a greater spoken vocabulary than the PARENTS of the welfare kids. In Figure 15.4 you can see how dramatic these graphs are. You can see that the babies are on divergent accelerating trajectories—the differences between babies get bigger and bigger over time. These children are on DIVERGENT ACCELERATING TRAJECTORIES in their very young lives. As you can see, we parents can make an enormous difference.

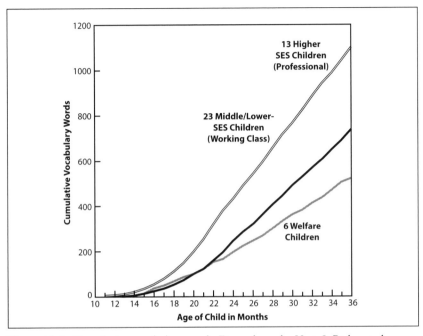

Figure 15.4. Cumulative vocabulary graph. Figure from the Hart & Risley study showing the three groups of children on divergent trajectories

Here's the reason Hart and Risley did this study. In the 1960s many investigators of kids' development went into research with the antipoverty program. They were trying to boost the cognitive development of disadvantaged preschool kids. John in grad school was the director of one such program with migrant worker high school dropouts at the University of Wisconsin. These dedicated and imaginative investigators found that they could indeed boost the cognitive development of these preschool children. In fact, they got large effect sizes. However, a few years later, by second grade, the differences between the kids in the control group and the experimental group had vanished. Apparently intervening with preschoolers was just too late. And their study shows why. By the time the kids are 4 years old, their cognitive and language development is already seriously compromised. Isn't that a depressing result?

Fortunately, Hart and Risley also carefully studied how the parents interacted with their children. That's the part we want to tell you about in our systems view of families. Most people who summarize the Hart and Risley study describe the differences between families by saying that the interactions of the professional and working-class parents were linguistically richer than the interactions of welfare parents. That is certainly true. However, it is not the major difference, in our view. The major difference in the three groups of parents was that the working-class and professional parents (to very different degrees) were emotion coaches for their babies. Here are just a few of these differences.

Reasons for Saying "No." All the parents said, "stop!" "No" and "Don't" equally often to their children. But the professional parents gave a reason for saying "No," "Stop," or "Don't." The welfare parents just said, "No," but the professional parents said, "No, no milk now because we're going to Grandma's and we are eating there."

Giving Babies and Kids Choices. The more educated parents not only gave more explanations for saying "No," they also gave their kids more choices. "Put on your coat now!" in the mouth of a professional came out as, "Do you want to put on your coat now or in 5 minutes?" Even very young babies, who were not producing many words, could understand their parents' words, and they could easily make these small choices. Kids can understand language pretty well by 10 months.

Talking to Babies and Kids About Their Feelings. The more educated parents talked more to their kids about their feelings. They described their kids' feelings: "Oh, you look so sad." They validated these feelings more and even helped the babies understand with words why they might be feeling a certain way: "Oh, that's so frustrating when you drop the Cheerios. No wonder you're angry" instead of, "No more Cheerios for you, for four months."

Fantasy Play Talk With Babies. The more educated parents engaged in fantasy play with their children. "Oh, okay, we're on a rocket ship. We're going so fast. How did you learn to drive this rocket? Are you the captain? Here we go!" "Oh, is your little baby doll sleepy? Is it time for her to go to bed?" The more educated parents also problem solved with their kids and elicited solutions from them. They were not impatient with their kids as they problem solved.

**Our conclusion: Emotion coaching starts VERY early
and it has huge potential consequences for reversing
the major harmful effects of social disadvantages.**

AFTERWORD

We see that nature is a vast, interconnected fabric. We have only to peer closely at a small part of nature, as we have done here, to understand her intricate order, whose depth inspires awe at the majesty of her beauty. We have presented a general systems theory and therapy for families, one that has the potential to create much larger effect sizes. The theory leads to a greater understanding of the system in couples, and how the system extends to families. We are at the threshold of a new couples and family theory and therapy, one that is solidly based on science. It is a work in progress, and we are anxious to continue this work. We strongly believe that healing love relationships and healing families is one important way to heal the world.

CHAPTER 16

Summary of Our Family Systems Therapy

Let's briefly summarize what we have learned so far.

1. What is regulated in couples?
   a. The balance of positive and negative affect *observed* during conflict and nonconflict interaction (5-to-1) is regulated.
   b. The balance of positive and negative affect *experienced* during conflict and nonconflict interaction (video recall rating dial) is regulated.
   c. The negative absorbing Markov state, which is the failure of repair, characterizes unhappy couples. We need to build repair processes in systems therapy.
   d. Autonomic physiology is regulated and remains calm in stable, happy couples. We apply Porges's polyvagal theory. The "smart" vagus nerve makes it possible both to stay calm and also to engage prosocially when the vagal brake on the heart is released. Couples need self-soothing skill, high vagal tone, and ability to take effective breaks. Use pulse oximeters, Heart Math's emwave device to build vagal tone in therapy.
   e. For many couples we see the pervasive spillover of negative affect, so therefore, the friendship/intimacy system also needs changing to get lasting change.

2. What causes the negative absorbing Markov state?
   a. Lack of trust, defined with game theory. The trust metric means

both partners are maximizing the sum of payoffs of both. Lack of trust is absence of a safe haven.

b. Lack of trust is caused by the absence of everyday emotional attunement in nonconflict, that is, negative emotion dismissing. Because they are disconnected emotionally, negative affect escalates during conflict. The therapist must teach couples the four skills of attunement during nonconflict interactions, like dates.

c. Lack of commitment, defined with game theory, indicated by a high betrayal metric, power struggles, win-lose interactions. Lack of commitment is caused by negative comparisons instead of cherishing. Rusbult showed that this results in investing less in the relationship, looking elsewhere to get needs met, real betrayal.

d. The carrying capacity for negative affect in the system changes in unhappily married couples so there is less tolerance for a partner's negative affect. Men have lower carrying capacity than women.

e. Regrettable incidents are inevitable. We need effective repair. Use the Aftermath of a Fight or Regrettable Incident intervention.

3. What needs to be changed in a couple to get lasting effects?

   a. A couple in phase space needs a strong positive attractor rather than a negative attractor. Can change the vector force field by changing parameters such as start-ups, accepting influence (low emotional inertia), lower threshold for repair.

   b. Interrupting relationship conflict with brief proximal changes such as taking a break, increasing fondness and admiration.

   c. Dismantling studies show that friendship/intimacy also needs changing, not just conflict.

4. What explains the demand-withdraw pattern, which characterizes unhappy relationships?

   a. Need to get partners to turn toward bids

   b. They have to turn toward in all seven Panksepp emotional command systems. Example given of couple's sex life: Everywhere on the planet people with a great sex life do the same baker's dozen things of turning toward.

c. Meta-emotion mismatches explain the demand-withdraw pattern. They need to be resolved by developing a common emotion culture in relationship: Understanding must precede action. This turns out to be not very hard to change in therapy.

d. The Art and Science of Love workshop works to build the trust metric.

e. We can treat difficult comorbidities such as some domestic violence (situational) with couples therapy where individual therapy fails. Currently doing research on couples treatment of PTSD, addiction recovery, affairs.

5. Can we extend to a family systems theory? Yes, we can.

a. Systems theory is extended to the family through coregulation of infant's affect through regulated parenting.

b. Porges's polyvagal theory is link between parenting and positive child outcomes, including extension to the child peer system. Actually teaches child emotional intelligence.

c. Unhappy couple relationships strongly affect the developing baby (and fetus).

d. When a baby arrives, it is a crisis for 67% of couples. Parent-infant interaction is affected with disastrous consequences for the child.

e. We can change all that in two days for 77% of couples! And Baby Makes Three workshop and support groups helps more couples than that.

f. The baby is the third axis in family phase space. Lausanne Triadic Play shows exactly how it is a family system. The family is the same fabric as the couple.

g. Family therapy is extended through emotion coaching in parenting, which includes nonderogatory interactions with scaffolding. Avoids coercive cycle. Tested in randomized clinical trials, works in UK, Australia, and South Korea.

h. The Sound Relationship House Theory. Interventions include:

    i. Gottman-Rapoport Conflict Blueprint

    ii. The Dan Wile Intervention

    iii. Aftermath of a Fight or Regrettable Incident for healing past emotional wounds

    iv. The Dreams Within Conflict Intervention for Gridlocked Conflict on Perpetual Issues

    v. Building friendship and intimacy with love maps, open-ended questions, expressing needs, and GottSex Kit

    vi. Building the shared meaning system through rituals of connection, shared goals, supporting roles

vii. Emotion coaching workshop for kids

6. WE ARE ON THE WAY TO A 4SD COUPLES AND FAMILY THERAPY!

ARE WE THERE YET? YES, WE ARE.

a. Some of our effect sizes are already 4SD.

b. But there is still a great deal of research to do.

c. We must merge research with clinical practice, so the samples in research are representative of what we see clinically every day.

d. We must do effective gold-standard unbiased measurement.

e. There must be a respectful collaboration between therapists and researchers, because both have important things to learn from one another.

f. We have to deal with the major comorbidities we encounter every day: Depression, addiction, trauma, other psychopathologies (manic-depressive disorder, borderline personality disorder), domestic violence, and extramarital affairs.

How Children Become Friends

We have had to abbreviate our writing about the world of children's friendships. In this appendix, we wanted to give you some idea of how ordered a world this is by summarizing some of the research that John did with his former student Jennifer Parkhurst. It's hard to believe, but back in the 1970s psychologists had no idea how children became friends with some kids, but not with other kids. Because of this lack of knowledge, we had no idea how to help kids who were socially isolated or rejected in school. Yet we did know that socially isolated kids, or kids with no friends, did suffer greatly in life.

To learn how children become friends, John and Jennifer conducted two studies. The two studies pinpointed a set of social processes that could totally explain unacquainted children's progress toward friendship, or their failure to hit it off. John discovered that kids who could do these things together had terrific fun with one another, while other kids' play would dissolve into conflict and tears.

In the first study there were 26 dyads aged 3 to 6 years playing in their homes either with a best friend or with a stranger for one session. The second study involved 18 dyads aged 3 to 9 years playing in their homes for three sessions. John created a behavioral criterion variable that indexed how well the unacquainted children hit it off. That criterion was generated and tested by requiring it to: (a) discriminate friends from strangers in the first study, and (2) correlate with a mothers' questionnaire assessing children's progress toward friendship in the second study.

John used an observational coding system with high reliability, and they used sequential analyses that measured:

- communication clarity and connectedness;
- information exchange;
- the exploration of themselves, their similarities and differences;
- the resolution of conflict;
- amity, consisting of great fun, excitement, joy, laughter, tenderness, and emotional support; and
- self-disclosure and empathy.

These process variables were able to account for over 80% of the variance in the criterion, and this result was robust. That means that these relationships were unusually strong. Furthermore, these findings were not strongly related to the ages and sex of the children. The importance of some social processes changed over the sessions. For example, self-disclosure in response to direct questions about feelings became important only in later sessions. Both studies produced 80 tapes that took 800 hours to transcribe and 4,200 hours for observers to code. Reliability was very high.

The following social processes were studied:

1. The children were very concerned about *connectedness* and *communication clarity*. A request for clarification was usually followed by a clarification, or—when the kids didn't hit it off—by its failure. For example, here's a clarification failure: "I need your dumb straw." "What's a dumb straw?" "I want the dumb straw!"

2. The children *exchanged information*. An attention-getting statement was usually followed by appropriate attention and then information. For example, "Hey, you know what?" "No, what?" "You can come to my house sometime."

3. The children *established common ground*. They found something to do together. One child might suggest something they

could do together, which was followed by agreement when the kids progressed to friendship.

4. The children experienced some *conflict*, and then they would try to *resolve the conflict* and repair the play. Effective ways of dealing with conflict were: (a) giving a reason for disagreeing, (b) complying with weak demands, and (c) avoiding a long disagreement chain. Example: "This is stretchy." "No, it's not." "Uh huh." "Yes." "Uh huh." "It's dirty too." "Uh huh." "Uh huh." "Uh huh." "It's not dirty." (d) There was also a nonverbal squabbling code.

5. The children engaged in *positive reciprocity*. They did this by engaging in (a) long chains of fantasy or (b) long chains of joking and laughter or (c) long chains of gossip in which they tried to understand other people together.

6. *Amity*: The children expressed great pleasure together, affection or sympathy for one another.

7. The children also did self-disclosure, and some even knew how to respond to it. They would have chains of asking about feelings and then expressing a feeling.

Overall, John and Jennifer discovered that the tasks of a first meeting are to interact with one another in a low-conflict and connected fashion, to exchange information, and to establish a common-ground activity. Over the three sessions, communication clarity became more important, as did information exchange and the establishment of common-ground activity. The children explored BOTH similarities and differences between them and found these comparisons fascinating. The resolution of conflict and self-disclosure, and positive reciprocity, especially of fantasy, were all very important in the children progressing toward friendship.

John and Jennifer discovered a hierarchy of play in friendship formation by examining sequences. They discovered that many play sessions among strangers began with less demanding interactions, and escalated as the children were successful. Here is the hierarchy:

1. The children often started with *parallel play* and used collective monologue. These were unconnected codes, where children were just narrating their own play, but taking turns. (A: "I'm making mine green." B: "This dolly is getting really sleepy.") Then they would move on to:

2. *Connected parallel play*, in which there were more connected dialogue chains. (A: "I'm making mine green." "How about if I draw also?")

3. *Narration* of other child's play. (A: "My skeleton is strong. Lots of other kids don't like him, but he's not mean." B: "I'm saying he is a friendly skeleton.")

4. *Asymmetrical exchanges*, in which at least one child has affected the other child's activity, with demands, compliance, and some noncompliance. (A: "Here, let's drive really fast 'cause we're race car drivers, right?" B: "Right. I want to drive this time." A: "Okay, you take the wheel." B: "Rummmbbbrrr.")

5. *Symmetrical exchanges* in which both children affect one another. (A: "Do you know how many things can kill you?" B: "How many?" A: "About a million. But the worst is the shark." B: "He won't get me. I will run to my room and slam the door." A: "No, no, no. He can bite the door down." B: "I'll use a METAL DOOR." A: "He can bite through metal." B: "What then?" A: "We have to hunt him down and kill him first.")

6. *Joint activity* (A: "Let's put these sharks in under water now." B: "They could bite you." A: "Yeah, especially your big gray shark.") (Or a failure: the initiation is ignored, and the activity does not develop for even a two-turn unit.)

7. An *escalation* occurs, in which an attempt is made to escalate the responsiveness demand of the common-ground activity. (A: "Okay, you hold the shark down while I kill him." B: "He's escaping. Quick." A: "Oh no, he can fly too!" B: "I better turn into Superman." A: "Yes, you'd better." B: "I caught him." A: "Bring him down here." B: "Gahhhh. He's drowning.")

8. *De-escalation.* Reducing the responsiveness demand.

9. *Conflict.* As evidenced by nonverbal squabble codes or disagreement chains.

10. *Conflict resolution.* (A: "Is it okay if I unbutton her?" B: "Why?" A: "Because she's just a baby and it's past her bedtime." B: "Sure then, go ahead.") Or a message clarification success. (A: "Which one?" B: "The blue one.")

11. *Gossip success.* (A: "Why does he come here all the time?" B: "Because he does, because my mommy asks him.")

12. *Similarity.* (A: "Mine is almost finished." B: "Mine too.")

13. *Contrast.* Kids note they are not the same. (A: "I'm gonna be five in my birthday." B: "Well, I'm five now.")

14. *Self-disclosure.* (A: "She didn't say anything about the dress. She said leave me alone." B: "Why did she say that?" A: "She doesn't love me.")

15. *Amity.* Validation or approval of the other person. Affirmation of the relationship, sympathy, offers, affection, wit, hilarity, shared deviance. (A kisses B. B: "Oh gosh." A: "What?" B: "You just kissed me on the cheek. Thank you." A: "I'll kiss you on the forehead now." B: "I'll kiss you too.")

Here are some excerpts from the play of two girls, which illustrate how orderly and connected this process is of becoming friends.

They engaged in parallel play, but commented on one another's play.

> **J:** I got a fruit cutter plate.
> **D:** Mine's white.
> **J:** You got white Play-Doh and this color and that color.
> **D:** Every color. That's the colors we got.

They escalated the responsiveness demanded.

> **D:** I'm putting pink in the blue.

J: Mix pink.
D: Pass the blue.
J: I think I'll pass the blue.

They moved toward a common-ground activity.

D: And you make those for when we get it together, Okay?
J: 'Kay.
D: Have to make these.
J: Pretend like those little roll cookies, too, Okay?
D: And make, um, make a, um, pancake too.
J: Oh rats. This is a little pancake.
D: Okay. Make, make me, um, make two flat cookies. 'Cause I'm, I'm cutting any, I'm cutting this. My snake.

The next escalation included offers.

J: You want my blue?
D: Yes. To make cookies. Just to make cookies, but we can't mess the cookies up.
J: Nope.

THEN A JOINT ACTIVITY USING "WE."

D: Put this the right way. Okay? **We're** making supper, huh?
J: We're making supper. Maybe we could use, if you get white, we could use that too, maybe.
D: I don't have any white. Yes, we, yes I do.
J: If you got some white, we could have some, y'know.

They tried to escalate to fantasy, but failed.

D: I'm the mommy.

> J: Who am I?
> D: Um, the baby.
> J: Daddy.
> D: Sister.
> J: I wanna be the daddy.
> D: You're the sister.
> J: Daddy.
> D: You're the BIG sister.
> J: Don't play house. I don't want to play house.

She then de-escalates.

> J: Just play eat-eat. We can play eat-eat. We have to play that way.

But the de-escalation is unsuccessful.

> J: Look hungry!
> **D. Huh?**
> J: I said look hungry!
> D: Look hungry? This is dumb.
> J: Look hungry!
> D: No!

The children then moved to the previous play and had many amity codes at that level of demand.

For these two girls, examples included strong validation and approval ("How do you like this?" "That's pretty."), the expression of sympathy ("Don't worry about that, it'll come off. It was on before and it came off before. Just don't worry about it, 'cause I'm not worried."), support (we-against-others, as in, "We're not mad at each other like she is, right?" "Right."), affection, wit ("How do you do this stupid thing?" "You do it in a stupid way."), and hilarity and glee, in which both children are convulsed by their own wit, or silliness.

Some children engaged in self-disclosure, which did not just come from older children. These are two girls, A (5 years-0 months) and K (4 years-3 months).

SELF-DISCLOSURE IN WHICH A CHILD TRIES TO UNDER-STAND THAT MOMMY HAS A NEW BOYFRIEND.

> **A:** Like if Jimmy, he's a little boy and playing with us, he would take that brown if he needs it, right?
> **K:** Huh?
> **A:** He would take that brown, wouldn't he?
> **K:** Jimmy who?
> **A:** That big man downstairs.
> **K:** Your brother?
> **A:** He's not my brother. He's a friend of ours.
> **K:** Why does he come over all the time?
> **A:** Because he does. Because my mommy asks him.
> **K:** All the time?
> **A:** She even goes out, he even goes places without *me*.
> **K:** Where do you stay?
> **A:** Home.
> **K:** Why? You're afraid?
> **A:** No. Why?
> **K:** I'm afraid, 'less I stayed with you.
> **A:** Are you afraid to stay with me?
> **K:** Uh uh. I said I was afraid of my mommy, if she leaves me.

This leads to more self-disclosure.

> **A:** This one is too. . . . This one, I don't know what she says. I don't know what she says. I don't know what she says. She doesn't say. I guess I'll put it on.
> **Did she not say? Did she not say? Did she not say?**
> **A:** She didn't say anything about the dress. She said, "Leave me and Jimmy alone."

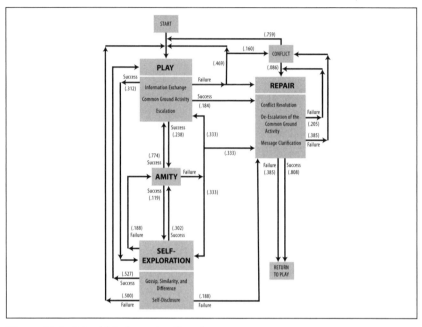

Figure A1.1. Friendship formation flow chart

> **K:** Why'd she say that?
> **A:** She doesn't love me.
> **K:** Why?
> **A:** 'Cause I get near you . . . my mom and Jimmy. Look how long these things are.
> **K:** Oh gosh.

Later they try to understand why A's mother and Jimmy are always taking naps.

> **A:** She said, "Never come in here with me and Jimmy."
> **K:** That's what she said?
> **A:** Her and Jimmy are sleeping.
> **K:** Huh?
> **A:** Her and Jimmy are sleeping.
> **K:** You aren't, are you?

A: We're not asleep.

K: But he is.

A: My mom is not asleep.

They are convinced of their superiority in requiring less sleep than this adult who always visits A's mother.

In John's monograph (Gottman, 1983) based on this research, he presented a flowchart that showed how complex and ordered he found children's play when it progressed toward friendship or failed to do so (Figure A1.1).

The diagram is a lot like the Markov diagram we saw earlier for the negative absorbing state of unhappy couples. The boxes represent states of child activity, and the numbers represent the probabilities that kids would move from one kind of activity to another. Play consisted of exchanging information while doing something together, and trying to escalate the amount of cooperation in a common-ground adventure, usually involving fantasy or pretend. Each escalation required something new of the other child, and it required managing their separate desires. If the escalation failed, they moved on to conflict and potentially toward repair of the play. To repair they might give reasons for what they wanted or didn't want, or they tried to persuade or accommodate their separate desires. They gave in and compromised, or they failed at it. If the escalated play was too demanding, they would de-escalate and try playing at a lower level of demand. They would explore themselves, by examining their similarities and differences, by gossiping about other people, and by self-disclosing. Sometimes that self-disclosure took place within a fantasy, where their play characters could safely express their feelings, worries, and doubts. Sometimes that self-disclosure was met with understanding and support, at times within the fantasy.

They soared like eagles; they became Mommy and Daddy and baby; they became mighty hunters and superheroes. They became powerful, or vulnerable. They became silly; they became "convulsed by their own wit"; they laughed with abandon. They expressed joy and delight, and great heights of connection, often not matched in intensity by the adults they lived with. Or, sadly, they failed to connect.

EXPERIMENTAL TESTS OF FRIENDSHIP SKILLS

To test these correlational results, John and his student Jeff Parker created an experimental setting in which an adult female experimenter narrated the play of an extraterrestrial doll. Her voice was projected wirelessly as she narrated the play of the extraterrestrial, who was introduced to a 4-year-old child as Panduit, the green visitor from outer space. For now Panduit was living at the university, and he got lonely, so he wanted to play. This experiment actually preceded Spielberg's movie *E.T.* John found Panduit in a toy shop in San Francisco.

As the children played with Panduit, the adult who was Panduit's voice demonstrated either competence or incompetence at the basic skills of play that were reported in the monograph *How Children Become Friends* (Gottman, 1983). She followed a flexible but scripted manual randomly demonstrating competence with some kids or incompetence with others. What John and Jeff were interested in measuring was the resulting play and the child's desire to return (as measured by a questionnaire the child's mom filled out). The results of these experiments were reported in the edited book *Conversations of Friends* (Gottman & Parker, 1986).

Parker and Gottman found experimental evidence that children wanted to visit Panduit more when he was better at making friends following the flowchart above. This was therefore an experimental test of the observational results. They had successfully identified the skills for friendship formation for young children. With Jennifer Parkhurst and Dorothy Ginsberg they studied the conversations of friends from age 3 through the college years. With Martha Putallaz, John studied what happens in school when a child is told by a teacher to join in the play of another group of children, what the child can do that determines whether he or she is accepted or rejected by the group. Martha's dissertation discovered how important parents were in building these essential social skills in a child.

Six Math Sidebars

MATH SIDEBAR 1: THE ACTUAL
INITIAL MATH MODEL

The model is presented in Gottman et al. (2002).

1. Had a START-UP term (reflects past history and/or personality variables),
2. Had a SELF-INFLUENCE term, how the past has influence, or inertia,
3. And a PARTNER INFLUENCE FUNCTION term.

The present = [start-up] + [self-influence of the past] + [partner influence].

$$W_{t+1} = a + r_1 W_t + I_{HW} (H_t)$$
$$H_{t+1} = b + r_2 H_t + I_{WH} (W_t)$$

The letter t = time.

How do we fit this INFLUENCE FUNCTION (our theory) TO THE DATA?

$$W_{t+1} = a + r_1 W_t + I_{HW} (H_t)$$

Simple. We algebraically solve for the influence function, as follows:

$$I_{HW}(H_t) = a + r_1 W_t - W_{t+1}$$

All we need to do now is just estimate a and r_1. Then we have the influence function's **data points.** Let's assume for now that we know how to do that. We said it was simple, but it actually took us two years to think of it. James Murray's brilliant student, Julian Cook, was the one who first suggested this method. He suggested using neutral affect points to estimate a and r_1. Ellen Hamaker later showed us that this wasn't necessary. But we used Cook's method effectively for years. We used the bilinear influence function, with repair and damping added to it.

MATH SIDEBAR 2: NULL CLINES

How we find the system's attractors. The idea is that the fixed points or attractors are where nothing is changing, nothing's moving, so both wife and husband are steady over time.

$$Set\ W_t = Constant = W^*$$
$$W_{t+1} = a + r_1 W_t + I_{HW}(H_t)$$

Now becomes

$$W^* = a + r_1 W^* + I_{HW}(H_t)$$

Solve for W^*:

$$W^* = [a + I_{HW}(H_t)]/(1 - r_1)$$

This is the wife's null cline, where she is not changing. CONCLUSION: The null clines have the same shape as the influence functions, except for a translation and a stretching. NOW WE DO THE SAME FOR THE HUSBAND.

$$Set\ H_t = Constant = H*$$
$$H_{t+1} = b + r_2\ H_t + I_{WH}\ (W_t)$$

Now becomes

$$H* = b + r_2\ H* + I_{WH}\ (W_t)$$

Solve for $H*$:

$$H* = [b + I_{WH}\ (W_t)]/(1 - r_2\ )$$

This is the husband's null cline. We didn't make up that weird name—it comes from the math. His null cline therefore has the same shape as the influence function, except that it is moved by the factor b and then stretched by the factor $1/(1 - r_2)$. It's easy to draw this on a computer.

Why is this so very cool? Well, where the two null clines (his and hers) intersect are the system's steady states, steady states that can be either STABLE or UNSTABLE. We look for the couple's attractors (and repellers). The attractors are the system's stable steady states. On a graph, this is the homeostasis set point where the null clines intersect.

Note that more than one homeostatic set point (attractor) can exist for a couple! That eliminates Wile's concern that homeostasis implies an adversarial relationship between family and therapist. Both the family and therapist now would seek to strengthen the positive homeostatic set point(s) and weaken the negative homeostatic set point(s). No worries.

MATH SIDEBAR 3: THE DIFFERENTIAL EQUATION FORM OF THE MODEL

In his book *Topics in Mathematical Modeling*, K. K. Tung (2007) extended our math model to differential equation form, which makes it far more tractable.

In differential equation form, the model is:

$$dx/dt = r_1(x - x_0) + I_1(y)$$
$$dy/dt = r_2(y - y_0) + I_2(x),$$

where x is the husband, y is the wife, t is time (as usual), and I is the influence functions. The rs are still the emotional inertia parameters, and x_0 and y_0 are start-ups at time zero.

MATH SIDEBAR 4: THE RICHARDSON ARMS RACE

The Richardson linear differential equations model for escalating military expenditures of the two nations that lead to war was:

$$dx/dt = k_1 y - ax + g_1$$
$$dy/dt = k_2 x - by + g_2$$

The parameters k_1 and k_2 represent the amount of menace each nation perceives the other nation represents, the parameters a and b represent the fixed current cost of arming, and the parameters g_1 and g_2 represent grievances that each nation has. Under most conditions, the arms race is unstable. This will be the case even if both nations have no grievances or even negative grievances. It is very difficult—hence unlikely—that the two nations can create a stable balance point in this model. So it is a runaway model, mostly leading to war.

MATH SIDEBAR 5

The two axes and Figure A2.1 itself come from an equation called the "characteristic equation," which we derive directly from the math model and its EIGENVALUES. The matrix A is the standard Jacobian matrix of partial derivatives, and we then solve for the determinant $(A - \lambda I) = 0$. The λs are the eigenvalues at each steady state. Abbreviations in the axes of Figure A2.1 are det = determinant and tr = trace of A). Don't worry about how to compute these; the computer program does these calculations for every steady state the couple has.

MATH SIDEBAR 6: THE COUPLE'S EIGENVALUES

What the heck are eigenvalues? The EIGENVALUES tell us what kind of steady state we have. Is it unstable, a repeller? Then a small perturbation away from the steady state will make the system drift away from

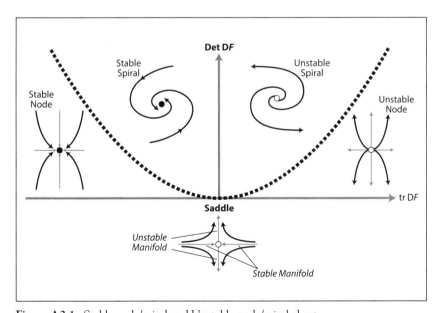

Figure A2.1. Stable node/spiral and Unstable node/spiral chart

the steady state. Or is it stable? Then a small perturbation away from the steady state will make the system be pulled back toward the steady state. Is it a strong attractor, kind of like the planet Jupiter? Or is it a weak attractor, more like the planet Mercury? The eigenvalues tell us all these things, and more. They define the nature of the steady state.

The History of the Eigenvalue Concept

Let's leave psychology for a moment and enter the world of physics. The beautiful familiar rainbow we often see in the sky is actually a spectrum of visible light. The spectrum consists of white light decomposed into its constituent parts; that is, we see its spectral signature. In the same way, every element in the universe has a characteristic spectral signature in the way in interacts with light. Astronomers use this signature to examine light from any star to tell them what elements compose the star. We think it's amazing that by just examining the star's light astronomers can tell what it's made of. Well, that spectral signature is all about the energies, related to the EIGENVALUES that the spectral signature of a star has.

In atomic physics, the very familiar planetary-style Bohr model of the atom, introduced by Niels Bohr and his mentor, Ernest Rutherford, in 1913, depicts the atom as a small, positively charged nucleus surrounded by electrons that travel in circular orbits around the nucleus—similar in structure to the solar system, but with attraction provided by electrostatic forces rather than gravity.

Bohr, for his doctoral thesis, succeeded in using his model to derive the spectral signature of the hydrogen atom (called the Rydberg formula). Later, the Bohr model was derived from the quantum mechanical energy wave equation of Erwin Schrödinger. John learned about the Bohr model as an undergraduate physics student in an introduction to quantum mechanics or energy-level eigenvalue diagrams. John thought it was extremely beautiful. Among other things, it provided an *explanation* for the Mendeleev periodic table of the elements. Isn't that totally cool?

Later, the genius Erwin Schrödinger developed one beautiful equation that elucidated the wave mechanics that explained these eigenvalues that the Bohr model of the atom described. Quantum mechanics was born with that magnificent Schrödinger wave equation that could derive Mendeleev's periodic table of all the elements.

All those magnificent accomplishments of physics are about energies, or eigenvalues. One of John's real dreams right now is to have therapists be able to talk comfortably about the eigenvalues of a couple's interactions. These values refer to the nature of the couple's attractors and to energies in their phase space force field portrait of their interaction.

How does this actually work with a couple? Well, in a couple's phase space diagram there are many different kinds of steady states. We can have cycles, or we can have spirals that spiral in or out of the steady state, or a variety of other shapes that the local force field produces.

The full picture gives us a deep understanding of the couple's state space. This diagram shows various types of stable steady states, also called attractors, and even the couple's potential repellers, which are the opposite of attractors.

- The stable node attractor is very simple. Everywhere the couple starts, they are drawn to this attractor.
- The stable spiral attractor means they are also drawn to it, but it takes time to get there.
- The unstable node attractor, a repeller, is also very simple. Everywhere the couple starts, they are drawn away from this attractor.
- The unstable spiral attractor (repeller) means they are drawn away from it, but it takes time to leave.

John's favorite shape is the saddle, for which the pattern is more complicated; some paths draw the couple toward, and some paths draw the couple away from the attractor. It's stable in one direction and unstable from another path. Figure A2.2 shows why it's called a saddle. Approach the middle of the saddle from one direction and it's a maximum of that

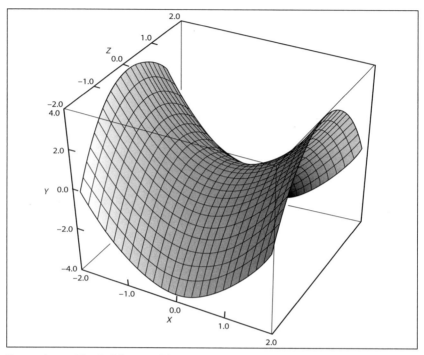

Figure A2.2. The Saddle Unstable Steady State

curve. Approach the middle of the saddle from another direction and it's a minimum of that curve. It's what we call a "minimax."

With these two parameters, the eigenvalues, we get two more process goals, 7 and 8. We didn't talk about this in the text because we thought that it might be too much to take in to hear about eigenvalues. Here's how we might use an understanding of eigenvalues in therapy.

Process Goal 7: Change the Eigenvalues of the Positive Attractor So It's Stronger

We want a strong positive attractor, not a weak one. This is about commitment (investment and cherishing), so you really believe that positive attractor is real—you can rely on it, lean back into it. The story of us is very positive, and we-ness is very high. Maybe put them through a challenge that they really succeed at. Something like the Ravich Train Game, or they use their combined EEGs to move a car around a track, or compete with other couples and win. Or play with a computer and think they win.

Process Goal 8: Change the Eigenvalues of the Negative Attractor So It's Weaker

This is about trust. You don't think that negative state will last very long. Your story of us is very clear that you can get through anything together. Put them through experiences where they have to trust one another and it's successful.

Simulation Sidebar

Here is an example of a simulation of a conflict-avoiding couple, but who have negative start-ups (Figure A3.1). You are quite likely to see a couple like this one in your clinical office. They are failed persuasion conflict avoiders. How did we know they were conflict avoiders? They have non-zero positive affect slope (husband 0.6, wife 0.35) and zero negative affect slope. That's a classic avoider pattern, and they're matched.

They have a stable steady state, an attractor, with eigenvalues that show stability. It's nice and dark BUT IT IS in the negative-negative quadrant. Their attractor is in the negative-negative quadrant. He's at −6.8 and she's at −5.2. That isn't very good as a stable steady state.

OUR QUANTITATIVE FANTASY

What if we simulate this couple, but this time have them start positively? Of course, we're just pretending we can accomplish that. This is just a simulation. Let's see what they might look like in phase space, assuming we can accomplish a miracle like that (Figure A3.2).

That's so much better! Now we have moved them so that they have a positive instead of a negative attractor. And hooray, the eigenvalues tell us *it is a stable attractor*. Of course, we have assumed that we *can* create such a massive change, moving the husband from a start-up x_0 of −6.8 to a start-up of 10.3, and that we can move the wife from a start-up y_0 of

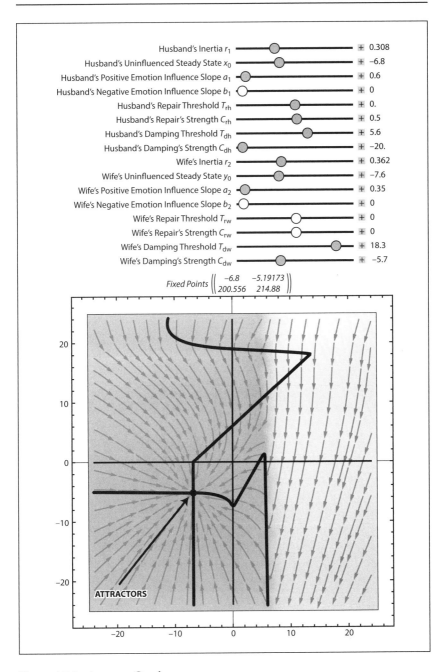

Figure A3.1. Attractor Graph

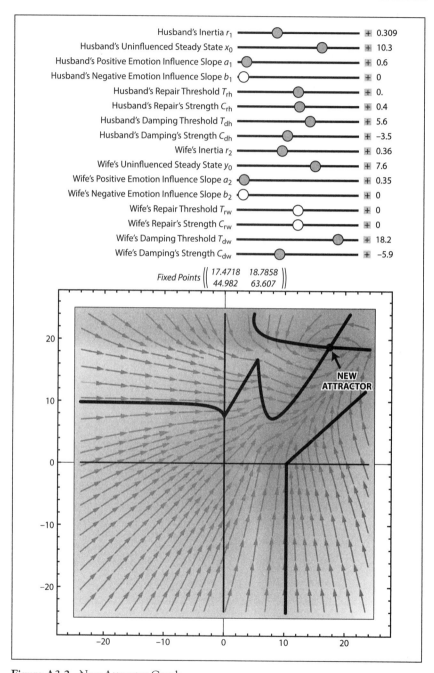

Figure A3.2. New Attractor Graph

−7.6 to a start-up of 7.6. That would be a very big change in start-up. The steady state for him is now at 17.5 and her steady state is at 18.8.

QUANTITATIVE FANTASY #2

So maybe we can try to be a bit more realistic and see what would happen to this couple if we just changed their start-up so it was a bit more positive, just close to neutral. Let's move the wife so she's *totally* neutral, instead of negative, and let's make the husband only slightly positive, at 0.4. That's more modest, and pretty easy to accomplish. We know from our proximal change experiments that we can get those kinds of effect sizes just by a physiologically soothing break.

Let's look at their new (imagined) phase space portrait (Figure A3.3). The result is still better. Their steady state is now at 5.6 and 4.6. Pretty good. Uh oh—let's look at the shading around this steady state, and we can see that this new steady state is a little lighter on the right side, so it's a stable state if you approach the steady state from the left, but unstable if you approach it from the right. That's a classic *saddle point* (John's favorite). So the situation is better, but not as good as we'd like. Still it's improved for sure, but we are hardly done. In this case the attractor is stable *only when it is approached from the left side*—that side is dark brown. It is a stable valley, but only partly. When the attractor is approached from the left, it is very light and the arrows draw the system away from stability. This is an unstable system, a saddle. This tells us that we need an intervention for this couple that is powerful as in Figure A3.2.

Can you see where we are going with using the math in this way? All these computations were made with just a few lines of code in the program Mathematica. Once one gets the hang of this kind of simulation, it's pretty easy to do. The diagrams inform the therapy! All we need to be able to do is understand the graphics. That is the beauty of Poincaré's nonlinear math.

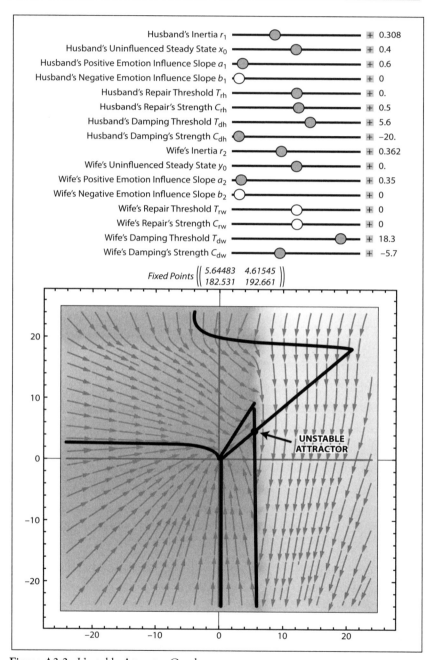

Figure A3.3. Unstable Attractor Graph

If the reader is interested in how the mathematics work for creating these lovely force field phase space diagrams, see Appendix 2.

Notice also that this simulation thinking means that we have a clear therapeutic goal in couples therapy:

GOAL: Every couple needs a stable positive attractor.

Note that we may not be able to help a couple move from having just a negative attractor to having a stable positive attractor by just changing the parameters of their phase space diagram. That means that we may not be able to help everyone.

References

Achenbach, T. M., & Edelbrock, C. (1983). *Manual for the child behavior checklist and revised child behavior profile.* Burlington: University of Vermont, Department of Psychiatry.

Achenbach, T. M., & Edelbrock, C. (1986). *Manual for the teacher's report form and teacher version of the child behavior profile.* Burlington: University of Vermont, Department of Psychiatry.

Ainsworth, M. D. S., Bell, S. M., & Stayton, D. J. (1971). Individual differences in the strange situation behavior of one-year-olds. In H. R. Schaffer (Ed.), *The origins of human social relations.* London: Academic Press.

Asher, S. R. (1983). Social competence and peer status: Recent advances and future directions. *Child Development, 54*(6), 1427–1434.

Asher, S. R., & Coie, J. D. (Eds.). (1990). *Peer rejection in childhood.* New York: Cambridge University Press.

Asher, S. R., & Gottman, J. M. (Eds.). (1981). *The development of children's friendships.* New York: Cambridge University Press.

Axelrod, J., & Reisine, T. D. (1984). Stress hormones: Their interaction and regulation. *Science, 224*(4648), 452–459.

Azrin, N. H., Naster, B. J., & Jones, R. (1973). Reciprocity counseling: A rapid learning-based procedure for marital counseling. *Behavior Research and Theory, 11*, 365–382.

Babcock, J. C., Gottman, J. M., Ryan, K. D., & Gottman, J. S. (2013). A component analysis of a brief psycho-educational couples workshop: One-year follow up results. *Journal of Family Therapy, 35*, 252–280.

Babcock, J. C., Waltz, J., Jacobson, N. S., & Gottman, J. M. (1993). Power and violence: The relation between communication patterns, power discrepancies, and domestic violence. *Journal of Consulting and Clinical Psychology, 61*, 40–50.

Bach, G. R., & Wyden, P. (1983). *The intimate enemy.* New York: Avon.

Bakeman, R., & Gottman, J. M. (1986). *Observing interaction: An introduction to sequential analysis.* New York: Cambridge University Press.

Bateson, G., Jackson, D. D., Haley, J., & Weakland, J. (1956). Toward a theory of schizophrenia. *Behavioral Science, 1*, 251–264.

Baucom, B. R., McFarland, P. T., & Christensen, A. (2010). Gender, topic, and time in observed demand-withdraw interaction in cross- and same-sex couples. *Journal of Family Psychology, 24*, 233–242.

Baucom, D. H., Epstein, N., Rankin, L. A., & Burnett, C. K. (1996). Assessing relationship standards: The inventory of specific relationship standards. *Journal of Family Psychology, 10*, 72–88.

Belsky, J., & Kelly, J. (1995). *The transition to parenthood.* New York: Dell.

Berkman, L. F., Kawachi, J. K., & Glymour, M. M. (2014). *Social epidemiology* (2nd ed.). New York: Oxford University Press.

Berkman, L. F., & Syme, S. L. (1979). Social networks, host resistance, and mortality: A nine-year follow-up of Alameda County residents. *American Journal of Epidemiology, 109*, 186–204.

Bernard, C. (1927). *An introduction to the study of experimental medicine.* New York: Macmillan.

Birnbaum, G. E., Reis, H. T., Mizrahi, M., Kanat-Maymon, Y., Sass, O., & Granovski-Milner, C. (2016). Intimately connected: The importance of partner responsiveness for experiencing desire. *Journal of Personality and Social Psychology, 111*, 530–546.

Blumstein, P., & Schwartz, P. (1983). *American couples: Money, work, sex.* N.Y.: William Morrow & Co.

Boccia, M., & Campos, J. J. (1989). Maternal emotional signals, social referencing, and infants' reactions to strangers. *New Directions in Child Development, 44*, 25–49.

Bradley, R. P. C., & Gottman, J. M. (2012). Reducing situational violence in low-income couples by fostering healthy relationships. *Journal of Marital and Family Therapy, 38*, 187–198.

Brazelton, T. B., Koslowski, T. B., & Main, M. (1974). The origins of reciprocity: The early mother-infant interaction. In M. Lewis & L. A. Rosenblum (Eds.), *The effect of the infant on its caregiver* (pp. 49–76). New York: Wiley.

Buehlman, K., Gottman, J. M., & Katz, L. (1992). How a couple views their past predicts their future: Predicting divorce from an oral history interview. *Journal of Family Psychology, 5*, 295–318.

Bullock, B. G. (2016). *Mindful relationships.* Edinburgh, Scotland: Handspring.

Burnay, C., & Cordovil, R. (2016). Crawling experience predicts avoidance of real cliffs and water cliffs. *Infancy, 21*, 677–684.

Campbell, D.T., & Fiske, D.W. (1959). Convergent and discriminant validation by the multitrait-multimethod matrix. *Psychological Bulletin, 56*, 81-105.

Cannon, W. B. (1932). *The wisdom of the body.* New York: Norton Library.

Cassidy, J., Ehrlich, K. B., & Sherman, L. J. (2014). Child-parent attachment and response to threat: A move from the level of representation. In M. Mikulincer & P. R. Shaver (Eds.), *Mechanisms of social connection: From brain to group* (pp. 125–143). Washington, DC: American Psychological Association Press.

Cervantes, M. de. (2005). *Don Quixote* (E. Grossman, Trans.). New York: Harper Perennial.

Chrisler, J. C., & McCreary, D. R. (2010). *Handbook of gender research in psychology* (Vol. 1). New York: Springer.

Christensen, A., Doss, B. D., & Jacobson, N. S. (2014). *Reconcilable differences* (2nd ed.). New York: Guilford.

Christensen, A., & Jacobson, N. S. (1988). *Acceptance and change in couple therapy*. New York: W.W. Norton.

Coan, J. A., Schaefer, H. S., & Davidson, R. J. (2006). Lending a hand: Social regulation of the neural response to threat. *Psychophysiology, 17*, 1032–1039.

Cohen, J. (1992). A power primer. *Psychological Bulletin, 112*, 155-159.

Cowan, C. P., & Cowan, P. A. (1999). *When partners become parents*. New York: Routledge.

Cummings, E. M. (1987). Coping with background anger in early childhood. *Child Development, 58*, 876–984.

Cummings, E. M., & Davies, P. (1994). *Children and marital conflict: The impact of family dispute resolution*. New York: Guilford.

Cummings, E. M., Goeke-Morey, M. C., & Papp, L. M. (2003). Children's responses to everyday marital conflict tactics in the home. *Child Development, 74*, 1918–1929.

Cummings, E. M., Goeke-Morey, M. C., & Papp, L. M. (2004). Everyday marital conflict and child aggression. *Journal of Abnormal Child Psychology, 32*, 191–202.

Cummings, E. M., Lannotti, R. J., & Zahn-Waxler, C. (1985). Influence of conflict between adults on the emotions and aggression of young children. *Developmental Psychology, 21*, 495–507.

Cummings, E. M., Papp, L. M., & Kouros, C. D. (2009). Regulatory processes in chldren's coping with exposure to marital conflict. In S. L. Olson & A. J. Sameroff (Eds.), *Biopsychosocial regulatory processes in the development of childhood behavioral problems* (pp. 238–257). New York: Cambridge University Press.

Cummings, E. M., Zahn-Waxler, C., & Radke-Yarrow, M. (1981). Young children's responses to expressions of anger and affection by others in the family. *Child Development, 52*, 1274–1282.

Damon, W. (2006). Socialization and individuation. In G. Handel (Ed.), *Childhood socialization, 2nd Ed,* (pp. 3-9). New Brunswick, NJ: Aldine Transactions.

Davidson, R.J., & Begley, S. (2012). *The emotional life of your brain*. N.Y.: Avery Reprints.

Dawson, G., Klinger, L. G., Panagiotides, H., Hill, D., & Spieker, S. (1992). Frontal lobe activity and affective behavior of infants of mothers with depressive symptoms. *Child Development, 63*, 725–737.

de Becker, G. (2010). *The gift of fear*. New York: DeBecker.

Ditzen, B., Schaer, M., Gabriel, B., Bidenmann, G., & Ehlert, U. M. (2009). Intranasal oxytocin increases positive communication and reduces cortisol levels during conflict. *Behavioral Psychiatry, 65*, 728–731.

Doherty, W. J. (1997). *The intentional family*. New York: Harper Collins.

Doherty, W.J., & Simmons, D.S. (1996). Clinical practice patterns of marriage and family therapists: A national survey of therapists and their clients. *Journal of Marital and Family Therapy, 22*, 9-25.

Drigotas, S. M., & Rusbult, C. E. (1992). Should I stay or should I go? A dependence model of breakups. *Journal of Personality and Social Psychology, 62*, 62–87.

Driver, J.L. and Gottman, J.M., (2004). Daily marital interactions and Positive Affect During Marital Conflict Among Newlywed Couples, *Family Process, 43(3)*, 301-314;

Duncombe, M. E., Havighurst, S. S., Kehoe, C. E., Holland, K. A., Frankling, E. J. (2016). Comparing an emotion- and a behavior-focused parenting program as part of a multisystemic intervention for child conduct problems. *Journal of Clinical Child and Adolescent Psychology, 45,* 320–333.

Dunn, J. (1977). *Distress and comfort.* Cambridge, MA: Harvard University Press.

Eichler, S., & Kartkin, E. S. (1994). The relationship between cardiovascular reactivity and heartbeat detection. *Psychophysiology, 31,* 229–234.

Ekman, P. (2013). *Emotions in the human face.* New York: Malor.

Epstein, E.E., & McCrady, B.S. (2009). *Overcoming alcohol abuse problems.* New York: Oxford University Press.

Evans, G. W., Dongping, L., & Whipple, S. S. (2013). Cumulative risk and child development. *Psychological Bulletin, 139,* 1342–1391.

Faber, A., & Mazlish, E. (1980). *How to talk so kids will listen and listen so kids will talk.* New York: Scribner.

Faber, A., & Mazlish, E. (2012). *Siblings without rivalry.* New York: W.W. Norton.

Fals-Stewart, W., O'Farrell, T., & Lam, W. (2009). Behavioral Couple Therapy for Gay and Lesbian Couples with Alcohol Use Disorders. *Journal of Substance Abuse Treatment. 37,* 379–387.

Field, T. (1995). Infants of depressed mothers (International Society for Infant Studies). *Infant Behavior and Development, 18,* 1–13.

Filmore, J. M.; Baretto, D., Ysasi, N. A. Counseling gay and lesbian couples. In Marini, I (Ed), Stebnicki, M. A. (Ed). (2016). *The professional counselor's desk reference, 2nd edition,* (pp. 403-408). New York, NY, US: Springer Publishing Co.

Fisher, H. (2016). *The anatomy of love.* New York: W.W. Norton.

Fivaz-Depeursinge, E., & Corboz-Warnery, A. (1999). *The primary triangle.* New York: Basic Books.

Fivaz-Depeursinge, E., Corboz-Warnery, A., & Keren, M. (2004). The primary triangle: Treating infants and their families. In S. L. Olson & A. J. Sameroff (Eds.), *Biopsychosocial regulatory processes in the development of childhood behavioral problems* (pp. 123–151). New York: Cambridge University Press.

Frankl, V. E. (2006). *Man's search for meaning.* Boston: Beacon.

Garber, J., & Dodge, K. A. (Eds.). (1991). *The development of emotion regulation and dysregulation.* New York: Cambridge University Press.

Gendlin, E. (2007). *Focusing.* New York: Bantam.

Gianino, A., & Tronick, E. Z. (1988). The mutual regulation model: The infant's self and interactive regulation and coping and defensive capacities. In T. M. Field, P. M. McCabe, & N. Schneiderman (Eds.), *Stress and coping across development* (pp. 47–70). Hillsdale, NJ: Erlbaum.

Gigy, L., & Kelly, J. B. (1992). Reasons for divorce: Perspectives of divorcing men and women. *Journal of Divorce and Remarriage, 18,* 169–187.

Ginott, H. G. (1971). *Between parent and teenager.* New York: Avon.

Ginott, H. G. (1975). *Teacher and child.* New York: Avon.

Ginott, H. G. (1994). *Between parent and child.* New York: Avon. (Original work published 1965)

Glass, S. P., & Staeheli, J. C. (2004). *Not just friends.* New York: Attica.

Godek, G. (2012). *1001 ways to be romantic.* New York: Astrel.

Goleman, D. (2005). *Emotional intelligence.* New York: Bantam.

Gotta, G., Green, R. J., Rothblum, E., Solomon, S., Balsam, K., Schwartz, P. Heterosexual, Lesbian, and Gay Male Relationships: A Comparison of Couples in 1975 and 2000. *Family Process, 50(3)*, 353-376.

Gottman, J.M., Levenson, R.W., Gross, J., Fredrickson, B., McCoy, K., Rosentahl, L., Ruel, A., and Yoshimoto, D., (2003). Correlates of Gay and Lesbian Couples' Relationship Satisfaction and Relationship Dissolution, *Journal of Homosexuality, 45(1)*, 23-43;

Gottman, J.M., Levenson, R.W., Swanson, C., Swanson, K., Tyson, R., and Yoshimoto, D., (2003). Observing Gay, Lesbian and heterosexual Couples' Relationships: Mathematical modeling of conflict interactions, *Journal of Homosexuality, 45(1)*, 65-91.

Gottman, J.M., & Gottman, J.S. (2008) *And baby makes three.* N.Y.: Harmony (Random House)

Gottman, J. M. (1983). How children become friends. *Monographs of the Society for Research in Child Development, 48*(3), 1–86.

Gottman, J. M. (1993a). The roles of conflict engagement, escalation, or avoidance in marital interaction: A longitudinal view of five types of couple. *Journal of Consulting and Clinical Psychology, 61*, 6–15.

Gottman, J. M. (1993b). A theory of marital dissolution and stability. *Journal of Family Psychology, 7*(1), 57–75.

Gottman, J. M. (1994). *What predicts divorce?* Hillsdale, NJ: Erlbaum.

Gottman, J. M. (2015). *Principia Amoris: The new science of love.* New York: Routledge.

Gottman, J.M., & Tabares, A. (in press). Interrupting marital conflict. *Journal of Marital and Family Therapy.*

Gottman, J. M., & DeClaire, J. (2001). *The relationship cure.* New York: Crown.

Gottman, J. M., Driver, J., & Tabares, A. (2015). Repair during marital conflict in newlyweds: How couples move from attack-defend to collaboration. *Journal of Family Psychotherapy, 26*, 85–108.

Gottman, J. S., & Gottman, J. M. (2015). *Ten principles for doing effective couples therapy.* New York: W.W. Norton.

Gottman, J. M., Gottman, J. S., Abrams, D., Carlton Abrams, R., & Love, L. (2016). *The man's guide to women.* New York: Rodale.

Gottman, J. M., Gottman, J. S., & DeClaire, J. (2006). *Ten lessons to transform your marriage.* New York: Crown.

Gottman, J. M., & Katz, L. F. (1989). The effects of marital discord on young children's peer interaction and health. *Developmental Psychology, 25*, 373–381.

Gottman, J. M., Katz, L. F., & Hooven, C. (1997). *Meta-emotion.* Hillsdale, NJ: Erlbaum.

Gottman, J. M., & Krokoff, L. (1989). Marital interaction and satisfaction: A longitudinal view. *Journal of Consulting and Clinical Psychology, 57*, 47–52.

Gottman, J. M., & Levenson, R. W. (1985). A valid procedure for obtaining self-report of affect in marital interaction. *Journal of Consulting and Clinical Psychology, 53*, 151–160.

Gottman, J. M., & Levenson, R. W. (1988). The social psychophysiology of marriage. In P. Noller and M. A. Fitzpatrick (Eds.), *Perspectives on marital interaction.* Philadelphia: Multilingual Matters.

Gottman, J. M., & Levenson, R. W. (1992). Marital processes predictive of later dissolution: Behavior, physiology and health. *Journal of Personality and Social Psychology, 63*, 221–233.

Gottman, J. M., Levenson, R. W., Gross, J., Fredrickson, B., McCoy, K., Rosentahl, L., Ruel, A., & Yoshimoto, D. (2003). Correlates of gay and lesbian couples' relationship satisfaction and relationship dissolution. *Journal of Homosexuality, 45*(1), 23–43.

Gottman, J. M., Levenson, R. W., Swanson, C., Swanson, K., Tyson, R., & Yoshimoto, D. (2003). Observing gay, lesbian and heterosexual couples' relationships: Mathematical modeling of conflict interactions. *Journal of Homosexuality, 45*(1), 65–91.

Gottman, J., Murray, J., Swanson, C., Tyson, R., & Swanson, K. (2002). *The mathematics of marriage: Dynamic nonlinear models.* Cambridge, MA: MIT Press.

Gottman, J. & Parker, J. (Eds.) (1986). *Conversations of friends.* New York: Cambridge University Press.

Guerney, B. (1991). *Relationship enhancement.* San Francisco: Jossey-Bass.

Gunnar, M. R., Connors, J., Isensee, J., & Wall, L. (1988). Adrenocortical activity and behavioral distress in human newborns. *Developmental Psychology, 21*(4), 297–310.

Guralnick, M. J. (1981). Peer influences on the development of communicative competence. In P. Strain (Ed.), *The utilization of classroom peers as behavior change agents* (pp. 31–68). New York: Plenum.

Hahlweg, K., & Jacobson, N. S. (1986). *Marital interaction.* New York: Guilford.

Hart, B., & Risley, T. R. (1999). *The social world of children learning to talk.* Baltimore, MD: Paul H/ Brooks.

Hart, B., & Risley, T. R. (1994). *Meaningful differences in the everyday experience of young American children.* Baltimore, MD: Paul H. Brooks.

Havighurst, S. S., Duncombe, M., Frankling, E., Holland, K., Kehoe, C., & Stargatt, R. (2015). An emotion-focused early intervention for children with emerging conduct problems. *Journal of Abnormal Child Psychology, 43*, 749–760.

Havighurst, S. S., Kehoe, C. E., & Harley, A. E. (2015). Tuning in to teens: Improving parental responses to anger and reducing youth externalizing behavior problems. *Journal of Adolescence, 42*, 148–158.

Havighurst, S. S., Wilson, K. R., Harley, A. E., Kehoe, C., Efron, D., & Prior, M. R. (2013). "Tuning into kids": Reducing young children's behavior problems using an emotion coaching parenting program. *Child Psychiatry and Human Development, 44*, 247–264.

Havighurst, S. S., Wilson, K. R., Harley, A. E., Prior, M. R., & Kehoe, C. (2010). Tuning in to kids: Improving emotion socialization practices in parents of preschool children—findings from a community trial. *Journal of Child Psychology and Psychiatry, 51*, 1342–1350.

Hendrix, H. (1988). *Getting the love you want.* New York: Henry Holt.

Hochschild, A. R. (1983). *The managed heart.* Berkeley: University of California Press.

Hofheimer, J. A., & Lawson, E. E. (1987). Maturation and recovery from illness in neonatal cardiorespiratory regulation and behavior. *Psychophysiology, 24*, 593.

House, J. S. (2001) Social isolation kills, but how and why? *Psychosomatic Medicine, 63*, 237–274

Jacobson, N., & Gottman, J. (2007). *When men batter women.* N.Y.: Simon & Schuster.

Jacobson, N. S. (1984). A component analysis of behavioral marital therapy: The relative effectiveness of behavior exchange and communication problem-solving training. *Journal of Clinical and Consulting Psychology, 52*, 295–305.

Jaffee, S. R., Caspi, A., Moffitt, T. E., Pob-Tomas, M., & Taylor, A. (2007). Individual, family, and neighborhood factors distinguish resilient from non-resilient maltreated children. *Child Abuse and Neglect, 31*(3), 231–253.

Johnson, S. (2007). A new era for couple therapy: Theory, research, and practice in context. *Journal of Systemic Therapies, 26,* 5–16.

Johnson, S. (2008a). *Hold me tight.* Boston: Little, Brown.

Johnson, S. (2008b). *The practice of emotionally-focused couple therapy.* New York: Routledge.

Johnson, S. (2013). *Love sense.* Boston: Little, Brown.

Katkin, E. S., & Murraby, E. N. (1968). Instrumental conditioning of autonomic mediated behavior. *Psychological Bulletin, 70,* 52–68.

Katona, G. P., McClean, M., Dighton, H. D., & Guz, A. (1982). Sympathetic and parasympathetic cardiac control in athletes and nonathletes at rest. *Journal of Applied Physiology, 52,* 1652–1657.

Kehoe, C. E., Havighurst, S. S., & Harley, A. E. (2014). Tuning in to teens: Improving parent emotion socialization to reduce youth internalizing difficulties. *Social Development, 23,* 413–431.

Kehoe, C. E., Havighurst, S. S., & Harley, A. E. (2015). Somatic complaints in early adolescence: The role of parents' emotion socialization. *Journal of Early Adolescence, 35,* 966–989.

Keenan, K., Jacob, S., Grace, D., & Gunthorpe, D. Context matters: Exploring definitions of a poorly modulated stress response. In Olson, Sheryl L. (Ed); Sameroff, Arnold J. (Ed). Biopsychosocial regulatory processes in the development of childhood behavioral problems , (pp. 38-56). New York: Cambridge University Press.

Kelley, H. H. (1978). *Personal relationships.* New York: Distinguished Lecture Series.

Kiecolt-Glaser, J. K., Bane, C., Glaser, R., & Malarkey, W. B. (2003). Love, marriage, and divorce: Newlyweds stress hormones foreshadow relationship changes. *Journal of Consulting and Clinical Psychology, 71,* 176–188.

Kramer, L., & Gottman, J. M. (1992). Becoming a sibling: "With a little help from my friends." *Developmental Psychology, 28,* 685–699.

Kurdek, L. A. (2004). Are gay and lesbian cohabiting couples really different from heterosexual married couples? *Journal of Marriage and Family, 66,* 880–900.

Kurdek, L. A. (2005). What do we know about gay and lesbian couples? *Current Directions in Psychological Science, 14,* 251–254.

Larson, M. C., Gunnar, M. R., & Hertsgaard, L. (1991). The effects of morning naps, car trips, and maternal separation on adrenocortical activity in human infants. *Child Development, 62*(2), 362–372.

Lauw, M.S.M., Havighurst, S.S., Wilson, K.R., Harley, A.E., & Northam, E.A. (2014). Improving parenting of toddlers' emotions using an emotioncoaching parenting program: A pilot study of tuning in to toddlers. *Journal of Community Psychology, 42,* 169-175.

Lederer, W. J., & Jackson, D. D. (1990). *The mirages of marriage.* New York: W.W. Norton.

Levenson, R.W., & Ruef, A. M. (1992). Empathy: A physiological substrate. *Journal of Personality and Social Psychology, 63,* 234–246.

Lewis, M., & Rosenblum, L. A. (1974). *The effect of the infant on its caregiver.* New York: Wiley.

Liebovitch, L. S., Peluso, P. R., Norman, M. D., & Su, J. (2012). Mathematical model of the dynamics of psychotherapy. *Cognitive Neurodynamics, 5,* 265–275.

Locke, H. J., & Wallace, K. M. (1959). Short marital adjustment and prediction tests: Their reliability and validity. *Marriage and Family Living, 21,* 251–255.

Maccoby, E.E. (1980). *Social development.* N.Y.: Harcourt Brace Jovanovitch.

Mayer, J. D. (2004). *Emotional intelligence.* New York: Dude.

Minuchin, S. (1974). *Families and family therapy.* Cambridge, MA: Harvard Press.

Mischel, W. (1968). *Personality and assessment.* Mahwah, NJ: Erlbaum.

Murray, J. D. (2002). *Mathematical biology* (Vols. 1 & 2, 3rd ed.). New York: Springer Verlag.

Murstein, B. I. (1999). The relationship of exchange and commitment. In J. M. Adams & W. H. Jones (Eds.), *Handbook of interpersonal commitment and relationship stability* (pp. 205–219). Dordrecht, Netherlands: Kluwer Academic.

Murstein, B. I., Cerreto, M., & MacDonald, M. G. (1977). A theory and investigation of the effect of exchange-orientation on marriage and friendship. *Journal of Marriage and the Family, 39,* 543–548.

Nagoski, E. (2015). *Come as you are.* N.Y.: Simon & Schuster.

Northrup, C., Schwartz, P., & Witte, J. (2014). *The normal bar.* N.Y.: Harmony.

Olds, J., & Milner, P. (1954). Positive reinforcement produced by electrical stimulation of the septal area and other regions of the rat brain. *Journal of Comparative and Physiological Psychology, 47,* 419–427.

Olson, S. L., & Sameroff, A. J. (2009). *Biopsychosocial regulatory processes in the development of childhood behavioral problems.* New York: Cambridge University Press.

Olson, S. L., Sameroff, A. J., Lukenheimer, E. S., & Kerr, D. C. (2009). Self-regulatory processes in the development of disruptive behavior problems: The preschool to school transition. In S. L. Olson & A. J. Sameroff (Eds.), *Biopsychosocial regulatory processes in the development of childhood behavioral problems* (pp. 144–185). New York: Cambridge University Press.

Panksepp, J. (1998). *Affective neuroscience.* New York: Oxford University Press.

Parke, R. (1996). *Fatherhood.* Cambridge, MA: Harvard University Press.

Parker, J. G., & Asher, S. R. (1987). Peer relations and later personal adjustment: Are low-accepted children at risk? *Psychological Bulletin, 102,* 357–389.

Parker, J. G., & Asher, S. R. (1993). Friendship and friendship quality in middle childhood: Links with peer group acceptance and feelings of loneliness and social dissatisfaction. *Clinician Research Digest, 12,* 2.

Parkhurst, J., & Gottman, J. M. (1986). How young children get what they want. In J. Gottman & J. Parker (Eds.), *Conversations of friends* (pp. 315–345). New York: Cambridge University Press.

Patterson, C. J., Vaden, N. A., & Kupersmidt, J. B. (1991). Family background, recent life events and peer rejection during childhood. *Journal of Social and Personal Relationships, 8,* 347–361.

Patterson, G. R. (1982). *Coercive family process.* Eugene, OR: Castalia.

Paul, A. M. (2011). *Origins: How the nine months before birth shape the rest of our lives.* New York: Free Press.

Peal, N. V. (1952). *The power of positive thinking.* New York: Simon & Schuster.

Peluso, P. R., Liebovitch, L. S., Gottman, J. M., Norman, M. D., & Su, J. (2012). A mathematical model of psychotherapy: An investigation using dynamic non-linear equations to model the therapeutic relationship. *Psychotherapy Research, 22*, 40–55.

Perel, E. (2007). *Mating in captivity.* N.Y.: Harper.

Peterson, I. 1993). *Newton's clock: Chaos in the solar system.* N.Y.: W.H. Freeman.

Pinsof, W. M., & Wynne, L. C. (1995a). The efficacy of marital and family therapy: An empirical overview, conclusions, and recommendations. *Journal of Marital and Family Therapy, 21*, 585–613.

Pinsof, W. M., & Wynne, L. C. (1995b). *Family therapy effectiveness.* Washington, DC: American Association for Marriage and Family Therapy Press.

Pinsof, W. M., & Wynne, L. C. (2000). Toward progress research: Closing the gap between family therapy practice and research. *Journal of Marital and Family Therapy, 26*, 1–8.

Porges, S. W. (2011). *The polyvagal theory.* New York: W.W. Norton.

Putallaz, M., & Gottman, J. M. (1981). An interactional model of children's entry into peer groups. *Child Development, 52*, 986–994.

Putnam, R. (2000). *Bowling alone.* New York: Simon & Schuster.

Raush, H. L. (1974). *Communication, conflict, and marriage.* San Francisco: Jossey Bass.

Richardson, L. F. (1960). *Statistics of deadly quarrels.* New York: Boxwood.

Robinson, E. A., & Price, M. G. (1980). Pleasurable behavior in relationship interaction: An observational study. *Journal of Consulting and Clinical Psychology, 48*, 117–118.

Rogers, C. (1961). *On becoming a person.* New York: Houghton-Mifflin.

Rowell, L. B. (1986). *Human circulation: Regulation during physical stress.* New York: Oxford University Press.

Rusbult, C. E., Johnson, O. J., & Morrow, G. D. (1986). Predicting satisfaction and commitment in adult romantic involvements: An assessment of the generalizability of the investment model. *Social Psychology Quarterly, 49*, 81–89.

Sawilowsky, S. (2009). New effect size rules of thumb. *Journal of Modern Applied Statistical Methods. 8*, 467-474.

Salovey, P., & Mayer, J. D. (1990). Emotional intelligence. *Imagination, Cognition and Personality, 9*, 185–211.

Sameroff, A. J. (2009). *The transactional model of development.* Washington, DC: American Psychological Association Press.

Sameroff, A. J., & Emde, R. N. (1989). *Relationship disturbances in early childhood.* New York: Basic Books.

Sameroff, A. J., McDonough, S. C., & Rosenblum, K. L. (2004). *Treating parent-infant relationship problems.* New York: Guilford.

Sameroff, A. J., Seifer, R., Zax, M., & Barocas, R. (1987). Early indicators of developmental risk: Rochester longitudinal study. *Schizophrenia Bulletin, 13*, 383–394.

Sawilowsky, S. (2009). New effect size rules of thumb. *Journal of Modern Applied Statistical Methods. 8*, 467-474.

Satir, V. (1978). *Your many faces.* New York: Crown.

Shapiro, A. F., & Gottman, J. (2005). Effects on marriage of a psycho-communicative-educational intervention with couples undergoing the transition to parenthood, evaluation at 1-year post-intervention. *Journal of Family Communication 5*(1), 1–24.

Simmons, D.S., & Doherty, W.J. (1995). Defining who we are and what we do: Clinical practice patterns of marriage and family therapists in Minnesota. *Journal of Marital and Family Therapy, 21*, 3-16.

Spanier, G. B. (1979). The measurement of marital quality. *Journal of Sex and Marital Therapy, 5,* 288–300.

Stern, D. N. (1977). *The first relationship.* Cambridge, MA: Harvard University Press.

Tavris, C. (2010). *Anger, the misunderstood emotion.* New York: Simon & Schuster.

Tedeschi, R. G., Park, C. L., & Calhoun, L. G. (2008). *Post-traumatic growth.* New York: Psychology Press.

Thibaut, J., & Lelley, H. H. (2016). *The social psychology of groups.* New York: Forgotten Books.

Tolstoy, L. (2000). *Anna Karenina.* New York: Modern Library.

Tronick, E., Als, H., Adamson, C., Wise, S., & Brazelton, T. B. (1978). The infant response to entrapment between contradictory messages in face-to-face interaction. *Journal of the American Academy of Child Psychiatry, 17,* 1–13.

Tung, K. K. (2007). *Topics in mathematical modeling.* Princeton, NJ: Princeton University Press.

Vanhalst, J., Soenens, B., Luyckx, K., Van Petegem, S., Weeks, M. S., & Asher, S. R. (2015). Why do the lonely stay lonely? Chronically lonely adolescents' attributions and emotions in situations of social inclusion or exclusion. *Journal of Personality and Social Psychology, 109,* 932–948.

von Bertalanffy, L. (1968). *General system theory.* New York: George Braziller.

von Neumann, J., & Morgenstern, O. (1949). *Theory of games and economic behavior.* Princeton, NJ: Princeton University Press.

Vuchinich, S., Hetherington, E. M., Vuchinich, R. A., & Clingempeel, W. G. (1991). Parent-child interaction and gender differences in early adolescents' adaptation to stepfamilies. *Developmental Psychology, 27,* 618–626.

Watzlawick, P., Weakland, J. H., & Fisch, R. (2011). *Change.* New York: W.W. Norton. (Original work published 1974)

Webster-Stratton. C. (1992). *The incredible years.* New York: Umbrella.

Wedekind, C., Seebeck, T., Bettens, F., & Paepkae, A. J. (1995). MHC-dependent preferences in humans. *Proceedings of the Royal Society of London, 260,* 245–249.

Weinberg, M. K., & Tronick, E. Z. (1996). Infant affective reactions to the resumption of maternal interaction after the still face. *Child Development, 67,* 905–914.

Weiss, R. L. (1980). Strategic behavioral relationship therapy: Toward a model for assessment and intervention. In J. P. Vincent (Ed.), *Advances in family intervention, assessment, and theory* (Vol. 1, pp. 229–271). Greenwich, CT: JAI Press.

Wiener, N. (2013). *Cybernetics* (2nd ed.). New York: Martino Fine Books.

Whitton, S.W., Weitbrecht, E.M., Kuryluk, A.D., & Hutsell, D.W. (2016). A randomized waitlist-controlled trial of culturally sensitive education for male same-sex couples. *Journal of Family Psychology, 30,* 763-768.

Wilcox, W. B., Doherty, W., Glenn, N., & Waite, L. (2005). *Why marriage matters* (2nd ed.). New York: Institute of American Values.

Wile, D. (1981). *Couples therapy: A nontraditional approach.* New York: John Wiley.

Wile, D. (1993). *After the fight.* New York: Guilford.

Wile, D. (2008). *After the honeymoon.* Oakland, CA: Dan Wile.

Wilson, K.R., Havighurst, S.S., & Harley, A.E. (2014). Dads tuning into kids: Piloting a new parenting program targeting fathers' emotion coaching skills. *Journal of Community Psychology, 42,* 162-168

Yoshimoto, D. K. (2005). Marital meta-emotion: Emotion coaching and dyadic interaction. *Dissertation Abstracts International, Section B: The Sciences and Engineering,* 66(6-B), 3448.

Zak, P. (2013). *The moral molecule: How trust works.* New York: Plume/Penguin.

Zak, P. (2017). *The trust factor.* New York: AMACOM.

Index

mathematics
 nonlinear, 99–107, 102f, 103f, 105f,
 106f, 100f
 in systems theory, 99
math of systems that reacted to feedback, 2
math sidebars, 293–304
 actual initial math model, 293–94
 "characteristic equation," 297, 297f
 couple's eigenvalues, 297–301, 300f,
 302f–4f
 differential equation form of model,
 296
 null clines, 294–95
 Richardson arms race, 296
Mating in Captivity, 210
matrix
 described, 21–23
 game theory, 21–25 (*see also* game theory matrix)
Mayer, J.D., 261, 181
Mazlish, E., 252–53
McClean, M., 90–91
McDonough, S.C., 248
McFall, R., 5
McGraw, P., 147
meaning
 shared, 161, 157–58, 146f
*Meaningful Differences in the Everyday
 Experience of Young American Children,* 274
meditation
 mindful, 95
medulla
 adrenal, 89
Mendeleev periodic table of elements,
 298
mental health
 longevity effects of, 10–11
mentality
 in betrayal metric, 39
META. *see* meta-communication
 (META)
meta-cognition
 defined, 180
meta-communication
 described, 180

meta-communication (META), 4–5
meta-emotion(s), 177–200
 structure of, 180–84
meta-emotion concept, 182–84
meta-emotion interview(s), 251–52
 case example, 185–88
meta-emotion mismatch, 177–200
 case example, 184–99
 demand-withdraw with, 184
 treatment for, 199–200
meta-emotion structure, 180–84
 defined, 181
meta-emotion structure construct, 181
meta-emotion study
 parental types in, 253–54
metaphor(s)
 about emotion, 182
metric
 betrayal (*see* betrayal metric)
 commitment, 39–62
 fairness, 115
 self-centered, 39
 trust (*see* trust metric)
Milner, P., 53
mind
 flooding as state of, 92–94
 habit of, 125
mindful meditation, 95
mindfulness
 in attunement, 36
 during flooding, 92–94
Mindful Relationships, 95
mindset
 from negative to positive, 125
 negotiation, 45
minimal therapeutic interventions
 simulations for selecting, 119–20
"minimax," 300
Minuchin, S., 4, 7, 2, x
Mischel, W., 64
mismatched couple types, 225–26, 226f
Missteps in the Dance, 233
MIT
 lectures on cybernetics at, 2
modern culture
 managed emotions as part of, 178

safe haven (*continued*)
  in relationship, 39, 32–34
  trust as, 30
  trust metric in, 34
Salovey, P., 261
Sameroff, A.J., 272–73, 246–48
Satir, V., 4, 2, 131, x
Saturday Night Live skit
  about Olympic judges scoring couple
    for how effective they were at ruin-
    ing their relationship, 104, 102
Sawilowsky, S., 217
Sawyer, T., 135
saying "no"
  reasons for, 276
scent(s)
  sex, 51
Schrödinger, E., 299, 298
Schwartz, P., 215, 210
scientific assessment
  of couples, 145–46
second-order change, 96–97
security
  attachment, 247–48
self-centered metric, 39
self-disclosure
  avoidance in affair couples, 59
self-disclosure mode
  from attack-defend mode to, 86
self-editing
  positive, 125
self-report measures
  of treatment outcome, xiv–xv
Sellers, P., 26
"sensitivity to initial conditions," 101
sensualist
  as emotional command system,
    208–10
sentiment(s)
  negative *vs.* positive, 150–51, 146*f*
  in SRH, 150–51, 146*f*
sentry
  as emotional command system, 207, 206
sequence(s)
  information theory in discovering, 72
  in relationships, 68–70

serotonin, 52
set point(s)
  biological, 7–8
  as variables, 8
sex life
  building great, 210–12
  good, 210–12
sex scents
  in pheromones, 51
sexual infidelity. *see also* infidelity
  cascade toward, 46–49
  case example, 56–62
  predicting, 41–44
Shannon, C., 72, 70
Shapiro, A., 239, 234
Shapiro coding
  of LTP, 244
shared humor
  in high agreement-to-disagreement
    ratio, 74
shared meaning
  on Gottman Relationship Checkup
    questionnaire, 161
  in SRH, 157–58, 146*f*
Siegel, D., 36
Silver, N., 76
simulation(s)
  as quantitative fantasy, 118–20
  in selecting minimal therapeutic
    interventions, 119–20
  in testing predictors, 98
simulation sidebar, 305–7
Slattery, J., 240
Sleepless in Seattle, 52
sliding door moments
  defined, 203
  examples of, 203–5
  in relationships, 203–5
Sliding Doors, 202–3
Sloan Center
  at UCLA, 211–12
small-effect therapies
  evidence-based, xii–xiii, xiii*f*
smile(s)
  Duchenne, 178
  "unfelt," 178